1972

EMILY DICKINSON

*The Human Background
of Her Poetry*

From *Letters of Emily Dickinson* by Mabel
Loomis Todd. Little, Brown & Company

EMILY DICKINSON

EMILY DICKINSON

The Human Background
of her Poetry

by

JOSEPHINE POLLITT

COOPER SQUARE PUBLISHERS, INC.
NEW YORK
1970

Printed in U.S.A. by
NOBLE OFFSET PRINTERS, INC.
NEW YORK 3, N. Y.

TO MY MOTHER

CONTENTS

ILLUSTRATIONS

New Foreword 1970

" It is doubtful if Emily Dickinson will ever be famous," wrote Robert Hillyer in *The Freeman* in 1922. The successful literary debut of this strange new genius, in the early eighteen-nineties, had been followed by more than a quarter of a century of general neglect. She was too "special," too esoteric for the times. There came *The Single Hound,* edited by Martha Dickinson Bianchi in 1914; and the guns of a World War. Bookshops were being deserted for news-bulletins in the streets. It took a private war to break what the poet calls in her poem "Through the dark sod," the "mold-life."

Emily Dickinson was born in 1830. With the approach of the centenary of the poet's birth, Madame Bianchi, sole surviving member of the immediate family, again became active as family spokesman. Between 1924 and 1930, she published *The Life and Letters of Emily Dickinson, The Complete Poems, Further Poems,* and *The Poems of Emily Dickinson,* in that order, the last two with Alfred Leete Hampson as co-editor. In her republication of the letters and many of the poems, Madame Bianchi had not given personal acknowledgment to the original Dickinson editors, Colonel T. W. Higginson and Mrs. Mabel Loomis Todd. The old feud over editorial honors (and justice), and the rankling memory of a lawsuit, now erupted, with fireworks. The suit had been brought by Emily's sister Lavinia against Professor and Mrs Todd, over a piece of real estate. But the heart of the searing background of the court case was of a personal nature; and Lavinia was considered to have been the scapegoat. Lavinia won her case in court. For more than a

decade after the centenary year, volumes came from both sides
of the fence. Each volume added to our knowledge of the Dickinson poetry, but because of the feud, handicapped the independent biographer.

It was a new, a modern generation of readers that was now
finding Emily Dickinson. The poems were extraordinary. Her
readers wanted to know more about the poet. They asked questions. They met with contradiction, controversy, and lack of
information as to some of the turning points in Emily Dickinson's life. The events were too far past — as the events sometimes were when Emily Dickinson's brother and sister were
aiding the first editors in 1890. In the sudden pressure upon them,
forty years later, to "tell all," or at least to tell more, and in
the rivalry generated by the two hostile factions, each was forced
into becoming "the authority." Their friends took sides; and
unfortunately, used as sources by authors of rapidly succeeding
biographical works, there appeared the informant, anonymous
by request. For a short time, every book giving "new light" had
its Madame X. Of more significance, each of the opposing editors
had in her possession letters written by Emily Dickinson which
had been "edited," and not all the originals of the published
letters were forthcoming. Actually, in consideration of the time-
lapse, and the admitted manipulation of an occasional date by
Emily's brother or sister to protect what they considered to be
"well-bred reticence," there was some question whether they
could answer all that their interrogators wished to know.

The poet's Public had become engaged in insistent speculation as to "the lover"; so intense, so personal were many of
the poems. The official biographer, Emily's niece, gave unwav-
ering support to the idea that there had been a real renunciation.
From the beginning, both Madame Bianchi and Mrs. Todd had
indicated the subject of the Clarke letters as the friend who
meant most to Emily Dickinson. They did not identify him. In
my biography, I did identify him: as Dr. Charles Wadsworth;

though disagreeing with both editors as to their interpretation of that friendship.

More than twenty years after her mother's death, Mrs. Millicent Todd Bingham in her book, *Emily Dickinson's Home* (1955) devoted considerable space to a denial that Dr. Wadsworth was the subject of Emily Dickinson's intense love poems. "To turn a relationship such as that of Dr. Wadsworth and Emily Dickinson into a love affair is not only misleading; it is false." It was a "transcendental friendship." Wisdom suggests that it is not essential to have proof whether Emily Dickinson's lover, or lovers were real or imaginary. Acceptance of such an opinion, Mrs. Bingham thought, should not deter us from continuing to learn all we can about Emily Dickinson's friends, and to explore all her relationships for the light they might throw upon an inscrutable poem. "No relationship is too tenous to be investigated," Mrs. Bingham wrote. She herself the year before published *Emily Dickinson — A Revelation*: Emily's love, late in life, for her father's friend, Judge Lord.

But as Mrs. Bingham was preparing her final book, she had discovered in a repository overlooked, and forgotten, drafts of what have come to be known as the "Master Letters." For Emily Dickinson there had been a real person. Whether the man to whom Emily wrote the "Master Letters" ever saw them (the second indicates that he had seen at least one), whether the letters were ever sent, remain questions. The extent of the influence she had on him may continue to be a matter of opinion. Speculation was intensified as to the identity of the man who had inspired her great love poems. Regardless of newly discovered facts, the very weight of the Bianchi and Todd-Bingham prestigious positions tended to give continuing support to the theory of "the Philadelphia clergyman."

In the new Dickinsonia, some of it made available within the last decade, there are items that I find to be of special interest:

The publication of the full body of the Boltwood Papers, now in the Burton Collection of the Detroit Public Library, would give a valuable picture of "inside Amherst" in Emily's day.

"The Lyman Letters: New Light on Emily Dickinson," a long monograph, is important for an interpretation of Emily and particularly of her sister Lavinia. It is in *The Massachusetts Review*, Autumn, 1965.

Two dates given in the earlier biographies, which followed Madame Bianchi and Mrs. Todd, can now be corrected. The date of Emily's visit to Washington and Philadelphia was not the spring of 1854, even though both Madame Bianchi and Mrs. Todd cite Austin and Lavinia as their source for that date. Mr. Jay Leyda's researches have turned up clear evidence (correspondence of Sue — Mrs. Austin Dickinson) that Emily herself did not go South in the spring of 1854; but she and Lavinia were with their father at the Willard Hotel in Washington at the close of their father's term in Congress, in February — March, 1855.

It was assumed that Emily became acquainted with the clergyman while visiting in Philadelphia; and that he called on her in Amherst not long afterwards, when he was visiting in Northampton. But his first call, Emily Dickinson herself tells us, was while he was in mourning for his mother. I have found that the headstone in the Litchfield Cemetery gives the date of the death of Dr. Wadsworth's mother as October 1, 1859. His second call upon Emily Dickinson was twenty years later.

The records, now available in the National Archives, Army Engineering Department, place Captain Hunt (later Major) in Amherst for more than four weeks in August and early September, 1860; a town to which he was no stranger. Helen Fiske had brought him to the Amherst Commencement in August, 1852, two months before their marriage. (Palmer Letters, Huntington Library). In August 1860, the Hunts came from Boston to Amherst. Governor and Mrs. Banks were the house guests of Edward Dickinson and family for three nights, until they left on August 11th. There was a brilliant "levee" given by the President of the College on August 10th. On the night of August 10th, the Hunts stayed at the Amherst House. Lavinia Dickinson in 1895 (letter to the *Midland Monthly,* 1895) says that the Hunts attended a reception at the Dickinson home (presumably Edward Dickinson's annual Trustees reception, which Emily always took part in). "Emily was charmed with them both, and their mutual interest began from that date." Mr. Leyda dates the event 1860. It might have been in the previous year. On August 11th of 1860, the Hunts moved into the Amherst home of Mrs. Adams. In the comfortable quarters provided for them by the widow of Charles Adams, a former associate in the American Association for the Advancement of Science, Hunt found a congenial place in which to work under pressure. Helen wrote to her sister on August 12th that they had sat with the Dickinsons in church, and were going that Sunday evening to the Dickinsons. On August 29th, Captain and Mrs. Hunt signed the register at the Appleton Cabinet (fossil-track collection) on the Amherst College campus. On September 7th, the Hunts went to Brattleboro, Vermont, a pleasant drive from Amherst, to "take the cure" at the famous springs. From Brattleboro, Hunt sent an autographed copy of his *Modern Warfare: Its Science and Art* to the Reverend Wheeler, of Amherst. In November, Captain Hunt went to Key West, on his Army assignment; and Helen and son Rennie returned to Amherst, late in December, to rejoin Mrs. Adams. For the information in Helen Hunt's letters written from Amherst to her sister in Boston, I am indebted to Mr. Leyda's researches.

To my great regret, Margaret Maher, the Irish maid in the Dickinson household in the last years of Emily's life, had died in the late nineteen-twenties. Study of Maggie's influence upon the poet would be fruitful. I believe that Miss Maher has been artfully immortalized; that the off-rhyme, so charming and original, is the faithful sound of what Emily heard when Maggie was speaking to other members of the Dickinson establishment; the answering brogue laid upon the voice of one of the Dickinsons or of one of Emily's callers.

The life of Emily Dickinson as well as her poetry has fascinated people of artistic temperament. She has been a creative inspiration for a remarkable variety of forms in the Arts: notably, in drama, in music, in ballet and in decorative design. The problem of translating her into a foreign language is engagingly shown in *Choix de Poèmes* by Félix Ansermoz-Dubois. She has had an energizing influence upon American poets of this century, including such disparate writers as Jack Kerouac and Scott Momaday.

When I chose Emily Dickinson to be my special study in graduate work at Columbia University, I knew her only as a poet. I was not particularly interested in identification of the person, or persons, who inspired her love poems — until I undertook to write a biography. Were I rewriting this biography, I would make no changes in the essential outline of the story. It is still her poems that we treasure most; but for a full appreciation of the poems, a knowledge of the human background of her poetry is essential.

JOSEPHINE POLLITT POHL

April, 1970
Brooklyn Heights.

FOREWORD

The material for this book is entirely the result of research, verified, wherever necessary and possible, by responsible persons. My interpretation of Emily Dickinson and of the influences upon her, is offered as a suggestion. This short study of the human background of Emily Dickinson's poetry is incomplete without

> THE LIFE AND LETTERS OF EMILY DICKINSON
> by Martha Dickinson Bianchi
> Houghton Mifflin 1924

> THE COMPLETE POEMS OF EMILY DICKINSON
> with an Introduction by Martha Dickinson Bianchi
> Little, Brown & Co. 1924

> FURTHER POEMS BY EMILY DICKINSON
> edited by Martha Dickinson Bianchi
> and Alfred Leete Hampson
> Little, Brown & Co. 1929

from which I am not permitted by the copyright owners to make quotations..

For their interest and kind assistance, I am indebted to the nieces of Emily Dickinson's tutor, Miss Louisa E. Humphrey, and her sisters; Dr. William Scott Wadsworth; Mrs. Charles Wadsworth, Jr.; Mrs. George E. Thorndike; Mrs. Paul

Stewart; Miss Narcie Pollitt; and the Editorial Department of Harper & Brothers, particularly Mr. Eugene F. Saxton.

To my husband, Frederick J. Pohl, I am further indebted for assistance in tedious research during the last six months, and especially for critical advice and an enthusiasm for the subject which has helped to bring the book to completion. He has taken a special interest in the biography of Dr. Charles Wadsworth and he personally obtained some of the information relative to the early career of the clergyman.

I wish also to make kind acknowledgment to Houghton Mifflin for permission to make a quotation from THE LETTERS AND JOURNALS OF T. W. HIGGINSON, *edited by Mary Thatcher Higginson, 1921; to Little, Brown & Co. for their consent to my use of five poems from* THE COMPLETE POEMS OF EMILY DICKINSON, *1924; and to the Century Co. for permission to quote from* THE PRINCE'S LITTLE SWEETHEART, *by Helen Hunt Jackson, published in* The Century, May, *1885.*

JOSEPHINE POLLITT

EMILY DICKINSON

The Human Background of Her Poetry

*

Chapter One

A PEDIGREE AND A PARSON

*

ONE glaring forenoon early in June of 1840, the old Massachusetts stage-coach was making its way, as usual, along the road from Belchertown. In spite of the heat, the four black horses trotted at a good-natured pace which eased their driver into a semi-doze on his little box of a seat. The rattle of the works had become a rhythm almost musical to his ear. He flicked away a glutinous blue fly, and pulled the reins expertly at the approach of a hollow in the road; but for the most part the luxuriant country-side was to him a hazy vision through narrowing slits.

The coach had met the train from Boston at Palmer and had taken on several passengers. One by one these had been deposited at their various destinations, until now only two were left, both bound for Amherst. The elder of the two gazed appreciatively across the filmy fields; though not a native of western Massachusetts, he knew and loved that country well. The younger man, Aaron Colton by name, leaned against the weathered window frame and wished himself dead.

Through the open windows ahead of him, the green meadowlands were flooded with daisies and buttercups.

On either hand, above fertile farms lifted orchard-sweet hillsides higher and higher, swelling softly into heavily-wooded, low mountain ranges: the one on the east side of the valley, known as the Pelham Hills; and the other, a broken ridge that carried the eye beyond the " Notch " and across the Connecticut River to Mt. Tom, eight miles or more to the west. The touch of summer wind upon his cheek, the slow circling of crows above white birches and clumps of pine, the magical sunlight on the slopes toward Pelham, were good to know; but the young man in the rattling coach was restless, worried, almost inclined to spring out through the window and put his feet firmly on the road with his face toward Boston. . . . Well, he had given his word. He would take his fate by the bridle. . . .

This was not his first journey to Amherst. Three months before, he had undertaken the emphatic ride from Palmer over muddy March roads, in this same shell and shackle of a coach. The harness had given out three times before they reached the heights of Belchertown, but their Jonathan of a driver was well equipped with straps and strings against contingencies. The axle-deep mud and back-breaking jolts, with stark certainties of hill and spire, had made his first view of Amherst a whittled memory.

Now as the coach came down through the Gap, summer was bright upon one of the loveliest landscapes he had ever seen. The horses trotted along the rim of a great bowl of rolling farmlands and billowing hills. On a hill-top, almost in the center of this valley, were the towers of

MT. HOLYOKE RANGE, LOOKING SOUTH FROM AMHERST CAMPUS

Amherst. He recalled even now how clearly he had been able to distinguish details of color for miles away as he had first stood upon the college eminence and had looked far off to the silver ox-bow of the river. To live in Amherst was like living on a mountain and yet keeping miraculously about one the neighborly valley.

Amherst itself had proved to be little more than a village in the woods: a few stores on the main street, houses widely separated from each other by prosperous farms — with here and there a crossroad, a blacksmith shop, a grist mill, almshouse, tavern, and trees — trees everywhere, concealing even such fine dwellings as there were. Forests touched the very rear of the college buildings; they spread like an undulating sea across the bottomland between the village and Hadley; they swirled their green waves around the base and up the sides of the Mt. Holyoke Range; they overspread the Pelham slopes; they flooded vast tracts northward to the mountains at Sunderland and Deerfield.

As the coach turned from the rim and swung westward into the heart of the great bowl, the Gap seemed to close softly behind him and the young traveler was in a pocket, beautiful, sunny, open to the sky.

Aaron Colton was a student from Andover, and this was his first ministerial charge. A slender, gentle, sensitive youth, with bright eyes set in a face of slightly Scotch cast, he won friends easily and had no cause for distrust of himself or of his future. He knew the more metropolitan area of eastern Massachusetts and was of New England heritage. Yet that initial experience of last March, when he had come out into the western part of the state to act as supply in the First Church of Amherst, was frozen into his recollections.

He had, by direction, gone straightway upon arrival to call upon Edward Dickinson, Esquire. He had been kindly, even cordially received by Mr. and Mrs. Dickinson and had had tea with them: a gentleman of military bearing, with compressed lips and fine dark eyes; a dainty lady in bombazine, whose curls fell about her delicate face as she bent over the teacups. They were then living in one half of the house owned by Deacon Mack. The occasion had been a pleasant one, yet, he scarcely knew why, he had found himself becoming increasingly uneasy. It was, perhaps, a matter of suggestion. The deference with which Mr. Dickinson turned to him, the elder man's talk of char-rge and responsi-bil-i-ty, the slow striking of the clock, the strange views through the window-panes against which night was pressing, filled him with dread. To a sensitive temperament accustomed to the flatlands, the darkening of hills that lock one in for the night becomes depressing. Then a Mr. Luke Sweetser had come with a lantern and had led him up through a piece of woods to his own house among the trees. The next morning, Sunday morning, he awoke with a nervous headache.

Monday morning there had been a meeting of the parish committee in the office of Edward Dickinson, Esquire. The young preacher was asked to attend. He dared not do otherwise. In the solemn little group who meant to do him an honor, " he felt like a fish caught with a hook and hung up by the gills." He had not intended to stay. They protested. They wanted him as pastor. It took two hours of persuasion before he could decide to accept. Then he had worked in a fever all week, calling on families of the parish; had preached one more Sunday; then home to Andover. He had heard that Edward Dickinson had paid him a compliment: " That Colton's a marvel of a man to visit two hundred families in one week and tire out seven committeemen and pat every woman's baby. . . ."

Now he was coming back to be ordained. He was coming direct from the seclusion of student life in the seminary to be pastor to men who had built a chief New England college of which he had not been a member. He was assuming the care of a large parish. When he had visited those two hundred families he had paid his respects to exactly half the town, a town with a reputation for literary interests.[1] Would he be equal to it?

The wind rippled along the edges of a newspaper that one of the passengers had left behind him at Three Rivers. Aaron Colton's eye fell listlessly upon the dancing print of an editorial paragraph:

" Spring music. Our old friend, Robert Lincoln, Esquire, alias Bobolink, has already commenced his spring

[1] The *Springfield Republican*, March 11, 1843, in commenting on the high literary tone of Amherst, gives these statistics: " In the 400 families there were

concert. The following is a literal copy of the words of his last song: ' Oorioo — tudilink — bobolink, bobolink, Old Tip's coming in — cheer up — cheer up — sky clear — oorioo — Old Tip — three cheers — he'll sweep 'em out clean — yes, he will — blow 'em sky high — Van and Amos, Benton too — sky high — Mercy on 'em — cheer — cheer — Tip — O-hi-o — Clear the coast — sweet — sweet."

It was a Saturday number of the *Springfield Republican;* advertising parasols, Leghorn hats, Spanish segars, French collars, jackonettes; news of the Whig convention; the arrival of the steamship *Unicorn* on its eighteenth day from Liverpool, the six-hundred-pound cheese that a Connecticut farmer's wife was sending to Queen Victoria; and a Matrimonial Telegraph from a late London paper, " which may interest some of our readers. The general adoption of the system might save many a bashful lover a bungling or awkward éclairissement."

" If a gentleman wants a wife, he wears a ring on the first finger of the left hand; if he is engaged, he wears it on his second finger; if married, on the third; and on the fourth, if he never intends to get married. When a lady is not engaged she wears a hoop or diamond on her first finger; if engaged, on the second; if married, on the third;

---

636 subscribers to newspapers, 265 to periodicals, 550 to religious publications; 8,500 papers were received in Amherst, an average of 21 to each family," and adds that of the 515 voters in Amherst, 105 were bachelors.

and on the fourth, if she intends to be a maid. — When a gentleman presents a fan, a flower, or trinkets, to a lady with the left hand, this on his part, is an overture of regard; should she receive it with the left hand, it is considered as an acceptance of his esteem; but if with the right hand, it is a refusal of the offer. Thus by a few simple tokens, explained by rule, the passion of love is expressed."

Within seven years the paper was to undergo a change under the editorship of young Samuel Bowles. The pretty appeal of printed lawns, shawls, veils, and cutlery was to be peppered and splashed all over the front and back pages with advertisements of more gross but practical attraction; shower baths; sarsaparilla; cures for dysentery and deafness; and that most popular *Married Woman's Private Medical Companion* by Dr. A. M. Mouriceau, Professor of Diseases of Women (Third Edition — 25,000 copies sold in 3 months), especially intended for the married, as it discloses important secrets; poetry; the " most horrid murders "; suicides, usually of women; and political news in a style that crackled. But in 1840 the *Springfield Republican* was indebted solely to the politeness of one of its readers for particulars even of the most horrible murder.

Aaron Colton dropped the paper upon the seat beside him. There were ivory clouds above the hill-climbing daisies. If one were looking for mountain views, he would find here every variety, near or far. Peak by peak, a Polyphemus might have stridden from Amherst across the Berkshires and Green Mountains into Canada.

These Dickinsons who set the standard for their parsons had had the deciding voice in most of Amherst's affairs. They had built Hampshire County. They had enough mortar and timber in them to build a dozen shires. Their whole genealogical background is a great early American canvas of grim-faced Englishmen who had come forth from their Colonial progenitor Nathaniel, along powder-burned pathways in the French and Indian War and in Bunker Hill. There was a Dickinson intellect in the planning of every important Colonial rebellion. They were an unusually energetic people who drew their lines early from Massachusetts as far west as Kaskaskia, from Connecticut as far south as the hybrid colony of James Oglethorpe. Give a Dickinson the room and freedom which his spirit demanded, and he would achieve with distinction. Deny him that room and freedom and he would take it despite all obstacles.

Edward Dickinson's line could be traced back directly to the first of the name in this country, that sturdy Nathaniel, who had emigrated from England to the Massachusetts Bay Colony between 1631 and 1635, but did not remain. He had to have more land and greater independence of action. He forced his way through the wilderness to the Quenicticot River valley and settled there in Wethersfield between 1635 and 1640. In successive generations the families of Samuel, Ebenezer, and Nathan moved from Wethersfield to Hadley, Massachusetts, and on to Amherst, actuated in part by strong feeling due to religious disputes. It was a necessity of the Dickinson nature that he be permitted to make his own choice, though it be usually in favor of conformity. If in the genealogies one finds a remarkable record of Dickinsons diffused, in the little town of Amherst he has an even more impressive picture of Dickinsons concentrated. There was no more permanently flourishing family tree in New England history. In the regularity with which their strength was handed down from father to son, the Amherst Dickinsons court comparison with the Adams family; and there was greater variation.

As an example of the fiber of which they were made, we hear of Marquis Dickinson trained to hardness from his youth. When he was thirteen he went with a drover to take fat cattle to Boston, and came home alone on a dog trot. Starting from Cambridge at sunrise, he took off his shoes and ran all the way. He ate his supper in Leicester, spent the night in Spencer, and reached Amherst at two o'clock the next day, a journey of over ninety-five miles.

A Dickinson brain was at work in the planning of Shays' Rebellion. Daniel Shays himself lived only half a mile or so from " Conkey's Tavern " over in East Pelham, and he had found the old inn, off from the main travelways and isolated from all other habitation, to be a fitting place for a plot against the government. Amherst was in a neighborhood of independents.

The Dickinsons were from the beginning a power in the church, as there was always a Dickinson on the seat-ing committee. That power could be turned against the parson upon occasion, especially where politics were concerned, as the stanch Tory, Reverend David Parsons, could testify. Squire " Nat " Dickinson, an ardent Revolutionist, was a dominating figure in all Amherst and Hampshire County gatherings. It is recorded that when Reverend Parsons was compelled to read from the pulpit a proclamation issued by the authority of the new government, he added to the formal conclusion (" God save the Commonwealth of Massachusetts! ") his own views in a firm voice, " But I say, 'God save the king!'" Up sprang Squire Nat in his pew and, shaking his fist to punctuate his words, thunderingly shouted, " And I say you are a damned rascal!" His words rebounded from the walls and ceiling and fell in echoes like hail upon the transfixed people.

When Reverend Parsons died, in 1781, his son David, the Harvard graduate, was persuaded to occupy the pulpit for a time. The Reverend Parsons, Jr., had sparkling raven-black eyes and a beaming face, a friendly way with people, and the keenest nose for jokes, in which he indulged himself without restraint, sometimes even in the pulpit; nevertheless, his preaching was considered sensible and instructive. But the rumor went around that he was going to ballrooms to watch the dancers. Also, he was a Tory still. There was argument as to his fitness. Feeling ran high. Finally, one Sunday morning, his admirers and opponents passed out of the meeting-house and stood opposite to one another in front of it. The two lines were of about equal length, and so the Second Church was formed. The Dickinsons were in the revolting division.

Though there could always be assembled within the clan enough churchmen to stand together in a straight line of opposition, there were within the ranks such contrasts as Oliver Dickinson, who built and owned the original meeting-house at North Amherst, selling the pews and giving each purchaser a deed in which he described himself as "sole owner and proprietor of the meeting-house," and Walter Dickinson in the early half of the nineteenth century, who had never taken a journey and never gone to church, and who had long spells of not talking that worried his daughter.

When the Revolutionary War was ended, these energetic Amherst leaders turned their attention to the one thing which they had been compelled somewhat to neglect in those earlier years of action and disorder — their schools. Samuel Fowler Dickinson and Hezekiah Strong started the subscription for the Academy; Reverend Parsons gave the land. Nathaniel Dickinson and David Parsons, Jr., had been the first college graduates in Amherst — Harvard men. Before the founding of the Academy there were forty-two young men out of the population of sixteen hundred who were college trained, at Harvard or Yale or Dartmouth or Williams or Middlebury. Some years after the Academy had become established as a flourishing institution, the necessity for a college in Hampshire County was keenly felt. One fall morning Squire Dickinson donned his white beaver and great-coat

and drove off in his yellow gig down the Bay Road to get
a charter. Other towns wanted the college and it was only
through the persuasion and logical arguments of Mr.
Dickinson that Amherst received the coveted authoriza-
tion. Colonel Elijah Dickinson donated the land and the
people started to build, much in the spirit of the Jews
building their Temple. From Leverett, down from Shutes-
bury and Pelham, from Belchertown and the entire countryside, the farmers came driving their ox-teams laden
with building material of all kinds, with lime and sand
and lumber and stone, all bound for College Hill. The
farmers camped in tents upon the hill. Once, at night-
fall, when the lime had given out and the builders were
about to leave, a team from the north arrived with a load
of lime sent by a stranger who had heard of the undertaking, and the work continued into the night.

Even so it is doubtful whether the first college building
could have been completed if it were not for Samuel
Fowler Dickinson; for money was scarce. Time and again
when the funds were exhausted, the squire pledged his
private property at the bank that the work might go on.
When there was no money to pay for teams to draw the
bricks, or men to handle them, the squire sent his own
horses and his own laborers to help. He even boarded
some of the laborers and paid their wages out of his own
pocket.

He was a man of driving power who had never smiled
but once before his children, according to the testimony
of his daughter, "though he was always cheerful and

genial." It is recorded that he would walk the seven miles
to the county seat because he could not wait to ride, and
that he slept but four hours out of the twenty-four. His
generosity ruined him financially, and, like so many of
his clan, he went West, to become steward of Lane Seminary in Cincinnati, Ohio, and, later, steward of Western
Reserve College in Hudson, Ohio. He had built at the end
of Main Street the first brick house in Amherst, which he
now had left to his son, his professional as well as personal heir.

Edward Dickinson, educated at Yale, had quickly become the leading lawyer in Amherst and its vicinity,
though he had not so quickly joined the church in spite
of the fact that such an act would have warmed his father's heart. Edward Dickinson was a man who acted
only when impelled by his own reason; seldom, if ever,
by the wishes of another. He was now conspicuous in
state politics, and had been a member of the Governor's
staff. There may have been, on occasion, more warmth in
his eyes than in his handclasp, but there were unplumbed
depths of tenderness and sympathy in his reserve. In Amherst, he was " the foremost citizen " — the initial act, the
final word. He had lived in the brick house for a time.
His children, Emily, Austin, and Lavinia, had been born
there. Now he was living nearer the center of the town's
activities.

He had married, in 1828, Miss Emily Norcross, a daughter of Joel Norcross of Monson, a very wealthy man, likewise a leader and benefactor of his town and a founder

of the Monson Academy. There seems to be no printed
genealogy of the Norcross family, as there is of the Dickinsons. There is said to have been insanity in the latter
family, though we can find no documentary evidence,
and if there were, it would not be remarkable, as New
England records go. But indeed the early history of the
town of Amherst is singularly free of any cases of
dementia.

Most of the families of Amherst in 1840 traced their descent back to the first settlements in western New England — Windsor, Hartford, Wethersfield. Admixture with
families from elsewhere had been very small. Such in-
breeding is a factor probably contributory to the produc-
tion of genius, but though the number and quality of
individual achievements were unusually high and Amherst was one of the three most distinguished college
towns in New England,[2] the local historians had themselves remarked that as yet Amherst had produced no
great genius in any field.

The old Massachusetts stage-coach made its way, as
usual, into the outskirts of the town that contained " the
college on the hill." Several loungers stood at the door of
a blacksmith shop to watch it pass. A whistling boy with
a rod and pail gave the stage-driver a grave salute. The
coach rattled by the almshouse, the grist mill, the old
Strong place, and came to a stop at the Amherst House at

[2] In 1834 Amherst College had 260 students, and was thus larger than
Harvard and next to Yale in size.

Edward Dickinson

one end of the common, and here Aaron Colton and his companion put off their luggage and at 2 P.M. betook themselves around the corner to Amity Street, where the solemn council awaited them.

Next day, June 10th, his ordination day, Aaron Colton again woke with a violent headache, as he has recorded. He got through the services somehow. There were rigid rows of black-figured men, and rows of softly folded women. A high and lonely pulpit. Hard seats, a somber hush, and the voice of Dr. Humphrey, that learned expounder of the Moral Law, delivering his charge in words that struck the sounding-board with force: " When your pastor comes, receive him wherever you may be. Disturb no dust. Make no apologies. . . ."

" At evening twilight I was on my way to a wedding in Mill Valley. Met Judge Dickinson in the road opposite the president's house. Saw at once from his dress and unshaven face that he had not attended my ordination. Was it come to this at my beginning here? Deacon in the church; college education; one of the wealthiest men in town. No matter now for the reasons, if I ever knew them, of his holding back. Enough my grateful testimony that Judge Dickinson became in no long time . . . one of my best friends and helpers.

" Leaving the wedding party, I returned to the Amherst House to my room, south front, directly over the office. No sleep for me that night — nor lying down. *Two such days*. The strain was nigh to breaking. Once in the night

I said to myself, ' This is all a dream, and I shall wake, and be relieved.' But the curtain turned aside, and the full moon shining brightly, down there in plain sight were the signs on the offices and stores. This certainly is no dream. Then a more than half purpose to leave Amherst before morning. Knew and said, ' There will be a noise over this. Strange freak: man called and settled, and ran away the first night.' — Had thoughts of dark and desperate expedients. It is a blessed thing that morning follows night. — At 10 A.M., Mr. J. S. Adams called. Saw I was cast down. But his gentleness of ways and manner brought no easement. . . ."

The weekly prayer-meeting was held that afternoon, with a large attendance at the church. The newly ordained young preacher took his place behind the communion table. He invoked a blessing and read a brief Scripture. Then he began, " I had thought that in assuming a pastoral charge, one took upon himself a great burden, but I never *felt* it as I do now." His voice broke and he was unable to speak further.

Deacon Mack rose quickly and said: " Oh, our pastor mustn't think so; the burden is *mutual*. It is on us all as well as on him; and we all, pastor and people, will help each other all we can. Best of all, God will help us, and we shall be stayed up." Then he prayed for " Our pastor," and another prayed, and another, and the meeting closed. As Reverend Aaron Colton walked to his room, the terrible burden rolled off.

He remained in Amherst as the pastor of the Dickinsons for thirteen years (1840–53), during which time he saw Emily, Lavinia, and Austin grow to early maturity. When in his gentle old age he was asked to contribute his recollections to the history of the First Church of Amherst, his mind turned back to one ineradicable impression: Amherst, and a summer night in the south room of the hotel, the moonlight dappling the curtains and the flowered carpet; and between his smarting young eyes and the far-off magical blue-tipped mountain peaks, the wooden signs of his townsmen, hanging in sinister clarity, or painted precisely upon an emotionless windowpane: "Sweetser and Cutler," straight and secure; "Green and Sweetser," bold and clean; "Dorrance and Cutler," slightly tip-tilted; "Edward Dickinson," of irreproachable line and contour; — none of them stirring a whit as the June breeze swept through this loveliest of all valleys in western New England.

*

Chapter Two

ADVENTURERS

*

THROUGH the long summer afternoons Emily played by
the hour with her younger sister Lavinia and her favorite
accomplice, Helen Fiske. Helen was a little dynamo of
physical activity and leaping spirits; willful, impulsive,
suddenly throwing her arms around her friend tightly and
kissing and hugging her. She liked to play pranks, to im-
pose herself upon people in various forms. It was fun to
dress up in disguise and to hide her face and make people
guess, then to snatch aside the mask and clap her hands at
the mock surprise of her elders. She could tell fantastic
stories of what had happened to her when she was kid-
napped and bound in a corner of the pirates' den, until
the girls would cry breathlessly, " Oh, really! " Her ghost
stories must have laid an icy finger upon even the most
intrepid spine. How she would have loved amateur the-
atricals!

Distances attracted her. She was frequently found well
along a twisty road that led to some vague spire, and
she never went alone. She liked to fall in with strange
characters, the more tattered and torn the better, if

they had some flutter of color upon them, some glitter — of tins for sale, or earrings, or a gold front tooth.

She loved nature. Who could be growing up in Amherst and not love hills and skylands and warm field flowers! Even in that long New England winter that kept the brooding spirit huddled by his stove, she was exhilarated by the freezing temperature, and followed the footprints of the woodcutters with glowing face.

Of all her playmates, she spent the most time with Emily, two months younger than she. Did Emily ever run away with her? Did she, too, have a longing to find out what lay beyond that bend of the long brown neck in the distant range? There are, apparently, no such legends of Emily's youth; but " danger," " hazard," " peril," " secret," are familiar words in her vocabulary, and her niece's recollections of smuggled sweets, of anonymous baskets lowered to little " Indian " raiders, of many a wonderful " rich " supplied for the small nephew, reflect Emily's romantic spirit.

Adventure, equally strong in the young playmates, took its form and color from the degree of their vitality. In her childhood Helen seems to have been more robust. She took to the road of wayside brambles and hot sunshine, and met tramps and journeymen. Emily was physically very frail in her earlier years. "When I was a baby, father used to take me to mill for my health. I was then in consumption! While he obtained the ' grist,' the horse looked round at me as if to say, ' Eye hath not seen nor ear heard the things that I would do to you if I weren't tied.' " [1] Hers was a tremendously exciting adventure in the world of the imagination and of more eerie fact. She took a shadowy path into the dim and quiet woods, and for her, nature became a magician. She had been warned to beware, for in the grasses were snakes that would fasten their fangs in her, in fragrant places were flowers that would poison her, and the bushes were huts of crouching goblins in wait to kidnap her; but no sooner had she gotten well into the enchanted place than she slew the dragon of fear and walked boldly. The grasses and leaves and flowers were friendly and shy. The Indian-pipe, the orchis in the bog, the ecstatic puff balls, the mysterious apples on the river pinks, laid a spell upon her. All about her were choirs of birds who warned her against household Mimi's who would hold something from her.

On very hot days the girls laid their wild flowers in patterns within the shade of the lotos-like hemlocks and the syringas and talked confidingly. One grew sleepy with the warm, spicy smell from the kitchen windows, the odors of evergreen, of sweet-fern, of peaches, and new-mown hay. From east to west the encircling hills were a clear-cut green. The sharp blue sky was heavy with motionless clouds. Their world was close. But when a bee flew into the ring and over them, his careless coming, and the windy lines of his leaving, held infinite magic. How wide the world seemed, all at once; sky, and space, and undulating grassland, like a prairie.

[1] *Letters of Emily Dickinson,* edited by Mabel Loomis Todd, vol. ii, p. 274.

There was for both Helen and Emily a witchcraft in the summer air.

Over the bees and the blossoms swerved an orange butterfly, out above the hayfields, then up against a massive cloud, and on into that Nowhere toward which other phantoms were circling without purpose. Close by, at the rim of the gravel walk, there was a perpetual drama between the worm, the bird, and the beetle. No afternoon was ever long enough.

Tiring of the leafy shade, the children ran back behind the house and into the comfortable, pungent old barn. There they played in and out between the stately cabriolet and the bins and stalls, with many a cluck and delighted shriek, until through the cracks in the walls or the door, which they had left ajar, they saw the slow wheels of Professor Fiske's chaise, or the glint of a black beaver hat, and the slant of a cane just above the hedge, as Edward Dickinson neared his front gate with the measured motion of a pendulum.

While the sundown crept steadily, blotting out men and hayfield and butterfly and all the afternoon, and the barn was busier than the mill, the family gathered around the lamp-lit table for supper. It must have been a pleasant, tempered, regulated meeting. If there were a guest at the table, Mr. Luke Sweetser, or Deacon Mack, or Reverend Aaron Colton, he would pinch Vinnie's cheek, pat Austin's shoulder, and — remember Emily.

She had lovely auburn hair, a boyish and finely sculptured head, a well-developed brow, and large dark eyes the color of her hair. The thin, almost compressed lips, the lower slightly fuller than the upper, revealed perfect little teeth when she laughed. From the portrait of her, painted at the age of about ten years, one deduces that laughter did not always touch her lips and her eyes at the same moment, and thus her expression at times had something of an enigmatic Leonardine quality. Her mouth curved upward at the corners, marking her sense of humor, and there was a tiny depression in her chin. She had a full throat, little hands, little feet — a daintiness of person.

Yet she was not a child over whom everyone grew enthusiastic. An Amherst woman wrote in a reminiscence published in an Oregon newspaper after Emily's poems became famous, " She was never an attractive child to me . . ." She was not regarded as a pretty little girl. Her features were irregular, her manner at times shy, at times a bit " old "; the type of child who sometimes embarrasses elders by a long searching look. To some, she lacked that precious quality of childhood which sparkles happily regardless of its audience.

Her elders spoke of things that troubled her. Not of poison, snakes, or goblins, for nature very early had trusted her. Threatening bog and dangerous thicket had yielded secrets of breath-taking beauty. True, nature had caused her intense grief, for beauty withered and died. For the death of the flowers, especially, she was inconsolable. She had no fear of externals, but from the lips of awful, black maturity fell utterances that brought her baffling problems.

She dared not ask. This anxious silence was due not to fear of the consequences to herself so much as to the effect upon her elders. She had the shyness of sensitive childhood, such as produces in one an inadequacy of expression or a shocking precipitation of speech. In either case the effect was unhappy. There was, for instance, the matter of the clock. Years later she informed Mr. Higginson that she could not tell time by the clock until she was fifteen, because when she was little her father had tried to explain it to her and she had not understood. She had not dared to ask him to repeat, and had been afraid to ask anyone else lest he hear of it. She would not have him believe that her mind was less than he had supposed it to be.

Every morning in the tolling of family prayers, and even more terribly on Sunday from the high, unfriendly pulpit, she heard of a threatening God of flint, and of a perdition which chilled the heart. Her own pastor, Reverend Colton, was gentle and kindly, but his serious sermons were sometimes replaced by wild and woeful ones of visiting clergymen. Once when she was very young, her parents had taken her with them to a funeral. " Is the arm of the Lord shortened, that it *cannot* save? " thundered the minister. Emily had been startled. Was there, then, a doubt of immortality? No one else troubled over the thought. She dared not ask, and the problem lay heavy on her mind for forty years. Solitary solution became a habit. Sometimes she went to the church service with her affectionate little cousin, Louisa Norcross, and the two fell asleep to the music of the bees in the vines outside the windows. Once she had wakened just in time to hear the final words, " For Thine is the kingdom, and the power, and the glory, forever and ever." The words were suspended in the air before her. She pondered them and decided that hers should be " the power." . . . With kingdom and glory for neighbors it seemed young and wild and striding.

Nor were her fears allayed by reading in the Bible for herself. There were stories of simple folk among the hills. These she could understand. There was beauty in the story of David, in the tragedy of his love for Absalom; there was excitement in the story of Moses and the Red Sea. There were also threats and warnings. One verse in particular frightened her: " From him that hath not shall be taken even that which he hath! " Did it cast a menacing shadow upon her own doorstep?

Her speculations upon God were to undergo a change, but her family seemed to be unalterable. Helen Fiske ran home to tell her mother and father all about each throbbing hour; but for Emily, running to mother and father would have been like encountering a thin mist or the imposing dark. Emily's mother was at her best, soft, sweet, and dutiful; at her worst, a feeble neuralgic moan. Emily could not touch her father, whose presence was perpetually a sort of concentrated absence. And so, the ways of childhood seemed to bring her always to some threshold of fear or wonder.

In addition to the woods and the barn, there were the attic and the hillsides, in which enchanted places she could forget that the world was hollow, that the flowers

Photograph by L. W. Barnes, Amherst, Mass.

THE DICKINSON HOME

in the parlor were made of wax, and that dolly was
stuffed with sawdust. Nature, furthermore, was compensation for that parental " sometime " which invariably
never occurred. There were, also, her devoted little sister
and her spirited elder brother. Even he, closer to her than
any other, seemed undisturbed by the deeper fancies which
often came to her. And there were her friends, like the
perennials in a hardy garden.

In spite of the fact that for one with a greedy young
mind it was a terrible thing to be growing up in a " godly "
village, to be a boy or a girl in itself was enchanting. Emily
wrote to her brother in the springtime of her twenty-third
year that she wished her childhood might be perpetuated
forever. Just what was it that made people ever grow up?

*

Chapter Three

ADOLESCENCE

*

WHEN she was fifteen years old, Emily put up her luxuriant auburn hair under a net cap, looked into her mirror, and saw that she was growing handsome. On her bureau were perfume, a fortune-teller, and a pair of candy hearts; for according to the fashion of 1845, Emily was now "a young lady," and expected to pay attention to such fashion hints as that in the *Springfield Republican,* to the effect that no lady should wear more than seven distinct colors in her dress at the same time, that being enough to form a rainbow; nor clouded stockings with a white dress; nor a pink bonnet; nor the hem of her gown above her ankles — if she hoped to be married.

Five years had brought other changes. Helen Fiske no longer lived in Amherst. Her mother had died, and Helen, now under the direction of her aunt, was going to school in Ipswich and proving to be a poor correspondent. Even though Emily sometimes received no reply from "that prodigal H——," she sent her a large, square, neatly written paper every week on Monday, a bombardment of

26

Amherst news and affection. Long after ten o'clock, when the rest of the family were sleeping, Emily's lamp was kept burning as she poured out her mind and heart in a fluent stream of confidences to her friends. Her letters of 1845–46 sparkle with facetiousness and animated bits of local gossip. Everything interested her. Everything amused her. Her own family were mentioned scarcely at all. She had, in the last five years, apparently made up her mind against Morals in favor of Manners. She had become a Cavalier in a Puritan setting. Conscience must be met gaily; quotations from Scripture were handy, but to be apologized for. Her ambition was not to be a perfect model of propriety and good behavior, not to be a teacher's " satellite," but to be the belle of Amherst, with crowds of admirers.

As Emily poured for herself a dainty drop of attar of rose she wondered whether she were not " Eve," and determined to coax Abiah into sending her a copy of the romance which the latter had been writing in Amherst, for Emily was in a fever to read it. Ah well, she says, with a shrug for Miss —— who is applying herself seriously to her books, there's time and to spare for all that. And if she loses her character because she cannot recite with printed precision in the coming trustee examinations before the whole school, who will be the wiser a hundred years from now? What can books offer to compete with her new piano! In the cool and darkened parlor she plays " The Grave of Bonaparte," and " The maiden weeps no more," tenderly, pensively. Then swift as the passing of an expression upon her face the mood changes, and her letters bubble with jokes at the expense of the music-teacher with his soul in the clouds, the bride and groom who get tightly fastened in a big bow knot, a local matron's promising children certain to become ornaments of society because of their embryonic usefulness, and young ladies who aim to be poetical and send their friends bouquets to be pressed.

At times, the suppressed conscience succeeded in coming to the surface again, and Emily sat down quietly on New-Year's Day to make good resolutions — merely to break them. If life were only one long round of visits from her chosen friends! " You know what my talent for entertainment is," she adds to an invitation, in substance, by way of inducement. " You know what a hostess I can be! Such times as you and I are going to have will make the rafters ring! "

Though Emily would rather be courted than be learned, would rather write letters than compositions, school was interesting. The Academy had boarding pupils as well as those who attended as day students. Thus she made new friends from other New England villages. In epistolary vein, her thoughts skip lightly across the stepping-stones of her factual lessons, with swift shoots of lyricism over the wild flowers and the trees. Mental philosophy, geology, Latin, botany — (such big studies, how large they sound!). Was Abiah making an herbarium? She deftly draws a word portrait of one of her classmates who was always whizzing about, but who was a girl of kind heart, the principal virtue, after all. Had Abiah noticed the trees?

It was Emily's flair for personality and her sense of humor that first drew her to Abiah Root (later, Mrs. Strong), one of the confidantes of her girlhood. Seven years afterward Emily wrote:

" You were always dignified, e'en when a little girl. . . . I used, now and then, to cut a timid caper. That makes me think of you the very first time I saw you and I can't repress a smile, not to say a hearty laugh, at your little girl's expense. . . . One Wednesday afternoon, in the days of that dear old Academy, I went in to be entertained by the rhetoric of the gentlemen and the milder form of the girls. I had hardly recovered myself from the dismay attendant upon entering august assemblies, when with the utmost equanimity you ascended the stairs, bedecked with dandelions, arranged, it seemed, for curls. I shall never forget that scene, if I live to have gray hairs, nor the very remarkable fancies it gave me then of you, and it comes over me now with the strangest, bygone funniness, and I laugh merrily. Oh, A., you and the early flower are forever linked to me; as soon as the first green grass comes, up from a chink in the stones peeps the little flower — and my heart fills toward you with a warm and childlike fulness . . ." [1]

The summer of 1845 was a high peak in the curve of Emily's happiness. She was in good health and abounding

[1] *Letters of Emily Dickinson*, vol. i, p. 61.

spirits. While Vinnie was "gaping at the sights" and starting at the sounds in the great city of Boston, escorted by her father, Emily took long walks in search of wild flowers, and reveled in her glamorous world. Let Amherst be Victorian in the winter, if it must, but in the summers of '45 and '46 the spirit of the Elizabethans swept all the countryside.

The leader of the expeditions was Professor Hitchcock; his band of cohorts, the geology class; their Indies, as much of the earth within sight of the college tower as their stout limbs could cover. Believing as he did that scenery exerts an important influence upon the education of youth in cultivating taste and inspiring noble sentiments and purpose, the professor often took his class out to name the mountains and the significant geological formations in the Connecticut Valley. Nor did the professor confine these adventures altogether to his class. He tried, so far as possible, to make them community affairs. The Fourth of July, especially, was made the occasion of a great civic celebration. There can be little doubt that Emily Dickinson was part and parcel of all the fun. Was not her father the leading citizen of the town, always in the high seat of distinction at the cattle show, the church, and commencement? Did she not have a lively brother who was to be a freshman in the college within a few months? Were not the Academy girls allowed to attend lectures in the college? Above all, was not Professor Hitchcock their neighbor?

One day in the early summer of 1845, the professor was

walking alone in the woods near the termination of the path down from Holyoke Mountain. He was startled out of his absorption by a crash through brittle branches, followed by the thud of a tumbling body and cursing near by. The footpath was almost at right angles to the base of the mountain, and was most precipitous and rough. With another ripping of brambles and uprooting of rocks, there emerged a disheveled, scratched, and bleeding stranger, who complained bitterly that people tolerated such a neck-breaking path. Professor Hitchcock made a careful scrutiny of the mountain-side and conceived the idea of building a road to the summit obliquely. Then he went for support, not to the leading preacher, nor to the town treasurer, nor to the local judge. He spoke to Miss Mary Lyon about it, and she, "with unfailing enthusiasm," offered to meet his party at the foot of the mountain with a dinner provided by her pupils after the proposed road was completed.

This was a larger undertaking than one class could handle; and so the geology class (almost all seniors) invited the juniors to help them, and through the local newspaper, the Amherst citizens and all the community round about were invited to participate. At first there was great enthusiasm among the townsfolk, but when the proposition was more fully understood, objections, doubts, and remonstrances began. The citizens "could see that it would take two weeks instead of two days" to build such a road (for which they could spare no such time), and they grew cool toward the idea, "not wanting

to take part in any enterprise which would be a failure."
Whereupon, the professor called his two classes together
early on the morning of the appointed day, and after a
rousing speech by him, interspersed with much stirring
Latin, the students went to work with a vengeance. Before eleven o'clock the road was so far opened that a
gentleman rode horseback over it, and by twelve o'clock
the young men had the work finished, had made their
toilets as well as they could with rocks for mirrors, and
were ready to descend to meet the Mt. Holyoke ladies,
who had dinner ready by the spring.

Such excursions made existence sweeter for Professor
Hitchcock himself, for his life was not without its weather.
There was opposition to these absences of his class from
the campus. There were jealousy and bitter rivalry on the
part of his fellow scientists. In the assembling of his world-
famous ichnological collection, which was a passion with
him, he had met with meanness, ridicule, and insult. Once
when he had found some precious bird tracks in the soft
mud near Amherst, he had returned breathless from his
search for a helper, only to find that a rival, and one
whom he had supposed to be his friend, had deliberately
stamped out all of the delicate tracings with his own feet.
Again, as he was walking with bent head along a side-
walk in lower Manhattan, he had seen some remarkable
tracks in the flagstone. Excitedly, he called upon a plas-
terer near by to take an immediate impression. He hov-
ered over his booty. A crowd quickly collected. There
was much lifting of eyebrows, nudging of elbows, and

Photograph by L. W. Barnes, Amherst, Mass.

Amherst College, from an Old Engraving, Probably 1840–50

rising chuckles. Put the old man where he belonged! Off with him to the asylum! But up went a window, and out leaned the careless head of a bright-eyed young lady, who calmly viewed the scene below her and called down to " let the old gentleman alone. She had been a student in his class in Amherst College and would testify that he was no crazier than most professors." She might have indicated to the New York crowd that he was actually beyond comparison with most professors. Dr. Hitchcock was the originator of the American Scientific Association and its first president. He received more honorary appellations than any contemporary American save Edward Everett. Nor was admiration for Dr. Hitchcock confined solely to his countrymen.

One day in the late summer of 1835, the historian, Mr. George Bancroft of Northampton, tied his horse to the Amherst College fence and escorted his distinguished English guest, Miss Harriet Martineau, into Professor Hitchcock's lecture-room. The Englishwoman gazed with astonishment upon the class of daughters of farmers, mechanics, and lawyers seated with the college boys and all listening closely to a lecture on geology. Miss Martineau declared that she doubted whether such a sight could be found outside New England. She also declared that Amherst was in the most memorably beautiful region of all her New England travels.

Made president of Amherst College in 1845, Dr. Hitchcock found that only by taking a drive with his old sorrel horse, Tobias, every morning, and by eating a bowl of

arrowroot for breakfast, could he endure the protracted
sessions of the trustee and faculty meetings that made his
head feel as though " bound by a hoop."

Emily Dickinson wrote to a friend, in her maturity, that
she had been comforted in childhood by Dr. Hitchcock's
book on the *Flowers of North America.* She had been
unable to reconcile herself to the death of the flowers until
she read Dr. Hitchcock's story of how the flowers continued to live in spite of their seeming mortality. (Letter
to Mr. Higginson, 1876.) We do not find a book of precisely this title, but Dr. Hitchcock's exposition of immortality as illustrated in the return of spring is given in the
publication of his *Religious Lectures on Peculiar Phenom-
ena in the Four Seasons,* published September 1, 1849.
These lectures were given in Amherst College in 1845-49,
and were heard by the townsfolk generally. In Dr. Hitchcock's philosophy of a natural religion as opposed to the
purely scriptural doctrine, Emily's mind took its first
stride. Dr. Hitchcock's lectures on *The Triumphal Arch
of Summer, Euthanasia of Autumn,* and *The Coronation
of Winter* were more conventional in theology and in
document than *The Resurrections of Spring,* though interspersed with some poetic description, especially of winter in New England. For a child, one value of his exposition lay in his enthusiastic advocacy of a study of nature
as an exhaustless source of happiness of which nothing
else in life can rob one; he spoke of nature's soothing
power upon the lonely heart. As emblems of the resurrec-

tion, he presented in a composite picture: a bird, a beetle, a tadpole, a frog, a moth, a cocoon, chrysalis, tree, mountain, and flower. He argued that the future organization must be widely different from flesh to make it immortal and incorruptible. Spring presents marvellous developments of structure and changes of condition in the organic world. Who, from looking at the seed, could predict the character of the plant to spring from it? Yet anemones, violets, gnaphalium, trifolium, leontodon, hepatica, trillium we recognize each spring. There was a corresponding metamorphosis of insects. So individuality will survive death. He believed that "the spiritual body will transcend the natural body; that it will have means of receiving knowledge far more delicate, certain, and rapid; that it will be possessed by an activity incapable of fatigue and eminently fitted for abstraction; that the memory will be perfect . . . an organization so exquisite as never to mislead or allure from duty. . . . There will be recognition in heaven, all marriage vows dissolved, and the lover and his beloved will become but angels of God." Such a sermon (delivered in the college and then printed), supported by illustrations drawn from science by a botanist and geologist, was too convincing, too striking, when heard or read by a young school girl, for her ever to forget it.

Emily was almost sixteen. There was a new note in her letters. She was growing serious, and was not only busy, but "hurried every minute." Then she confided in the faithful Abiah. She had an ambition. Would Abiah laugh? Emily, who had had no other purpose in life than to be happy, was giving serious thought to the improvement of her time. She was fitting to go to South Hadley Seminary a year from next fall, if her health were good. She had been dreaming about it by day and by night. Was not Abiah astonished to hear such news?

The summer of 1846 had been very hot. Emily drooped. The frailty of her babyhood had persisted. She took cold and her colds were not easily thrown off. Her parents became anxious. Perhaps a change would be beneficial. And so, in August Emily made a four weeks' visit in Boston. It seems to have been her first journey by rail. She writes to Abiah enthusiastically about her ride in the train. She has never seemed more thoroughly natural and alive to all about her. She went everywhere, enjoyed everything. But more than the concerts, or the flower show, or Bunker Hill, or the panorama from the roof of the State House, she was impressed with bits of human drama — the people in the cars, the cypress-shaded graveyard, the story of self-denial told by two Chinese who were trying to break the opium habit.

But even at sixteen, life for Emily was not all entertaining realities. She was beginning to pay for hours of ecstasy with a reaction of deep depression. She seemed always to anticipate more than she realized. On Christmas Eve it was difficult to put to sleep the visions of what Christmas could be. Abiah always had had a big fête — holly, and a houseful — oh, so many of them — a brimming sleigh,

MT. PLEASANT INSTITUTE, 1827

and dancing, and laughter. Emily awoke on Christmas morning. The house was still and cold. There hung her stocking, filled with presents. Her little sister and her young brother might come running in to share the fun of inspecting them, but with the assembling of the family around the breakfast table a solemnity settled like a thin pall upon the day. There was a sermon, a stately dinner, a nap, a tune on the piano, callers perhaps, possibly relatives for the day, but if Emily went to an evening party, it was always, apparently, at the home of some one else. It was a bit difficult, though not impossible, to become a belle when one can seldom invite the crowd to one's own home, and one's dancing steps and graces must be practiced in secret. In the geography there were names of places that set one to dreaming: Cashmere, Circassia, Golconda, Buenos Aires. But places, it sometimes seemed, were primarily for the housing of Whigs. On a late summer's afternoon she would come running in, all aglow with iridescent fancies, her arms filled with branches and trailing flowers — to meet some Medusa-like household reality.

In her sixteenth year she was becoming increasingly introspective. In childhood, " sometime " had never come. Each star upon which she had fixed her hope glittered, and waned, and glittered again until she sometimes had a swift premonition. Would there come a day for her when the stars would all go out? Would some caprice of the future overthrow all her airy plans and aspirations, and leave them in a crumbled heap? She tried to find the cause for these fitful moods. It was her nature. That was all. Though she was social rather than domestic by instinct, she docilely took lessons in bread-making and sewing, and resolved that she would, in the next months, study very hard indeed. For the first time, she kept her resolution. Also, in this summer of her sixteenth year, she began to make serious references to poetry, of the popular religious and moral type.

Throughout the following spring and summer, Emily devoted herself to her studies. Between her and her goal stood the public summer-term examination in the Academy and the written entrance examinations at Mt. Holyoke Seminary. Upon his high seat of ruling master sat the young principal of the Academy, Mr. Leonard Humphrey, with personal oversight of each department; the English Department, in which Emily and Vinnie were enrolled; the Classical Department, in which their new friend, Susan Gilbert, was a student; and the Teachers' Department, in which there were older boys and girls. Emily had always been in love with her teachers, but her feeling for Mr. Humphrey was different from that inspired by Miss Adams and Mr. Taylor, and the present preceptress, the affectionate and lovely Miss Woodbridge. She did not analyze it. She did not think about it at all. He was only twenty-two, gentle, sympathetic, winning. He taught his young pupils that in the mind lay the hidden gold of one's being, that to neglect the mind or to abuse it was treacherous, despicable. He talked to them, read to them from some of the great books of the masters, and his pupils believed. Under his inspiring guidance something that had been lying still in Emily's brain was beginning to stir and to stretch itself. There was in her now an absorbing ambition for application to her books. She wanted nothing so much in the whole world as to succeed.

Spring came slowly in New England. It seemed just to touch the hillsides and woodlands and then to vanish, leaving elfin beauties beside the thawing rivers and the ponds. But summer was a certainty of luxuriance. Summer-time in Amherst was socially the gayest season of the year. Students and visitors thronged the streets. The very heart and soul of the staid little village seemed to stir, awake, take flight, and spend itself each summer's end in a burst of oratory, music, and mass meeting, of hand-shaking and tea-drinking. The town common took on the appearance of a circus, with its barkers and its tenpenny shows, its auctions and oyster carts. The tents drove a brisk trade, and the man who kept a table where one turned a pointer and " allers won a prize " took in numberless dimes. Indeed, local entertainment went so far that the *Springfield Republican* in cold surprise felt compelled to administer a public reproof to the more youthful Amherst for its annual loss of dignity.

On hot summer evenings when the air was heavy with fragrance and the stars were close, Emily and Mattie and Eliza and Abby forgot their mathematics and their ecclesiastical history, even though the examination date was at hand. They strolled together along the gravel paths beside the high green hedges, or sat on the front steps and talked. For Emily, life never seemed so full. Her whole being tingled with expectancy. Sometimes on the morning after, her emotions overflowed into sentimental letters to Susie or Abiah: of how she and one of the girls had sat together on the steps and had talked about life and love until the moon was high. In spite of a shadow that fell at times across her expectations, each day was a new ecstasy. She had determined never to let her free spirit be chained. She held the world against her heart.

*

Chapter Four

MT. HOLYOKE

*

IN September, 1847, Emily Dickinson came under the influence of the most forceful woman in the educational world of that time. Mary Lyon had received a scientific education in the Amherst Academy and had lived in the home of Professor Hitchcock, for whose instruction this energetic, intellectual, homespun girl had three times come to Amherst, after intervals of earning her living elsewhere as a teacher. It is said that Professor Hitchcock himself had one day suggested to Miss Lyon that plan for a woman's college to which she so wholly dedicated herself. It is certainly no exaggeration to say that Mt. Holyoke Seminary originated in the fertile mental life of Amherst College and that Professor Hitchcock, more than any other single person, was the builder of that life. Miss Lyon had been indefatigable, and as a result of her unfaltering enthusiasm and the resourceful mind with which she had met every challenge, her college was a success. She had at first planned to call it " Pangynaskean," but the name had been ridiculed; and so in 1837 " Mt. Holyoke Female Seminary" was opened, in one of the loveliest locations in the entire country. The Seminary was housed in one large building, " tastefully furnished and arranged "; and there are many testimonials to the fact that visitors were pleased with their reception and entertainment.

When Emily climbed out of the stage-coach at the front gate of the Seminary, kissed her father good-by, and had her trunk put into the strange room with her cousin Emily, who was a senior in the school, she was almost ill from fatigue, excitement, and the cold which she had contracted. She gazed about her with interest and poise, and decided that she liked it. This was to be her home for a year and she had determined to make good. For Emily, that settled the matter. She had thought the problem through before she came. She foresaw that she would undoubtedly encounter rough and uncultivated manners, just as she had met them in the public school and the democratic Academy classes and college-student gatherings. She knew that she would miss her old friends, Abiah, Susan, and Eliza, but she welcomed experience. She wanted to learn. Going away to school meant enlargement of life. It was her first real test of her ability, and her father had taught her never to disgrace herself.

Although her nervousness over the entrance examinations must have somewhat dampened her ardor for a studious life, Emily worked hard, wrote the very best biweekly compositions that she could, took music lessons, made friends, and broke rules, especially rules in regard to correspondence. Though she stayed away from the popular circus party, because it was a good opportunity to be alone, she chafed at isolation, which was an entirely different matter. It was rather terrible suddenly to be shut up in a mental nutshell when there was the excitement of Mexico, and of Amherst Whig activities under her father's direction. But on the whole, she was getting along nicely, and was contented in her new environment, in spite of the frequent appearances of Austin and Vinnie, who told her that the house in Amherst was now like a funeral, and in spite of the visits of her mother and father, who made several trips over the Range to tell her that nothing could be the same for them until she returned. These pulls upon the heart-strings were a bit upsetting, but Emily had made up her mind that she would not be homesick and thereupon buried all such troublesome feelings. When the Thanksgiving vacation came around, she stood all morning at the rainy windowpane, watching for Austin's familiar horse and carriage; and as she and her roommate drove with him down the mountain on the Amherst side of the Notch, the slashing of the torrential rain against the curtains, the howling of the wind over their heads, and the rush of wild, overflowing brooks gave her a welcome that no one else was hearing.

Mrs. Todd, who in 1894 edited many of Emily's letters of this period, notes that " intellectual brilliancy of an individual type was already at seventeen Emily's distinguishing characteristic. . . . Traditions of extraordinary compositions still remain; and it is certain that each was an epoch for those who heard, whether teachers or pupils. An old friend and schoolmate of Emily's tells me that she was always surrounded by a group of girls at recess, to hear her strange and intensely funny stories, invented upon the spot."[1]

We must not take the social Emily too seriously when we find her writing to Abiah on November 6th that she had not expected to discover anyone in the Seminary who was likely to become an intimate, and that she was much surprised to find ease, and graceful manners, and general good will in this place of which she had been dreaming by night and by day for a year; for Emily was very happy throughout the year. Perhaps in the South Hadley Seminary of 1847–48 Emily developed that " upside-down philosophy " (a habit of discounting disappointment by anticipating it) which she continued for years to use as a fender.

Mary Lyon could have had very little influence upon this young girl, for several reasons. Though Emily was never a snob, she was an aristocrat, to the manner born; a girl of innate taste and refinement. The Seminary principal's most loyal friend, Professor Hitchcock, records in his memoir of Mary Lyon that " she was not schooled to observe nice customs; the getting a thing done so engrossed her thoughts, that none were left for the manner in which it should be done. She had a constitutional indifference to dress, and was sometimes seen in the drawing-room when every hair did not know its place, and some article of her apparel would not bear the closest scrutiny." Miss Lyon had engraved upon her heart,

1 *Letters of Emily Dickinson*, vol. i, p. 35.

Mt. Holyoke Female Seminary

" Blessed is the power to do," and from the flagstaff of her
school there floated an invisible banner, " Duty," which
was never taken down at sunset. " Fun," she said, " is a
word no young lady should use." " Learn to sit, with
energy." Her chief consideration was that a " lady " should
have a mind which would command respect, and such
health that she could use a spare hour whenever it came.
She was constantly warning the girls against squandering
golden moments by indefinite musings and needless speculations. " A young lady should be so educated that she
can go as a missionary at a fortnight's notice." Emily had
herself chosen " power " in preference to the kingdom
and the glory, but Emily's was the power to be.

Her most rewarding recreation from close application
to her studies Emily found in long walks, often alone.
There were widths of green fields and lovely streams of
clear water with rustic bridges, and if one went far into
the woods he found the anemones and the arbutus and
even the rare pink Indian-pipe. No lover of the beautiful
could languish in springtime at Mt. Holyoke Seminary.
When Miss Lyon became brain weary from long and
close application, " it was her practice at this period of
her life to sink voluntarily into a state of partial stupor
for one, two, or three days, as the case might require,
keeping to her bed most of the time, and taking very little
food. From such seasons of rest she would come forth
rejuvenated, and ready for a campaign that would ex-
haust anybody else. She would arrive at that state in which
she seemed to lose the power of stopping the wheels of

thought." According to her biographer, Mrs. Gilchrist, the most that she drew from the hillsides in their seasons was "patience and the value of soundless work." When the January thermometer was below zero, Miss Lyon could take some warm food, wrap a buffalo robe about her, commend herself to God, drive most of the day, and declare that she had never suffered less from any journey. But Emily shrank from the New England chill, and yearned for a life of perpetual summer-time.

There were points of contact between these two, however. Emily was thoroughly accustomed to the type of curriculum which Miss Lyon offered, and during her year in South Hadley she even got so far involved in her chemistry and her algebra, and infected by Miss Lyon's afternoon advice, that she wrote sternly to Austin, who was indulging in *The Arabian Nights,* to develop his other powers in proportion as he allowed imagination to capture him. Also, so long as Emily continued to attend church, she did get an emotional thrill from a good old-fashioned evangelical preacher, as she testifies in letters to her brother.

During the great "awakening" of 1847 (before Emily's arrival), there had been a Sabbath-like silence throughout the Seminary building. Everybody walked with hushed footsteps, and some of the young ladies even requested to be excused from their studies "because of their deep feelings." But during Emily's year Miss Lyon was having a rather troublesome experience. There was a small but determined minority of the prayerless and the non-conformists in her school. She felt, as she wrote later of a parallel situation: " Our vacation is near. Its disturbing influence I very much fear." The previous year, she had met the whole school in the hall on the day of fasting. Now, with the approach of that important annual day of fasting for the conversion of the world, she was uncertain of her following. As it happened, according to Mrs. Bianchi's well-known story, Miss Lyon carried every one with her in her determination that Christmas should be observed as a fast day — every one, that is, except Emily Dickinson, who stood up alone before the entire school to express her disapproval of converting a holiday into a day of abnegation, and was sent home on the afternoon stage-coach.

Emily kept no journal of these months, so far as we know, but a Miss Tolman did; and quotations from it are of interest:

" *Sept. 29, 1847* — Our school met today for the first time. A very large number present. Miss Lyon's subject of remark to them was in regard to absent or deceased friends. She addressed in her own peculiar manner the strange ones who had come among us. There were many tearful eyes. The examination of our new candidates is progressing rapidly.

" *Oct. 5* — Miss Lyon regrets very much our number is so full this year. At least 250. She had done all she could to avoid it. She had more than 500 applicants.

" *Oct 12* — Examinations nearly finished. Six left this

forenoon because they found themselves unprepared. Miss Lyon's health is improving daily. Her soul is full of benevolence.

"*Dec. 14* — At our family meeting this afternoon. Miss Lyon made some remarks upon the duty of preserving health. Theme suggested by one of the notes of criticism, 'wearing thin shoes and cotton hose.' She spoke of the inclemency of the New England climate and necessity of additional clothing. She then told them that when they became members of this school it was expected they would have maturity of character and moral principle enough to do what was right without a formal command. If they had not, they had better by all means go to a smaller school for younger persons, where they could receive the peculiar care needed by little girls. As she pursued the subject, her vivacity increased, and she said, 'There are two things, young ladies, that we expressly say you must not do. One is, that you must not violate the fire laws; the other is that you must not kill yourselves. If you will persist in killing yourselves by reckless exposure [in cotton stockings], we are not willing to take the responsibility of the act. We think by all means you had better go home and die in the arms of your dear mothers.' She said such exposures were a direct violation of two commands of God, ' Thou shalt not kill — and — steal,' for a violation of the first involved a violation of the second, as by it they robbed the world of the good they ought to do.

"*Dec. 16* — For a few mornings past at devotions, Miss Lyon has been dwelling upon the great doctrines of the Bible, total depravity, nature of sin, etc. Then she took up the Commandments in their order. . . . There has been fixed attention.

"*July 4*— In the hall this afternoon, Miss Lyon amused us with some of her most playful remarks. Miss Whitman had heard that the village lads were going to have fireworks this evening, and thought it not well that our family should lose their sleep to witness the display. So she remarked upon the probable splendor of the scene with such mock sublimity as to quell every vestige of excitement, had there been any. She then gave to all the remarkable permission to look out of their own windows, though not to leave their rooms. Miss Lyon added her contribution of merry words, and all joined in a hearty laugh.

"*Dec. 14, 1848*— Miss Lyon spoke on mutual influence. She illustrated remarks by examples from chemistry. Some of the rankest poisons were made by the union of the most valuable and inoffensive elements; as, for instance, oxygen and nitrogen, whose value and importance were so well known, were constituents in nearly all of them. So, many young ladies, if brought together, would make nicotine or strychnine."

It is to be hoped that this talk on mutual influence, dated soon after Emily's departure, had been given also during the preceding terms; for Miss Lyon's scientific illustration would have been of special value to Emily when she faced that host of " Jebusites and Hittites " now known as " Dickinson relatives," who so often sought her father's doorstep.

Although Emily had not been feeling well all winter as a result of such close application to her work, she carefully omitted any references to her fatigue in letters to her family; but a friend proved traitor and Austin appeared one day in May with peremptory commands to bring his sister home. She stormed, she wept, but Austin won, and she was led off in triumph, away from the teachers and companions with whom she much wanted to stay — to be dosed by her father, and to receive a daily visit from the family doctor, and to be called upon and condoled with by all the old ladies in Amherst. There was nothing to do but to make the best of it, of course. Her parents showed their clinging delight in her presence, her young sister followed her about and listened with awe and admiration to Mt. Holyoke wisdom, and Emily took this time for a "feast" in reading: *The Princess, Evangeline, The Maiden Aunt, The Epicurean, Twins and Heart.* There were the old-time parties and the long rambles through the woods and out to Orient Springs. When she was pronounced well enough to resume her studies, her friends lamented her departure, but the roosters and the singing birds were on her side as she again climbed into the stage-coach bound for South Hadley. This last term was, however, to be the end of it. Father had decided against the Seminary for another year. He wanted her to stay at home until her health was fully restored, and then he would probably send her away again, to a school not yet selected.

*

Chapter Five

"MY EARLIEST FRIEND"

*

HER year at Mt. Holyoke brought to Emily Dickinson a revelation of herself. She had dreams and determination, an invincible combination; but she did not know the impulsion of her own true nature. At Mt. Holyoke she had stood up against flagrant misuse of a holiday; had stood up alone against her whole spiritual environment there. Henceforward, though she was not quite certain to what purpose her life was tending, she knew what she must not, could not make of it. Not for her the way of the reformer, the uplifter, the doer of good. Throughout her girlhood, one impulse had been in the ascendancy. She would keep her free spirit unbound. Mt. Holyoke had shown her capacity for holding to a purpose. Her soul had strength to rely upon itself in opposition to everyone; it would never be divided against itself. Her dramatic act of defiance in the Seminary presaged far more than anyone there could see.

She was quite content to remain at home, which now seemed bright and shining after her nine months of boarding with Duty. If Emily were not actually the belle of

Amherst, she at least had all the admirers that her heart could wish. The most attractive young men of the village strolled with her along the shady, gravel pathways, went driving with her, danced with her at the contraband poetry-of-motion meetings. There were jolly "sugaring off" parties on the outskirts of Sunderland, arbutus treasure hunts at Orient Springs, chowder parties in the depths of the forest. For two years life was a busy matter, if not exactly a carnival.

"Emily was not beautiful, yet she had great beauties," her friend, Mrs. Emily Fowler Ford, said of her. "Her eyes were lovely auburn, soft and warm, her hair lay in rings of the same color all over her head, and her skin and teeth were fine. . . . At this time she had a demure manner which brightened easily into fun, where she felt at home, but among strangers she was rather shy, silent, and even deprecating. She was exquisitely neat and careful in her dress, and always had flowers about her. Emily was a free talker about what interested her, but did not express personal opinions of her mates, her home, or her habits. . . . There was a fine circle of young people in Amherst, and we influenced each other strongly. . . ." [1]

The young people organized a Shakespeare Club, said to have been something rare in those days. The men were troubled lest Shakespeare be a little too Rabelaisian for mixed company, so one of the tutors proposed that he collect from the club members their copies which were to be used at the meetings, and that he mark out the

[1] *Letters of Emily Dickinson,* vol. i, p. 130.

passages which might prove embarrassing. At the first meeting his proposition was put to a vote. The young men warmly supported their leader, but the girls voted " No," in unison. They " did not want the strange things emphasized nor their books spoiled with marks." The men were firm. There seemed to be a deadlock. Finally the girls said: " Do as you like. We shall read everything." One of them remembered long afterward how Emily Dickinson had tossed her head as she departed from the meeting with the remark, " There's nothing wicked in Shakespeare, and if there is I don't want to know it." For two or three sessions the men read modestly from their censored editions, while the girls gave a free rendering whenever their turns came. Then the young men yielded, and the unexpurgated text was read boldly.

There is, in her letters to her intimates of these years, an increasing tendency to weigh values in human intercourse. Even between two, conversation did not always give what she had hoped for. She dreamed of Abiah's approaching visit. There would be so much to talk about, so much of give and take. Abiah came and went. The opportunity hadn't fulfilled its promise. Why didn't we say more to one another? There was plenty to talk about. Too many beings within two persons tried to get themselves expressed. The Emily and the Abiah who had most to say to one another couldn't get themselves heard. One day, after some outdoor party from which they were returning together, Emily Dickinson had walked in silence for a little while; then she turned to her friend, Emily

Fowler, several years her senior, and remarked, " Doesn't
it make you shiver to hear a great many people talk? They
take all the clothes off their souls."

At sixteen, realization had seemed always to fall somewhat short of anticipation. Emily had tried to analyze the
situation, and had decided that she was made so. That was
all. Now she was aware of a contributory cause.

One bright, warm Sunday noon in May of her twentieth
year when Emily was busy with household tasks, there
came a rap at the door. One of her favorite friends had
come with his horse and buggy. The air was fresh and
sweet. " Come out for a drive through the woods," he invited. She could not go. Her mother had the neuralgia.
Emily must have looked longingly past him. He saw tears
in her eyes. He turned quickly. She *could* go and she
should go; he was for carrying her away then and there.
But there came a whiff of camphor from the darkened
room behind them, and a faint moan. Emily kept a stiff
lip and remained firm. When she heard the turning of
the wheels upon the gravel she began to hum a little tune,
until she saw that her mother seemed to be asleep. Then
Emily Dickinson put her head upon her arms and cried.
Why did some people have to be perpetually sick when
the world was warm and blossomy? Why did people ever
have to grow old and prey upon youth? All the old ladies
in town seemed to look forward to dying as if it were
some sort of pleasure — the supreme object of existence.
How was one to endure a lifetime of kitchens, thick shoes,
preachers, and the Moral Law; of the continual admoni-

tion of a shocked mother, " O Emily! won't you please be *sensible!* " and an exasperating father who passed from his house like an elegant stovepipe, in displeasure at his daughter's wayward fancies. At least there were ways of relieving one's feelings. She remembered the plates she had hurled upon the stones by the kitchen doorstep, and how once she had cracked the silence of her astonished and tight-lipped family with a slam of her bedroom door and the click of a key after a seven-mile buggy ride with her favorite cousin from the open grave of their relative; and there was always letter-writing for one's relief. Emily cautioned her confidantes never to worry over these re-citals of her woes, for her imprecations were really very harmless and they cooled her off so comfortably.

Her father — son of Samuel, son of Nathan, son of Ebenezer — had not wished his children to read anything but the Bible. Their young friends were astonished at the ignorance of current literature which they found in Emily and her brother. However, all the youthful Dickinsons needed was a little direction. It was well for all concerned that Edward Dickinson was not inclined to sit on his own door-step beside the great bush of old-fashioned box-tree, or to seek relief from his briefs in the evenings by strumming upon the parlor piano keys; for between 1845 and 1850 there had been more than one suspicious-look-ing package left in the bush as Mr. Bowdoin disappeared down the walk beneath the Dickinson hedge, and there was many a slight bulging of one corner of the piano cover as Austin made signs to his sister and retreated. In such

hiding-places Emily found the *Letters from New York*
by Mrs. Child, and *Jane Eyre,* for which she wrote excited
little notes of thanks, inclosing box leaves to the young
attorney in her father's office; Austin and she surrepti-
tiously read *Kavanagh,* published in 1849, and they had
many a hearty laugh at the village lady's man, that perfect ring-dove, Hiram A. Hawkins. He was, so Longfellow
said, a dealer in English linens and carpets, whose love
for himself, for Miss Vaughan, and for the beautiful had
transformed his name to H. Adolphus Hawkins. His
waistcoats were made like Lord Melbourne's, and his
shiny hair went off to the left in a superb sweep, like the
hand rail of a banister. He wore many rings, breastpins,
and gold chains, and on his bland physiognomy, as on his
linen, was stamped, " Soft finish for family use." He was,
moreover, a poet, so much a poet that " he spoke blank
verse in the bosom of his family." " A pyramid of mind
on the dark desert of despair," he had, at the age of twenty-
five, drunk the bitter draught of life to the dregs and
dashed the goblet down. His productions were being
published in the Poet's Corner of the *Fairmeadow Adver-
tiser.* This popular paper also carried announcement of
the publication of *Symphonies of the Soul, and Other
Poems,* by Clarissa Cartwright. The Cambridge author's
satire upon Fairmeadow was read with particular delight
in the Connecticut River Valley. For a time after the appearance of Adolphus Hawkins, even the most sincere of
youthful poets felt a reluctance to advertise his musings.
Longfellow had meant to hit hard at the three or four

hundred poseurs who were infesting the Poet's Corner of many an American newspaper and magazine of the decade; it was merely unfortunate if a sensitive and genuine poet were caught in the undertow of his laughter. Some of the Amherst readers remembered his *Defense of Poetry* in the *North American Review* seventeen years earlier. Longfellow had then urged American poets to be more original, more characteristic, more national in their writing; to follow Sidney's maxim, "Look in thy heart and write." He had advised them to express their own feelings and impressions of what they saw around them; not to write with preconceived notions of what poetry ought to be, caught by reading many books, and imitating many models. "Let us have no more skylarks and nightingales. For us they warble only in books," he had declared. "We hope that erelong some one of our most gifted bards will throw his fetters off, and relying upon himself alone, fathom the recesses of his own mind, and bring up rich pearls from the secret depths of thought." But the Longfellow of 1849 had little to say to Emily Dickinson; for four years Adolphus Hawkins was italicized in her consciousness, as a letter from her to Dr. and Mrs. Holland indicates.

She was, in her twentieth year, beginning to put her pen to paper with pointed brilliance in amplifying the simplest theme. For a clever diatribe on colds, and another on snakes, see her letter to Abiah in January, 1850. We find here the first evidence of the unusual in Emily's prose. She is said to have sent a poem, *In This Wondrous*

Sea, to Sue Gilbert two years earlier, and we know that she was very fond of composing valentines, of which we have a sample in the long and spirited one sent to Mr. Bowdoin in 1849. As she cast about for a more ambitious theme upon which to expend herself — after all, what should it be? — a garden, a strawberry bed, a school-house, an attorney-at-law? At some time during these unsettled years Emily Dickinson's young friend and tutor helped her to a realization of her destiny.

Leonard Humphrey had for eight years been a member of most of the social gatherings of Amherst young people. He had belonged to the college fraternity, Alpha Delta Phi; and he, with six other freshmen, had formed a free-masonry of their own. Each wore a bracelet made of their seven shades of finely braided brown hair, fastened together with a golden clasp on which was engraved the initials of the devoted group, and the date, 1841. These intimates shared one another's food, thoughts, sufferings, and ecstasies. They were the masculine counterparts of Emily, Abiah, Eliza, and Susan. They kept their lamps burning late into the night as they filled their notebooks with indexed material on every conceivable subject. They donned starched, beruffled waistcoats, and Byronesque ties, and took a proud peep into the mirror at their short but fashionable beards. Then they gave an apparently in-different second glance at Mason's *Manual of Rules for Conversation,* and sallied forth in graceful leisure; for, ac-cording to Mason, "it was inelegant to be hurried." They carried the precepts of the indispensable manual with them to every party at the homes of Professor Haven or Tyler or Fowler, where most of them forgot all about Mason's rules, until on the stiff-backed sofa conversation lapsed and there was dreadful silence. Then the well-trained youth would recall that Mr. Mason had fortunately reduced conversation to a science, and they were saved by Rule Number Three! " When the conversation droops, revive it by introducing some topic so general that all can say something upon it. Perhaps it will not be amiss to stock your mind beforehand with suitable topics." Or if, in the emergency, Rule Three could not be made to work, there was the blessed Rule Five: " Never be a cipher in company. Try to please and you will find something to say that will be acceptable. It is ill manners to be silent. What is trite, if said in an obliging manner, will be better received than entire silence; and a common remark will often lead to something valuable. Break a dead silence." Participation in social life was a purposeful undertaking with these serious young men, for they kept the spirit of Mason, Rule One: " Choose your company for profit just as you do your books. If you receive neither improvement nor entertainment from your company, furnish one or both for them. If you can neither receive nor bestow benefit, leave that company at once." Leonard Humphrey, if he ever had been in need of Mason's Rules, certainly became an easy, graceful conversationalist, and a young man of exceptional social charm.

While Emily was writing to Susan Gilbert in senti-

mental amatory strain, the young men were equally concerned with, " What is Love — true Love? " They talked
about it, wrote about it, copied out definitions by the
dozen. Young Humphrey found the most impressive description of love in the autobiography of Gibbon (the one
great man on his list who was disappointed in love), and
quoted painstakingly: " I understand by this passion the
union of desire, friendship, and tenderness which is in-
flamed by a single female, which prefers her to the rest of
her sex, and which seeks her possession as the supreme or
the sole happiness of our being." Then he read to them
from Dobson's *Life of Petrarch,* and they pondered anew
upon the nature and effects of Love. The members of the
free-masonry listened to him with respect.

Emily had known him first as a lover of nature. On
the Fourth of July, in her sixteenth year, he had, as president of his class, delivered to an audience of several hundred persons on the top of Mt. Norwottock, a brief but
enthusiastic speech in which he had given the mountain
its old Indian name. Six weeks later his valedictory had
helped to win for him the principalship of the Academy.
He was then only twenty-two and very popular among
the students. His valedictory was a plea for the supremacy
of the intellect, and for the free expression of an honest,
unborrowed opinion. With the vividness of a youthful
devotee of Carlyle, he gave verbal pictures of the British
treatment of India, the colonial treachery to the red men,
and the United States Government's current dealings with
the Mexicans, which thrilled his youthful listeners. Even

the older folk were moved by his argument for justice in the world, for the logical extension of their rooted personal morality to a morality of states; deeply moved by the kindling of the spirit in a frail body with life ebbing from it like a slow tide. For Leonard Humphrey suffered from a constitutional weakness of lungs and heart, and his intensive study brought on many an illness during his student days when it seemed that he could not survive. During his patient struggle against inroads of pain, he kept close at hand his Wordsworth and his Sir Thomas Browne, his Addison and his Carlyle; and he filled his Index Rerum as did the youthful Thoreau and Channing and Emerson. His will to live and his courage had endeared him to all his friends.

In the winter of her seventeenth year, Emily Dickinson became a pupil of Mr. Humphrey, " the last valedictory," as she designated him. She was not a good student, but she was original, eager, and piquant in her reactions. She was inspired by Mr. Humphrey to a more intense zeal in application to her books. He introduced to his pupils other writers than the curriculum provided. Living for eight years in the Bible-bound village of Amherst, he found it well to have arguments in support of profane works. He read Foster's essay *On the Hostility to Religion of Polite Literature;* Macintosh's views on the value of literature to moral science; and Abbot's thesis, *Fiction: is it allowable?* Then if by chance his young pupil Emily came into the Academy library to rent a book some calm summer afternoon when the windows framed details of cloud and roof-top, he was prepared to support with apt argument his recommendation of *The Princess, The Culprit Fay, The Faerie Queene,* or Mrs. Hemans. He could boldly meet even the prohibitory views of an Edward Dickinson.

Emily wrote in 1862 that in her early girlhood she had had a friend who had taught her the meaning of immortality. So close to it was her friend and teacher that early in their relationship he had gone too near and had never come back. Leonard Humphrey had attended Professor Hitchcock's lectures in the college, and he now interpreted further to his Academy pupils the professor's conception of a natural religion and of an immortality deduced from scientific illustrations. He may have given original views upon the subject, for his mind was constructive rather than purely receptive. There is, however, one very oblique suggestion in his private notebook that this reference may be actually to Wordsworth's *Ode on Intimations of Immortality.*

When Emily came home to reënter the Academy in 1848, Leonard Humphrey had also returned to Amherst from a year in Andover. In spirit at least, he too had " stood up " against the theological background; though not with the vehemence that had marked his pupil's triumph in South Hadley Seminary. Beauty had claimed him from the first, but he was only now beginning to realize the extent of his allegiance. His Index Rerum contained sensitive impressions of the loveliness inherent in each day, and particularly notes on poetry. He now determined upon a career devoted to philosophy, took his

LEONARD HUMPHREY

Master's degree, and was made a tutor in the college. He resided with Professor Hitchcock.

Mr. Humphrey was the earliest friend who penetrated to the root of Emily Dickinson's problem and whose mind was compelling enough to dominate hers. He, too, had had confusion of purpose, and had been divided in his aims. He, too, came from Puritan stock. His father had been a teacher, selectman, and representative; his mother was intellectual, and strongly religious. He loved his mother devotedly and found his father to be warmly sympathetic. It was not Emily's personal problem of the family that he shared, but the problem of her spirit in relation to her time. Yet he did not break his heart upon the ramparts of Jonathan Edwards. He sharpened his brain, polished his wit, and turned his intellect upon every difficulty presented to him. He could think further than she did, in every direction. He was precocious in his reading. He had taste. He who had eagerly absorbed the *Lyrical Ballads* could not have joined in the village guffaw at Longfellow's satire on the poet. To Leonard Humphrey, a poet was the rarest of all men. Neither *Kavanagh* nor *The Maiden Aunt* held his attention long. His conversations were of the English writers, largely, and he recommended his favorites. It was youth teaching youth.

Emily's tutor and friend was deeply interested not only in literature, but also in literary men, primarily in those with handicaps; for he, too, had literary aspirations, being particularly inclined toward the essay and poetry. Certain questions were recurring as he read and thought and jotted down notes. What is the character of true greatness? Does marriage help or hinder genius? Is lack of health an insurmountable obstacle to literary achievement? Does lack of conversational ability handicap a writer? Is society worth while? Why has poetry endured?

His Index Rerum contains a list of successful writers who never married: Michelangelo, Boyle, Newton, Locke, Shenstone, Leibnitz, Hobbes, Voltaire, Pope, Adam Smith, Swift, Thomson, Akenside, Arbuthnot, Hume, Gibbon, Cowper, Goldsmith, Gay, Lamb, Washington Irving. He noted the effect of sickness upon men of genius as discussed in Carlyle's *Schiller*. He made a list of famous men who had lacked conversational power.

Of the sensitive heart he once noted: " To those who have suffered from the inexorable rule of Common Society, — who know the compulsory effort to talk, or the grievous burden of listening, — how delicious is that freedom of intercourse in which the soul is suffered to pause in the abundance of its thoughts, and need speak only when the thoughts overflow. It is said that if a silken thread be tied around a perfectly molded bell at the moment of sounding, the bell will burst asunder, and shiver into a thousand pieces. So is it when a heart of perfect and delicate harmony in itself seeks to manifest its life among other hearts; the slightest revulsion is enough to destroy the expression forever."

He acquainted himself with the hardships and the vices of literary life, and with the necessity of the solitary. Of special interest to him was the case of Edward Payson, the Portland preacher, who gave up society entirely "lest it extinguish the glow of devotion and entirely banish seriousness." "For myself," wrote Mr. Payson, "when I go into company, if it is pleasing and agreeable, it has a tendency only to fix my thoughts on earth, . . . and to give me a distaste for serious duties, and to render me desirous of the applause and approbation of those with whom I associate. I have at length obtained satisfaction respecting my doubts about society; not, however, till I was brought to give it up. After I had done so, it appeared so plain and proper, that I wondered how a doubt could ever have arisen on this subject. Now, I shall hardly see a person in a week, except our own family; and I have no doubt of being much happier for it." Yet Payson craved congenial friendships and said that he would give almost anything that he possessed for an experienced friend.

Leonard Humphrey had by study, insight, and arrowy sympathy come to recognize the literary temperament. His mind was vigilant. He early had made his choice between truth and repose. Especially was he thinking his way through to a philosophy of the literary principle, to a conception of the nature of true poetry as exemplified in Wordsworth. "Imagination is a higher intellectual faculty than is reason," wrote a champion of that poet in the *New York Review* in January, 1839. "Imagination has been cramped in the narrow definitions of the schools of metaphysics — teaching that its office is to dissect what nature offers, and then culling its materials to build up a new nature of its own. No — its chief duty is rather to take

nature as it is, and to disclose the moral and spiritual asso-
ciations of all that is palpable to the eye and ear, — to
show not only the outward world of sense, but the inner
world of the human soul — and to give them unity."
Together with this article in the *Review,* Humphrey noted
approvingly the *Preface to the Lyrical Ballads.*

When Emily Dickinson was between her sixteenth and
her twentieth birthday, her tutor talked to her of these
things. We do not know how much or how little he may
have said, but his mind could not have touched another
young mind without some such impress. One day, under
circumstances of which we have no dated record, he told
Emily Dickinson that she had in her the making of a poet.
He may have said it only once; we cannot know. But he
did not jest. He may have read some of her verses, but
he would have recognized Emily as a poet had he never
read a line of her writing. He had seen her reactions to
nature in the hills and the fields and the deep woods. He
saw in her the dream-power. Already she had, at times, a
unique turn of phrase. He spoke intuitively.

Whether it was the climax of a long conversation, or
only a passing remark, his words became to her a matter
of terrific import. They brought to a focus the warring
moods, the restless mind, the questing spirit, that exquisite
response to music and color and curve in a Beauty which
was like brothers and sisters to her. She had sometimes
wondered whether she were not a *femina insania.* Her
tutor had said that he wished he could live to see that day
when Emily would be recognized for what she was — a

poet! Years later when Mr. Higginson praised her poems she answered that she had had a taste of such intoxication long before.

During her mother's indispositions Emily prepared food for the family, set the table a little absented-mindedly, dusted vigorously, and often fell to dreaming dreams with color of gold, and her eyes open all the while. She was, just before her twentieth birthday, also dreaming of romance; but there was less of the sentimentalist in her now. Already she is writing thoughtfully to Sue that matrimony is something of a gamble. To the bride everything seemed rose-tinted, but what of the wife, mused Emily — the wife forgotten, perhaps!

One leafless November afternoon in 1850, when the hills were crusted with snow and windows shook and rattled in the wind, Leonard Humphrey went home to spend his Thanksgiving vacation in Weymouth, where his father was building a new house that would face the sunrise. He never came back. He had been stricken suddenly, and died on November 30th, in his twenty-seventh year, from congestion of the brain.

The news of his death was a profound shock to the young people of Amherst. Emily's letters indicate that she had received a note from her friend shortly before his death, in which he had declared that he intended to return to the lovely hill region whether he lived or died. His books: the Greek lexicon, Addison, his Carlyle, were

given by the family to his Amherst intimates. He was, so
Mr. Humphrey's nieces now recall, engaged to be married to an Amherst girl of his own age with whom he
was reading German, a girl who later became the wife of
a professor in the college. The engagement had not been
announced, but was understood among the young people
of the town.

A month later, Emily poured out her grief in a letter
to Abiah:

[2] " I write tonight because it is cool and quiet and I can
forget the toil and care of the feverish day and because I
am feeling lonely. Some of my friends are gone, and some
of my friends are sleeping — sleeping the churchyard
sleep — the hour of evening is sad — it was once my study
hour — my master has gone to rest, and the open leaf of
the book, and the scholar at home *alone,* make the tears
come, and I cannot brush them away; I would not if I
could, for they are the only tribute I can pay the departed
Humphrey. *You* have stood by the grave before; I have
walked there sweet summer evenings and read the names
on the stones, and wondered who would come and give
me the same memorial; but I never have laid my friends
there, and forgot that they too must die; this is my first
affliction and indeed 'tis hard to bear it. . . . When the
unreconciled spirit has nothing left but God, that spirit is
lone indeed. I don't think there will be any sunshine, or

---

[2] The quotations in this division of the chapter are from *Letters of Emily
Dickinson,* vol. i, p. 50.

any singing birds in the spring that is coming. . . . I wish I were somebody else — I would pray the prayer of the ' Pharisee '; but I am only a poor little ' Publican.' ' Son of David,' look down on me! . . ."

That such grief at the loss of Leonard Humphrey was commonly felt, is shown in a letter written at about the same time to his brother, Mr. James Humphrey, by Francis March, of Amherst College:

" He was in many respects my most intimate and dearest friend. If you at home knew his social virtues better than any of us, his college associates, our opportunities for intellectual knowledge of and sympathy with each other were such as are not often enjoyed by kindred, and they were improved with ardor. For my own part, when I recollect how gradually his frank and upright manner won upon my own reserve and shyness, and when I think of the long days that week after week, and month after month, we used to spend together in the most unreserved expression of our thoughts and feelings, I am sick at heart as I think of the future. I never expect to know another man as I knew him. I never expect to be known by anyone else as I was by him. No shadow ever came between us.

" The tie of blood could have added little to the pain I felt at his death. My hopes and anticipations of this kind of converse, the half of my mind, fell away from me.

" He had lived so weak, so long, and had seemed to

be gaining strength of late that I had come to expect that he would outlive me — and the shock was utterly confounding. Neither philosophy nor religion can teach us to mourn for him.

" May I direct you to our friend's papers? I hope some one will examine them with a view to their literary merit, and to giving a portion of them to the public.

" His is the first death that has ever occurred among my intimate friends. I have not yet learned this mystery." [3]

If Emily Dickinson had fallen in love with her tutor, she did not realize it nor ever afterward think of him in that way. It was over the open book with the leaf turned down that she was grieving; pupil and teacher, her study hour, and all that the hour under his direction had meant to her. He had given something in anticipation that she could reach without interference, and all the hurry toward it only made it larger and more certain. He had read from the poets, his Wordsworth, perhaps, and she had read from the poets, Tennyson, certainly, and her spirit had begun to loosen, at first so softly that she did not know it. She found that words could be put together to make links of sound that made the mind quiver and kept her still; and that there were combinations of words that gave swift flashes of beauty that left her hot and cold in turn. " This, then, is a book, and there are more of them," she had remarked upon reading her first imaginative literature. Thirty-three years afterwards, when Emily had hun-

[3] Letter in the possession of Miss Louisa Humphrey.

dreds of poems to leave to posterity, she traced her development to its fountain-head in a letter to Miss Whitney. Emily wrote that in youth she had thought ecstasy but of the essence of natural living until the death of her earliest friend. With him gone she had come to realize that it was he who had unveiled the deeper meaning of beauty, nor did she discover the full measure of what he had given until long afterwards.

Now, in her twenty-third year, her nature shrank and brooded as she looked out of her frosted windowpane into the interminable white winter. She had lost, for the time, her spiritual ballast. The sharpness of his going left a scar on her memory forever. She refers to it again and again in later years. Her confusion drove her inward. "I do not care for the body. I love the timid soul, the blushing, shrinking soul; it hides, for it is afraid. . . . We are very small. I think we grow still smaller — this tiny, insect life the portal to another. We are growing away from each other, and talk even now like strangers. To forget the ' meum and tuum,' *dearest* friends must meet sometimes, and then comes the ' bond of the spirit ' which is ' unity.' "

Had Abiah urged her to marry and *not* to be an old-maid writer of verse, that Emily replies: " You are growing wiser than I am, and nipping in the bud fancies which I let blossom — perchance to bear no fruit, or if plucked, I may find it bitter. The shore is safer, A., but I love to buffet the sea, — I can count the bitter wrecks here in these pleasant waters, and hear the murmuring winds,

but oh, I love the danger! — You are learning control and
firmness. Christ Jesus will love you more. I am afraid he
won't love me *any!* " ?

And Emily cries out to Abiah, who is also slipping from
her, " We are not so young as we once were, and time
seems to be growing long."

*

Chapter Six

THE YOUNG POET

*

ONE stormy summer night in July, 1851, the Dickinsons
took the stage to Northampton to hear Jenny Lind.
Just past the blacksmith shop the horses began to kick
and plunge, while the driver alternately filled their ears
with honeyed pleadings and their hides with smart lashes
from the whip. It was only a six-mile drive and the concert did not commence until eight, but the Dickinsons
needed the full two hours which they had allotted for
their journey. The most cantankerous of the beasts finally
refused altogether to proceed. Everyone got out, advanced
to the hotel, and for a season halted. Finally the driver
reappeared and invited his party to take their seats in
the coach, as he had succeeded in procuring another
horse; but Edward Dickinson refused to let the ladies
budge until the animal was " warranted." This done, they
all got in. They rode through thunder and cataracts of
rain into Northampton, paused at Warner's Hotel, but,
since the rain did not abate, they walked on in a speechless procession to the church. Jenny Lind sang her sweetest for this audience of Northampton friends and their

neighbors; she intended to reside here upon her marriage. But though bouquets were tossed upon the platform and the roof was rent with the applause of hundreds of their townsmen, the Dickinsons sat in disapproving silence. They had been piqued by the praise heaped upon this foreign singer. They were prepared not to like her. Her personality was pleasing to them, but her Swedish accent and coloratura voice gave little satisfaction to the provincial ears of Edward Dickinson and his family. Even Emily boasted that she did not care a fig for Jenny Lind. She got more pleasure from the drama of a little fruit-vender and a big ticket-seller swaying among faded people in a Boston railway coach, or from lectures by the famous men who came to town: Henry Ward Beecher, Edward Everett, Charles Sumner, Richard Dana, and even European savants.

But Emily was finding it difficult fully to enjoy anything now that Austin was away. He had gone to Boston to teach some little Irish boys in the Endicott School, and seemed to be having a jolly time of it. His gorgeous letters were filled with the fun of a life that embraced people and places and doings of all sorts. Austin was full of big hurrahs. Austin loved books and managed somehow to find out what was interesting and new in reading. Austin had cut capers in the outlined silences of the old house. Where he was he made things stir. With him away, all feelings must be kept under. Emily hated the stillness. On Sundays, while her parents napped or perused such papers as they were sure had nothing in them fleshly and unsanctified, and Vinnie conformed by singing above her unsteady piano accompaniment, "Are we almost there?", Emily wrote long letters to the brother whom she deeply loved, laughed in solitude over pages of his old letters, or read *Ellen Middleton* and the poems of Alexander Smith, which he had selected for her, and about which he had asked her opinion. Yet even Austin sometimes failed her, sometimes poked fun at her emotions. Once when she had spent a particularly long time in writing to him of her inmost thoughts and philosophy of life, Austin had not comprehended, had demanded a simpler style. Very well, thought Emily, in exasperation, I'll pull a hood over my thoughts and tie a tight bow under my longings; I'll have a bee in my talk and flaunt a rose in my hair and become but one more little fish in our social lake.

In a lecture on the personality of her friend, Emily Dickinson, Mrs. Mabel Loomis Todd has told how Emily in young womanhood had noticed with increasing resentment the tendency of the young men to pass by the more serious girls for the cuddly, fluffy type of sweetheart; that the girls who wanted to exchange ideas with their partners had fewer partners, even in Amherst. It was not a case of "sour grapes" with Emily. We know that she had such admirers as Thomas — who sent her valentines, ardent Mr. Bowdoin, brilliant William Howland, Henry Root, a friend who was determined that she should go for a drive through the May woods, and there had been her tutor who had compelled the girls to develop their minds. One of Leonard Humphrey's favorite stories had been the *Philosophia Minutiæ,* by N. P. Willis. It was the story of a young philosopher who became tutor to a girl in her teens. She was not beautiful, but she was an engaging child, contemplative, inquisitive, shy. He led her to cultivate a love for study. As he talked to her of her mind, its grandeur, capacities, and destiny, he was impressed with the charm of a woman's face upon which thought had cast its reflection. He taught her poetry, conversed with her on the probability of a future existence, revealed hidden beauties of nature to her. Tutor Humphrey wrote in his private notebook, after entering a brief comment on the story, " Beautiful. Intellectual women! "

But Thomas and William Howland and Henry Root had gone off to make their fortunes, and her tutor's voice had been choked with snow. As Emily made a survey of the social life in the village of her day, she observed the regularity with which strong-minded men were mating with weak-minded women. She saw a New England spinster in almost every household, an intellectual woman, usually, who had no true outlet for her mental energy. It was not polemics that Emily asked for. It was honesty, and less of sheer cruelty. She resented the fact that a girl often had to become something less than she was in order to win the passionate devotion of a man; that she had to put up her brain as well as her hair under a net cap. Emily knew what it would have meant to a daughter to have a mother who cared for thought. And she is said to have concluded, To perdition with such a society !

At about this time Emily seems also to have been disillusioned in some of her friendships. Here and there one had failed her in whom she had put her trust. Doubt had arisen in her relations with another friend. Such experiences were particularly harsh for one of Emily's affectionate and introspective nature. She began instinctively to come to anchor in her home. Perhaps in the familiar, one could find release, even though it be a plain, hard backdrop before which all fun and jokes would rattle unapplauded.

In her letters to Austin the cleverness and intensity of her girlhood, the bustle and bubble and brightness of a life crowded with people give place to a quiet sensitiveness to beauty, color, smoothness and grace, and the projection of personality into nature. When her father's house was filled, as it so often was, with visitors and relatives who cast a film over the day, Emily did one of two things as soon as she was free from her part in the domestic routine. She went out into the hills and fields, and carried parts of them home in her arms; or she withdrew to her room and sat by her window in the late afternoon when the sunset was full of heavy gold. The angularity behind her seemed to soften and to color. . . . When your cocoon begins to tighten and something is teasing you to come out, better not let them see it — those minds as ponderous as prayer. They'll lay something heavy upon you. They can't stop themselves. It's the Law of the Heavy. They'll close the fingers of their minds around you. They want to feel something warm and beating against their cold palms. They want to feel something struggle, and weaken. Bet-

ter lie still until the room is empty if you want to get free
with your wings unbroken. . . .

"If you were to be exiled upon a desert island, what
books would you take with you?" The old question was
put to a group of twentieth-century intellectuals. "My
Shakespeare, my Iliad, my Dante, Wordsworth, Goethe,
Emerson — " The scholars began to count their precious
wares. "My dictionary," said the only poet in the crowd,
whose notebook was filled with fifty poems written in a
little Spanish village where he had been isolated for a few
weeks. "If I were alone upon a desert island, I'd put my
mind to work."

This is what Emily Dickinson did in the level years
following the death of her friend and teacher. Her lexicon
was her sole companion, so she told Mr. Higginson later.
What did she gain from it? A very good time, for one
thing; as much fun as Eliza Coleman was having over the
flower and lace and ribbon counter in a Philadelphia emporium, or as Sue Gilbert may have had in a theatre in
Baltimore, or as Helen Fiske, at a West Point ball. Only
her fellow poets would understand, perhaps, how much
fun Emily may have had in this beautiful hill country
when alone with her mind and thousands of magical
words to strike upon it. In the second place, she would
gain speed and precision in selection when her power as
a writer became fully developed. The exact word would
slip into its place. Definition would help her to clarify her
thoughts. She would have distinction of vocabulary. A
study of the dictionary would not prevent awkward

FRONT OF THE DICKINSON HOME, THE OPEN WINDOW INDICATING
EMILY'S ROOM

sounds and obscurity in expression; but was it not a good foundation for a poet whose unit was to be the idea?

Was Emily Dickinson writing poems at this time? Such practice work, no doubt, as she would disclaim, even destroy, ten years later. At least we know that Emily had something of a literary history. In her Academy days she had written chiefly for fun. The boys and girls had admired her turn of wit and her swinging, spirited verse. They came to expect something from her. She acquired a reputation when some of her work was copied by local papers. Mrs. Bianchi tells us that Emily wrote " In this Wondrous Sea " when she was eighteen years old. Possibly this is the poem published in the *Complete Poems of Emily Dickinson* as " On this wondrous sea." Tutor Humphrey had left her dreaming, and (we must feel certain, though we cannot prove it) with a sheaf of verses upon which she had expended no little secret ambition. In 1852 something noticeably stimulating had happened. A valentine which Emily had sent to William Howland, who was now practising law in Springfield, had been given by him to Dr. Holland, the literary editor of the *Springfield Republican*. The editor had not only published the poem with its full thirteen stanzas on the editorial page on February 26th, but he had prefaced it with the paragraph: " The hand that wrote the following amusing medley to a gentleman friend of ours as ' a valentine,' is capable of writing very fine things; and there is certainly no presumption in entertaining a private wish that a correspondence more direct than this may be estab-

lished between it and the *Republican*." This was close to
being fame. Though her name was not given in the paper,
Amherst readers knew it. This public invitation, received
three months after her twenty-first birthday, was greater
editorial encouragement than has fallen at such an age
to the lot of many of the world's greatest poets. Emily
did not become a contributor to the paper, but she seems
now to have tried her hand at prose pieces for practice.
On May 9, 1852, she was at work by her window on a
"Lyceum lecture," while her mother slept and her father
and sister were at meeting. In the *Hampshire Gazette* of
this time one reads that "papers were submitted anonymously by Amherst ladies" and read before the Lyceum
in Northampton. There were several Lyceum groups in
the Amherst neighborhood.

Emily ran out with flying face in the late March snow-
storm to meet her father as he was alighting from the
stage-coach. "Was Austin coming?" When her grave-
eyed parent replied that of course Austin was coming, since
his father would consent to no other arrangement, her
face was like a star and her heart so light that it could
gallop around the world on a grasshopper.

Soon after the editorial recognition of her valentine,
Emily was seized with a wanderlust. She half made up
her mind to say good-by to her flowers and her piano and
the box-leaf bush, to slip a little bundle of earthly posses-
sions over her shoulder and saunter off down an uncertain
road. But hers was a household from which people did
not travel without some very definite and practicable ob-

jective. Her parents, who held the purse strings, were not the ones to be told that she was about to take a train and not very sure where she was going, or was off down the highway with no time set for returning. Then would come a blue, flowering day, or great cream-colored storm clouds that swept the earth with wind and rain, and left it cool and glistening as with a golden dew. Her dwelling became a palace; the far-away city, a wheel of dust and din.

There came a day in June, 1853, when the whole town was full of buzz, and carriages flew here and there " like sparks." Edward Dickinson, marshal of the day, led the procession with the air of an old Roman to see the new railroad " a-workin'." While the townsfolk cheered the turning of the spokes, Emily sat among the ferns and the humming grasses in the wood behind Professor Tyler's house. There was a new sound in the summer air. Sleigh-bells had melted into bird notes. Frogs by the pools and crickets in the trees had drowned the noise of the bees; but now above them all, even above the steeple-bells, there arose another, in long, rebounding curves of music, the sound of a bell from a passing train. There was a traveling whistle, and echoes in shells of smoke. . . .

Even Carlo, the large dog that her father had bought for her, was sometimes not enough, though he was preferable to people because he could understand without having to speak. Sometimes she felt a desperate longing to talk. The more people there were around her, the worse it became. Perhaps they, too, were lonely, each in his way;

but hers was a sharper kind, a closer kind in proportion to the riches for one who has found his best friend to be nature, or thought. Nor was Emily Dickinson without her living kinsmen, though she was separated from them by the high range of hills.

Three days after the appearance of her valentine in the *Springfield Republican,* over in Concord, young Ellery Channing,[1] on a footstool, pipe in mouth, by the stove, staring in, remarked to his visitor, Thomas Wentworth Higginson: "Nobody has any knowledge of beauty; it's the rarest thing. People all go along, just like dogs, without seeing anything in nature. It separates you directly from men, if you care anything about it, — you are unsocial and puzzle them. . . . There is Thoreau; he knows it, — give him sunshine and a handful of nuts, and he has enough. . . . Do you feel as though these New England people were your countrymen? I do not. Every New Englander looks as though he were just stopping here a minute on his way to parts unknown."

Though she had declined the invitation of a former schoolmate, Emily was overjoyed at the prospect of a visit to Dr. and Mrs. Holland in Springfield. The mere thought of it made her wild, and she began to check off the days like a counting-out game. Saturday she would sew, and Sunday she would fold her hands and sing Hallelujahs, and Monday was the day before Tuesday!

[1] *The Letters and Journals of T. W. Higginson,* edited by Mary Thatcher Higginson, p. 42. Houghton Mifflin, 1921.

It was stimulating to visit the Hollands. There one did not have to keep one's heart under. One could release all one's feelings and speak all one's thoughts. The doctor, only ten years older than Emily, was a strikingly handsome man with dark, olive complexion and black eyes and hair, which gave him a Spanish look. He was a man of sweet nature, with a strong moral sense which expressed itself in well-developed clerical attributes. Dr. Holland, moreover, was a poet. He had married in 1845 the petite and lovely Elizabeth Chapin, whose strong practical judgment offset his more imaginative temperament. The atmosphere of their home was like draughts of fresh spring water to Emily. She enjoyed even the doctor's family prayers, for they were to a friendly God. There were laughter and joking around the lamp-lit table. The doctor would smile at Adolphus Hawkins, Esquire, but not at poetry in general. Poetry was an art toward which he earnestly aspired, — successfully, many thought. He declared his great confidence in Emily's ability. He treated her as a fellow writer. Before their hearth fire there were tales of the Southland as far away as where the ships of Evangeline and Gabriel passed in the night. For Dr. Holland had, since his marriage, been teaching in Richmond, Virginia, and then in Vicksburg, Mississippi, and had spent some time with Mrs. Holland on a remote Louisiana plantation, heavy with dreams. He was, even now, engaged in writing stories of plantation life, when he could take the time from his duties on the paper. Since 1850 he had been assistant editor of the *Springfield Repub-*

lican under young Samuel Bowles, who was six years his junior. The editor and his assistant were said to have been never intimate, never more than " Mr. Bowles " and " Dr. Holland " to one another; for to Dr. Holland, Mr. Bowles was " a bit of a heathen," and Bowles thought Holland " something of a prig." Yet the instinct of the editor had placed the talented doctor in his office to give a literary tone to an otherwise political paper, and the literary department was proving popular, especially the Timothy Titcomb letters. Emily heard stories concerning many a literary personality, and experiences from editorial lips. The Hollands were tonic to her.

She rode home from Springfield in a glow of mind and heart. From the train windows she saw the beautiful Connecticut River, the curves of color, and the hills of green; willows edging the bottom lands, blackbirds dipping over the blue-white stones in the clear canals. The train ran close along the water with its ripples of light and shadow. A spire or two, cows, and a farmhouse yonder. And then the train swung into the hills and toward the rich spur of the range and the faint blue mountains.

She kept the afterglow for days. The memory of a visit to the Hollands seemed to shake out all the bells within her heart and sent waves of warmth over her. For a time thereafter her letters might have been ascribed to Adolphus Hawkins himself, so Emily declared to Mrs. Holland; but no sooner did she release her soaring fancies than an Amherst rooster gave a crowing recall, or she got a whiff of something left to burn upon the kitchen stove. After a trip to Springfield there were certain to be some bits of a broken dish around the stones by the back door-steps.

She and Vinnie sewed together and talked of their visit, until Emily exclaimed, "How far away from us they are!" but Vinnie answered, in surprise, "Only a little way." Then Emily took up the *Republican* and made such vivid, sprightly stories of the gentlemen in factories who get their heads cut off quite informally and the funny accidents where railroads meet each other unexpectedly, that Vinnie wept that the world had not been all accidents the day before. Sometimes in these little sewing-bees Emily and Vinnie tried to talk together about "life and things," but both sisters became shy and the conversation was steered back deftly to the Hollands. So freely could she express herself to these friends in Springfield that more than once her letters to them ended with a bit of prose that was really poetry (cf. letter, autumn, 1853), and in the same letter Emily inclosed the poem, "Truth is as old as God." Her allusion to a holiday of the heart and bells within in a letter during this year suggests a stanza in her poem, "Unto my books so good to turn." These verses of 1853, written a year after the valentine that was typical of Emily Dickinson's earlier work (so far as we have seen it), show that she had somehow found the form which was to be hers in the years to come. Dr. Holland praised her poems and occasionally sent her one of his, as author to author. There is a definite change in her handwriting at this time, we are told by Mrs. Todd, who edited the letters.

Upon the future Emily banked heavily. Sometimes her thoughts went riding off in an air bubble. They saw a hill down which a man in armor was riding toward her. The hill was hot with sunshine. Again the air bubble took her off in another direction, a very long way, at the end of which nothing was clear, but Sue and Austin were looking at her proudly. That it would take a long time for her to reach that goal which her tutor had set for her, Emily Dickinson knew. A hill, a sunset, and a dog may be enough for a poet in his middle years, but they were not enough for an Emily Dickinson of twenty-three.

*

Chapter Seven

WASHINGTON

*

In March, 1854, the Honorable Edward Dickinson, now Congressman, wrote from Washington for his wife and Lavinia to come down to the capital for a visit; and sent a peremptory command to Austin (a senior in the Harvard Law School) to escort the ladies. He added that Emily was invited but not compelled to take the journey. She seems to have made up her mind reluctantly, for she writes on the 17th of March that her mother and Vinnie are preparing for a trip to Washington, — with no reference to herself. But it would not have been in character had Emily refused ultimately to go, for she had never yet missed an opportunity for genuine mental or social stimulus. Was not her childhood playmate, Helen Fiske Hunt, now living in Washington since Lieutenant Hunt had been assigned to the Coast Guard service in the superintendent's office at the capital? And would she not see Emily Fowler Ford and her aunt and uncle in New York, perhaps, and Eliza in Philadelphia? These were cities with which every cultured person of the times had some acquaintance.

87

Careful preparations were made for the trip. Her mother and Vinnie worked ceaselessly. They must have new dresses, new hats and slippers, boxes and bags and a strong trunk or two; for they were to be away for several weeks, and traveling in 1854 was not so simple as now. From the dates given to the published letters we conclude that they left Amherst near the end of March and were in Washington throughout the first three weeks in April.

They probably left Amherst on the nine-o'clock train and arrived in Springfield at noon. They might have proceeded by train directly to New York, but this was, in 1854, the more tedious way. It would have been easier to continue by rail to New Haven and there catch the mid-afternoon steamboat to New York. It is to be hoped that Emily took the ride through the Sound and the East River. She would have had as keen a relish for the panorama as did the traveling " Boz," who recorded gleefully how he had crossed the Sound and passed Hell Gate, Hog's Back, Frying Pan Channel; had viewed sloping banks on either side of him, pleasant villas, turf, and beautiful trees; had steamed past a lighthouse, past a madhouse where the lunatics flung up their caps and roared in sympathy with the headlong engine and the driving tide; past the jail — and emerged into a noble bay whose waters sparkled in the sunshine. Then there appeared before them a confused heap of buildings, with here and there a spire or steeple, and here and there a cloud of hazy smoke; in the foreground, a forest of ship masts, flapping sails, waving flags. From among them the New Haven boat emerged and sped toward the shore, and the passengers were landed amid a jumble of steam ferryboats laden with people, coaches, horses, wagons, baskets, boxes. Beyond were the outlines of low and scattered houses in dusk and softly twinkling night lights. Here the Dickinson party may have remained overnight and proceeded next morning by railroad and two ferries to Philadelphia. From Philadelphia by steamboat they traveled toward another railroad station three hours distant; then on by cars and out again to cross a wide river in a ferry, whereupon they were landed at the continuation of the railroad on the opposite bank; on by cars, over wooden bridges which spanned two creeks upon which were drifting canvas-back ducks, and so into Baltimore. Here they may have stayed over a second night and gone the next morning by train directly to Washington, which they would reach before noon. This was exactly the way young Henry Adams traveled from New England to Washington four years earlier.

From Amherst to New York Emily journeyed through the familiar beauty of Massachusetts and Connecticut landscape. From New York southward, a change came over the world. There were a number of negroes in Amherst and there was intense feeling over the whole national problem. A goodly quota of Amherst families were preparing to take the trail to Kansas. They were determined that Amherst should have a part in poulticing that slave-bitten outpost with the mustard of a New England conscience. Emily's father had thrown himself with no little mental violence into the Whig cause in Massachusetts. He was even now serving on the Congressional Committee to investigate conditions at the arsenal in Springfield and the one in Harper's Ferry. He had been president of the Taylor Club in Amherst, had attended the recent Whig convention in Baltimore, had taken up the cudgels against the Anti-Whigs of western Massachusetts, and had snapped off his subscription to the *Amherst Express,* when that independent little paper put the Free Soil candidates, Martin Van Buren and Charles Francis Adams, on the faces of their editorial banners. Mr. Dickinson had written a long and clear-cut letter to the editor on the political situation, a letter which was reprinted in the *Springfield Republican.* Samuel Bowles' newspaper often gave considerable space to the Honorable Edward Dickinson, who could so impressively state " certain plain truths in a plain way." From the age of fifteen, Emily had reflected her father's political views as though she had been his pocket mirror, but she had never before been in a slave state. Slave states were dirty, cluttered, poverty-stricken, ignorant, vicious, according to New England Whig training and the eye's evaluation. Yet the picture had another side. There was a raggedness of outline that carried the imagination into careless places. The railway, about the size and character of the modern trolley, rambled haphazardly through unfenced fields and woods, or through village streets, among a medley of pigs, cows, sties, and negro babies who sprawled over the doorways of blowsy little cabins and in nests of gourd and potato vines.

In Washington, the air was reeking with the thick odor

of cherry trees and catalpa bloom. Amber sunshine and leafy shadows were on the earthen roads and the streets with their meandering wheel tracks. Even such permanent department buildings as had been started were unfinished and uninhabitable. The Post Office and the Patent Office faced each other in the distance " like white Greek temples in the abandoned gravel pits of a deserted Syrian city." Here and there wooden houses were scattered along streets that held patches of pavement and no lamp-posts. The open squares destined for beauty spots were as yet densely over-grown with weeds. From her window in the Willard Hotel, then very new and the finest hostelry in town, Emily Dickinson looked out into a world that was altogether strange to her. The mellifluous indolence of a warm climate heavy with color; the burly sensuousness of a negro population; the freedom, " the swagger," the drawl; the lackadaisical listing of nature; the roaming of pigs in the streets; the scarlet bandanas above moist black faces; the colored cab-drivers calling softly from waiting cabs; servants drawing water from wells and springs; the warm, full figures of Southern women in billows of sprigged flounces; the handsome figures of cavalier swains in their light trousers, ruffled waistcoats, and tall beaver hats — were soothing to a nature that shrank instinctively from New England cold. Washington in the spring of 1854 gave the warmth of a hothouse and the romance of the undefined.

At night the streets were dismal, dark, and dangerous. Only Pennsylvania Avenue was lighted. From a neigh-

boring window a traveler pushed out a shutter as a distant
clock struck twelve, and leaned over the sill. The night
watchman was approaching on his beat. The traveler
gazed uncertainly down the thoroughfare, then called
softly to the night watchman and dropped down a letter to
be posted by the obliging public servant.

The Senate Chamber in those days was said to resemble
a pleasant political club; the tempests seethed under the
surface. Southerners were in control. Only a few days
before Emily's arrival Cutting had challenged Brecken-
ridge. The political battle lines were tense. In the House
of Representatives Congressman Dickinson flung himself determinedly into the fight against the Nebraska bill.
It was strange to hear the Honorable Edward Dickinson
declared " not in order " by the chair and to have hisses
mingled with applause when a vote upon his request for
a reading of the bill was announced. It was exciting to see
him in the center of the body calling upon Honorable
Jefferson Davis, the Secretary of War, for information respecting applications for the position of Superintendent of
the Armories at Harper's Ferry. Not unfamiliar, however,
to hear him voting " Nay " on measure after measure —
honest votes.

Emily writes with special enthusiasm of their trip to
Mt. Vernon. One April day her party had boarded a
brightly colored boat for the leisurely passage down the
Potomac. They went gliding softly past the old land pa-
tents: Bully's Disappointments, Billingsgate, Arrel's Folly.
How Emily must have loved the mention of names be-

tween Georgetown and the river: Noise Enough, Water
Piece, Conjurer's Disappointment, Frogland. The Potomac
was held in its channel by raw, earthen bluffs. The moment the boat had moored, Emily and Vinnie leaped
ashore and wandered along an overgrown pathway to the
tomb of General Washington, where they paused in silence
before going on to the beautiful old house itself.

Every evening there were brilliant assemblages in the
Willard corridors and the lounges. Most of the prominent
visitors to Washington stopped there. Edward Dickinson
had a large acquaintance in the capital's official life, not
only among the New England delegation, but also among
the Southern members with whom he served on commit-
tees. His wife and daughters were invited out to receptions,
dinners, and functions of one sort and another. There was
drama, color; there were flower-scented April nights;
there were conversations threaded with every conceivable
topic (except Puritan theology): the visit, two years earlier,
of Mr. Thackeray, Mrs. Stowe's novel, dueling, Mr. Sumner, Mr. Douglas, Cuba, Mrs. Pierce's levee. A Washington woman writing in the *Springfield Republican* at the
time remarked that one could talk more freely in Washington than in any other American city.

Emily was gayer than her family had ever known her
to be; — unforgettable. In Amherst she had known college
boys of keen mind and personal charm; she had known
professors, lawyers, clergymen, all of the New England
type. Now she saw the New England type contrasted with
another. There are legends of how she was quickly rec-

ognized as quite unusual by men many years her senior. Her biographer tells that she created a sensation by her knowledge of affairs of state, her wit and repartee. She was at home in the *salon*. In Washington in the spring of 1854 Emily Dickinson was like an exquisite blue-and-orange butterfly released from its chrysalis, that darts here and there with rapid shimmering testing of its wings.

She writes to a friend of the wonderful times; the distinguished companies, the glitter and courtliness. But better than anything that has yet happened to her, she adds in a note to Sue Gilbert, is her approaching reunion in Washington with a friend of her youth.

One evening not long after her arrival in Washington, Emily was summoned to the drawing-room. The cards which had been sent up had thrown her into a tremor of excitement. She made her way eagerly through the jostling throng and exchanged rapturous greetings with the vivacious, sweet-faced girl who bore her matronly honors well. The latter introduced her escort, who placed upon a convenient receptacle his scarlet military cape and his dark-blue hat with its pompon and its emb..n of a turreted castle. He joined the ladies easily in conversation. His uniform of gray trousers with red side stripe, dark-blue coat with brass buttons, the bar on his shoulder, and his scarlet sash and tassel, offset strikingly his unusual physique. He had strong features, a serious face, lighting easily with flashes of humor. Though he was only thirty-two years of age, he had already attained distinction. He proved to be as

Photograph by Handy, Washington, D. C.

THE OLD WILLARD HOTEL

charming a man personally as one could meet, brilliant in
mind, as colorful in his entire personal background as in
figure. In any conversation he very soon embarked upon
an exchange of ideas. Though his interests were universal,
and indeed there was no subject upon which he could not
contribute something, his special absorption was in the
field of science; he had a delightful way not only of pre-
senting his ideas, but of probing the mind of his companion.

He had been born in 1822, a poor boy in a back county
of western New York, the youngest of a family of nine.
As a child he was never known to play, but was always
ready to work with alacrity at anything. And there had
been enough to do. His remarkable physical strength and
the intense pleasure which he found in using his hands had
been well measured in pioneer life; but in study lay his
chief interest. It was, from the first, an absolute necessity
of his nature that his hand or his head be at work. His
brain never knew satiety. So avidly did his mind crave
knowledge that he almost totally lacked a capacity for
recreation. As he hoed and weeded and chopped wood,
and hunted and fished, he came to love Nature for
her facts as well as for her fancies. Everything interested
him and he trained himself from infancy to think. Until his eighteenth year, his education had been almost
entirely self-acquired. For only a limited period of two
or three terms had he been able to attend the village
academies, yet so thoroughly had he prepared himself,

that when he did take his place in a classroom he at once took the lead of his classmates. This complete freedom of his formative years had been of immense influence. He was original, and he had the whole universe for his mental hunting-ground. When he was nineteen years old, his brother, Washington Hunt, who was then a Congressman, had secured for him an appointment to the Military Academy at West Point. He entered that institution July 1, 1841. He was ambitious to attain a perfect record, and although he had as classmates the selected youth of the country, he was always well up toward the head. He had an eye upon himself rather than upon his rivals. His record each year indicates something of his aim. In mathematics, philosophy, ethics, chemistry, geology, and engineering, he was each year third or second in his class. Only twentieth in conduct during his first year, he advanced to third, first, and fourth in his later years; he was second in general scholastic record in his senior year, graduating in July, 1845. Promoted to the army as brevet second lieutenant, he was made assistant to the Board of Engineers in New York City. On December 29, 1845, he was made second lieutenant, and a year later he was asked to return to West Point as acting assistant professor of engineering (August, 1846–August, 1849). In 1852 he was transferred to Boston, where he became assistant engineer in the construction of Fort Warren, and on October 26th of that year, at the age of thirty, he married in Boston a charming girl of twenty-one. Better than anyone else he had ever known, she reacted to life in that careless, laughing, adventurous way which was so foreign to his own nature. She could play enchantingly, even with hearts. No stronger testimony to his personal attractiveness could be given than the fact that it was Edward Bissell Hunt who had won the heart of the romantic Helen Fiske, a belle from childhood.

Any man who was so attractive to Helen would certainly be of equal interest to Emily. Emily was personally fascinating when stimulated, and had an individual brilliance of mind which her childhood playmate had not yet shown, though Helen was very animated, witty, and amusing. Helen had become a great social favorite, with charming taste in dress, but no one as yet dreamed of her as a literary woman. She was, at twenty-three, devoted to her infant son and to her husband. The Hunts had cards to the White House, to the homes of Secretary Davis and William W. Corcoran, and to other exclusive places, in all of which, elegant entertainments were being planned for the American Association for the Advancement of Science, which was to meet in Washington on April 26th. The Willard Hotel was to house as many of the delegates as possible. Professor Hitchcock, Professor Snell, Professor C. B. Adams of Amherst College all attended these annual meetings, and it was of interest to Emily and to her family that Lieutenant Hunt was to read a paper before his fellow scientists. There was everything for Emily, Helen, and the lieutenant to talk about together. Emily must also have had conversations apart with Lieutenant Hunt, for undoubtedly they met several times during these three weeks in Washington, — at the Willard, at those large receptions attended by everyone in the relatively small group of officials in Washington in 1854.

Lieutenant Hunt had a magnetic appeal for Emily. She was accustomed to meeting governors, congressmen, judges, but Edward Hunt opened a new world for her. The army, between 1848 and 1861, was small and stationed at widely scattered posts. Arsenals and forts were objects of visit for the curious. The military was not a popular service. The active men and those stationed on the frontiers were the engineers who were building forts and surveying the route for a railway to the Pacific, or cleaning out and enlarging the channels of our waterways and our harbors. To this girl from the hill-encircled New England village, Lieutenant Hunt in his colorful way revealed a new vocabulary. In his assignment to Professor Bache's Department of Coast Survey (then a subdivision of the Treasury Department), Lieutenant Hunt was especially charged with the engraving of the charts. He must, of course, have explained to Emily something of the Coast Survey service, about which she would show a natural curiosity. He must have told her of the object of the survey, a systematic, continuous, and accurate sounding out and delineation of the marine bottom along our entire coast line. The plan was to obtain and publish accurate maps of the shore line, in all its ins and outs, from Maine to Texas, from San Diego to Fraser's River, omitting no island, tidal river, harbor, bay, branch, or lagoon; to make frequent soundings abreast of this coast line so as to secure a picture of the ocean bottom along our coast. The unveiling of the mysteries of the great deep was to be extended so far seaward as to furnish every practicable aid to the navigator in identifying his position.

Lieutenant Hunt had invented the interranger, an instrument designed to facilitate the running of sounding-boats on lines between signals. He was also especially interested in a self-registering tide-gauge. So keen was his understanding of the scientific aspects and values of such things, that he was frequently chosen by Professor Bache to explain the instruments to the scientific world. He sent long, closely written reports to the superintendent, and wrote articles for scientific journals. As a mathematical physicist, Lieutenant Hunt was at thirty-two considered one of the most promising in the country; though in his speculation upon cause and first principles he was somewhat inclined to neglect or disregard practical applications or results in detail, and so was in danger of being considered fanciful rather than substantial. His doctrine of molecular physics was considered to be of great potential importance to science.

He is said to have chafed at the necessity for having to earn his living, and passionately desired to free himself for a life given over wholly to study and invention. He would often spend the entire night in concentrated thought upon a point; and one morning, after a night of such concentration, he announced that he had solved a problem that had puzzled him for years.

But he was not a man of one passion in his interests. He

had knowledge in every direction. He believed that " the man of science who assiduously cultivates a chosen specialty becomes therein preëminent, but in so doing he is in great danger of losing his grasp on those generalities which transcend his particular field, and of becoming not only impotent but bigoted relative to those branches which he has not pursued. The power to generalize and the power to specialize must coexist in the true magnate of science. Great things may be done by men strong in either; but not the greatest. Whoever neglects general culture in his eager pursuit of the special, harms his own nature." [1] In a paper on Lithography (1853), he protested against "chromatic glories on muddy backgrounds of sooty ink. . . . Lake-faced Dulcineas and green-haired Corydons that glare down from the most sequestered cabin walls, in suspense between the rifle and the red peppers . . . are enough to arouse the Jacobinic spirit in one to whom art is a thing of sanctities." He proposed that copies of well-selected masterpieces should be made by lithograph in order to improve the national taste.

His conversation, charming in its expression, entertaining and even amusing at times, was inclined to be usually of a serious nature. He hated trivialities, gossip, and petty argument, and when he had a congenial companion, he liked to indulge in philosophy. Though he knew his Bible well, he was not a " religious man." He refused to affiliate with any church, for he had a great dislike of the theologian's narrowing effects upon the mind. His argument

1 *On an Index of Papers on Subjects of Mathematical and Physical Science.*

was that " science interprets God. He has wrought into the fabric of material nature those ideas and designs which he has chosen to adopt. The inorganic and organic worlds are thus records of divine thought and intent. Science reads these records. Through long historic ages the mind of man has been accumulating knowledge and slowly gathering to itself the means for deeper and clearer insight. The work of interpreting nature goes on with increasing success, and with ever-expanding faith in the Designing Author. Intelligent communion with Him augments and grows intimate. Loftier views and grander insights throng upon us. The higher scientific mind of to-day has learned to see in and through ' the invariable order of occurrence ' which prevails in nature, a grand expression of God's supreme will unfolding itself by a secular progress. What once was Fate is now our Father's will." [2]

He was particularly absorbed in a study of Infinity. " It has seemed to me a correct criticism on the usual modes of considering the subject of infinity, that they regard it too exclusively under its metaphysical or speculative aspects, and too little in its physical or actualized forms. When we consider that a mathematical formula is the nearest possible approach to a literally divine thought, we shall bow with reverence before the suggestion shadowed forth by the sublime symbol of infinity after all created limitations are eliminated from its significance. This symbol affords no basis for the commonly received idea that infinity means an absolute unboundedness, a quantity absolutely

[2] *Union Foundations.*

without end, a quality of nature transcending all boundaries. Such an idea has no right in the mind of man, for
the limitations of human perception forbid our attainment of any knowledge either of the extent of the absolute
cosmos or of the boundaries around what is abstractly
possible. The formula of infinity, so far from stating an
absolute boundlessness, endlessness, or illimitable magni-
tude, states simply the limitations of finite perceptive
power. It is the expression, not of the immeasurableness of
nature or of the Deity, but of the finite limitations of the
human mind. It stands for a negative, and not for a positive; it symbolizes not knowledge, but ignorance. If we
group infinite attributes under a divine name, we have
not defined Deity, but we have defined the limits of our
own conceptions. The limits of our knowledge lie near
at hand; the limits of our ignorance are known only to
the All-knowing." [3]

When he delivered these ideas in papers before learned
societies, they were cameos of knowledge; when he enlarged upon them in his easy conversational way, with his
apt and sympathetic illustrations, they became the essence
of poetry.

That his personality, different from any that she had
known, and his philosophy, running counter to New England transcendentalism, made the profoundest impression upon Emily Dickinson, we know from an unpublished letter written by another. From Helen he learned
much of her history and her talents, but he did not need

[3] *On the Idea of Physical and Metaphysical Infinity.*

this assistance. His keen and trained intellect had always been quick to perceive origins and causes. He recognized in her an unusual mind. She had a piquant charm. She had wit. She was *vive*. In the friendly warmth of this exotic atmosphere, Emily was beautiful. He met her father and mother. He plumbed to the depths of her personal problem. When he liked a friend he took particular pains to show it. He would go out of his way to contribute to that person's happiness, the more eagerly in that by nature he could detest as heartily as he could admire. It seemed that Emily could not learn enough from a mind strong enough and rich enough to meet her own. For the second time in her life, she had found a " master," in her quaint usage of the term, and a friend.

The three weeks in Washington passed as in a dream. For once, Emily's pen seems to have lain idle. In the only published letter which we have, written apropos of this visit, she says that her friends in New England seem blurred, and sometimes she wonders if she has dreamed this visit, if the world is all a dream, and Amherst but a hearsay, Springfield a fancy on a phantom river. Dr. Holland, Minnie and the dumb-bells — she hopes they will remember her until she becomes — more sensible. Why didn't she think to ask if they were all well and happy. Strange to be — *forgetful* Emilie!

*

Chapter Eight

PHILADELPHIA

*

FROM Washington Emily Dickinson and her family journeyed to Philadelphia, a handsome city of clear definition, with the mental tone of the Vicar of Wakefield, in the opinion of Charles Dickens; but Samuel Bowles thoroughly enjoyed his trips to the orderly city. He admired the imposing stores, and Chestnut Street where the ladies promenaded, "magnificently dressed." The broad-brimmed hat, wide white collar, and sleek crop of the Quaker were much in evidence, and "Thee" and "Thine" fell strokingly upon the sensibilities, in every large emporium and thoroughfare.

In Philadelphia, the Dickinson family were guests at the home of Emily's girlhood friend, Eliza Coleman. Eliza's father, Reverend Lyman Coleman, had been for seven years pastor at Belchertown, and later for three years (1843–46) the classical instructor at Amherst Academy. He now conducted the Presbyterian Academy of Philadelphia at his residence, 1008 Chestnut Street. A widely-traveled man, of scholarly tastes, he was maker of the famous Coleman map of Palestine. He had been professor of German at Princeton, and was later to occupy the chair of ancient languages in Lafayette College. He was a writer on church history and author of *The Historical Geography of the Bible*.

He had a handsome, ruddy face and could have passed for father of the Greek gods. Known as a " weighty and impressive " preacher, something of the *Ernst* which he had acquired from his contact with Teutonic scholars had infected his younger daughter Eliza. As Emily once put it in a letter to Austin, E. C. had grown fearfully learned, was sending back to Amherst letters which were a mixture of Plato, Socrates, and Jove. Mr. Coleman's profession and reputation sufficiently recommended him to the exacting Edward Dickinson, while his sympathy and graciousness as host made the sensitive Emily feel at home in the four-story brick house on Chestnut Street.

" What Philadelphia most needs," he said to his guests, " is a hill or two. Those who are privileged to spend their lives in Massachusetts are much to be envied the daily view of mountains. In my private musings I am habitually traversing those hills and valleys." For the moment the Dickinsons were back in Amherst.

In social conversation Mr. Coleman was not so formidable as his scholarly attainments might suggest, but was affable and attractive, for he had a lively imagination and told stories, of which he seemed to have no end. He had acquired great freedom in society in New Haven and Hartford, and in Philadelphia was constantly meeting public men from all parts of the country, from whom he gathered information as to politics, finance, literature, and science. Eliza told Emily that "he understood about as well the mechanism of a steam engine or clock or furnace as though an expert." To the unmechanical Emily he seemed Jove indeed.

Though a clergyman, Lyman Coleman was skeptical as to the value of mass movements in religion. He had observed Mr. Nettleton, the New England revivalist, and had learned how to guard against the evils that would seem to be inseparable from revivals. He called himself a conservative on the subject, and so he must have heard with particular satisfaction how his one-time pupil, Emily, had stood up at Mt. Holyoke in resistance to Mary Lyon's plan for a Christmas fast in preparation for the annual prayed-for revival.

"What you did, Emily, reminds me that on Sunday I am going to take you all to hear the preaching of a man who has your independence of spirit. He is the pastor of Arch Street Presbyterian Church. When he was a freshman at Hamilton College, there was some injustice that roused a protest among the students, and he led ninety per cent of his class over to Union College, at Schenectady, New York. He is a most individualistic young man. He started as a teacher in Litchfield County, Connecticut. He was assigned to a school where the previous teacher had been hung out of a window by the leg. He told me the other day how he gained mental and moral ascendancy over these students." Mr. Coleman chuckled. "The first day, he assigned one page of Vergil and the students sneered at him, for they thought him too young to know more than they did. At night he shaded the lamp in his room so that they could not see how late he had to study to cover that one page himself. The next day he assigned two pages, and studied them himself until midnight. On the third day he assigned three pages and spent most of the night in study. The next day, four pages, and studied all night. The following day the students squealed for mercy."

"Who is he?" Emily whispered to Eliza. Before her friend could answer, Mr. Coleman proceeded:

"He comes by his independence of character naturally, by inheritance from Captain Joseph Wadsworth of Hartford, the man of ' Charter Oak ' fame. You know the story of how Sir Edmund Andros, appointed Governor of New England, attempted to read the proclamation by which the Connecticut charter was declared forfeited, and how Captain Jo ordered the drummer to ' Drum.' When Andros verbally assailed the drummer, Wadsworth drew his gun and threatened the drummer if he should cease drumming. Captain Joseph was said to be the chief actor in secreting the charter. There is a strain of fighting blood in all the Wadsworths. Philadelphia is proud of her Arch Street preacher, and strangers come from far to hear him. People stopping at hotels inquire for his church and are directed to it by the clerks. I am fifty-eight years of age and have listened to many sermons, but none that can compare with his. I remember two years ago about the time of the funeral of Henry Clay, there was the usual overflow crowd at Arch Street, but by chance one seat in the gallery of the church was not taken. After the sermon had begun, a tall young mountaineer from Kentucky took the seat, but as the preacher launched into a vivid and moving description of Henry Clay's body borne with torchlight procession through the city, the Kentuckian lifted himself up, with his gaze transfixed upon the preacher, seemingly so entranced as to have lost control over himself. The whole congregation saw him, but the preacher did not notice him. The people expected the listener to break into a cry, which would have been a relief to them, but soon the preacher's vibrant voice softened and relaxed and relieved the crowd. With that art to which his audience was accustomed, he brought his remarks to a conclusion with a few words that eased them all. The young Kentuckian sank into his seat, his pent-up feelings finding relief in low racking sobs." Emily might have wondered whether the sermon she was to hear on the coming Sunday would be as dramatic.

"Dr. Charles Wadsworth attended Princeton Seminary and came to us from his first pastorate at Troy, New York, where under his ministry one hundred young men joined his church. When he effected the present organization of the Arch Street Church, there were only twelve families associated with him. Before he had been there long enough to receive his first quarter's salary, the congregation crowded the building, and pews ever since have been almost unobtainable by those who have sought to rent them. The secret of his popularity — No, I will let you judge for yourselves. You will find him different from other clergymen. He never gets into doctrinal disputes. He says 'he has his opinion of fools.' He avoids dissensions of every kind, and does not care even to take part in the discussions at church meetings. Once the Arch Street people raised a fight over the question of having a paid choir. After hours of fruitless argument, they called on him. 'Dr. Wadsworth, will you please give your opinion?' He replied, 'So long as those who cannot sing, will, and those who will sing, cannot, I am in favor of paid choirs.' The argument was thus ended." The Emily Dickinson who ridiculed the singing in the Amherst meeting-house must have clapped her hands with delight.

With anticipations aroused to hear Philadelphia's greatest preacher, on Sunday morning the Dickinsons must have accompanied their host with alacrity in the walk of the three short squares from 10th and Chestnut to Arch above 10th. A number of Quakers, the women in gray bonnets, passed them, bound for the Arch Street Friends' Meeting. The church which the Dickinsons approached was an imposing building, with tall tower and spire. The façade and steeple were highly ornamental, exhibiting from base to summit the Doric, Ionic, Corinthian, and Composite orders of architecture. The Dickinsons must have entered the church long before the hour of service, for by then most of the seats were always taken. As minute after minute went by, more people poured in, until they filled every pew and crowded the emergency benches in the aisles. The latest comers choked the aisles and sat in solid phalanx "upon the stairs leading to the sacred desk"; they "stood in the galleries and in the vestibule and many went away unable to gain entrance." It was time for service; the organ had begun playing. Where was the preacher? Or rather, if the preacher were in the building, how could he possibly reach the pulpit? It would be more than difficult and intensely awkward were he to attempt to push through such a crowd. But these musings were cut short, for suddenly, a trap door opened in the floor of the pulpit, and the tall, slim figure of Dr. Charles Wadsworth emerged from the basement.

He was dark in complexion, with black eyes and black hair that hung to his collar in the fashion of the day. There was Italian blood in him. When Emily Dickinson first saw him he was exactly forty years of age.

Twenty years later she wrote that the most beautiful sermon she had ever heard was the story of Judas and Jesus which the preacher told as though it were an everyday narrative of two intimate young friends. The source of Dr. Wadsworth's power and the secret of his popularity was his love for Jesus. The climax of his eloquence was his ability to sway the people with a sense of the anguish inherent in a Christian life of power; the cross and its glory, Christ crucified and exalted. One who heard him felt that "behind all he said there must be years of conflict and agony, of trials and sorrows, of deep gloom and despondency, of strong cries and tears." This quality of identifica-

REV. CHARLES WADSWORTH

tion of himself with deep suffering was traceable a long way back. In his seminary days he had made an impression with his tender and forceful appeal to the heart and to conscience. In those days he was living in a room alone some distance apart from his fellow students. He seemed to have been born of moody waters, Emily herself concluded many years later. His pathos went to the heart. Yet he turned toward his hearers also the bright side of the cloud. He loved the old ways and could get out of them enough of piety, philosophy, and novelty to make even rugged duty, however rugged, a pleasure. It was said of him: "He could lay his hand on an audience as a harper, by his fingers, sweeps the full chords, until all the varieties of melody answered the master's touch. . . . Thought, argument, learning flowed out of him like a bird's song; poetry, pathos, eloquence were blended into a white heat. It was the poetry of preaching."

As Emily Dickinson listened to the sermon by Dr. Charles Wadsworth that Sunday morning in April, 1854, she had opportunity to realize that while the noted clergyman had reached the pulpit most surprisingly through the floor, he was not "a sensation preacher." He shrank from notoriety, demonstrations, applause. He sat down after the sermon with a sense of failure. The church was crowded, and yet so unconscious was he of it all, so modest in his estimate of his ability, that when the service was over he frequently asked the sexton whether there had been many people present. His was "humility unfeigned, allied with so much greatness and mellowness, no less than deepened by divine grace that it threw a great charm around his character and gave him an attractiveness seldom met in such a world."

Mr. Coleman took his guests a second time to hear the famous preacher. Dr. Wadsworth frequently preached on such untheological subjects as Stars, The Dignity of Labor, Reading, Life and Food, Looking (a sermon to children), Common Sense, Politics, and Poetry. On such secular subjects he was as free of fanaticism as of metaphysical intangibilities. Once when there almost occurred no-popery riots in Philadelphia, he was called out to help fight for the Protestant cause. He refused, saying, " When I am working in one field, it is not incumbent upon me to throw rocks over the fence into the next field where others are working." His style was bold, original, brilliant, suggestive. Through all he said ran a polished wit and effective sarcasm, used in good taste and with propriety. Literature with its riches and culture he laid under heavy requisition, yet kept it as " a servant of the sanctuary, not a divinity enthroned in its shrine. The ornaments of his style were not a painted rhetorical confectionery hanging like the appendages to a Christmas tree, but the spring blossoms and autumn fruits clustering on a tree planted by the waters of life. Men found in him not a dreamer weaving poetical fancies, but a voice of the Spirit dwelling in this temple." He was as powerful and persuasive a preacher as there was in this country at that time, not excepting Mr. Beecher.

Through the kindness of her host, who was in a position to introduce his guests to Dr. Wadsworth, Emily Dickinson met the clergyman, whose dark countenance seemed to her to hold a hint of mystery. She found in him a friend. His wife was a Bostonian by birth, an intellectual woman, socially attractive and exceptionally beautiful. Though he was very expressive when preaching, Dr. Wadsworth was reserved, almost shy, in social intercourse. He had a Wordsworthian love for nature and a talent for writing verse not to be unexpected in one whose genealogy contained the names of Henry Wadsworth Longfellow and William Wordsworth himself. The clergyman was so near-sighted that he could not readily distinguish the faces in his congregation. When first he secured a pair of spectacles which gave him practically normal vision, he had stayed out all night to look at the stars.

It was natural for Emily Dickinson to talk with him of poetry and immortality, and sweet reasonableness in the affairs of earth. In all probability he spoke to her much as he expressed himself in his sermons: " Dying? What is dying? See that little worm, rolled up in a kind of little cobweb, fastened to a twig? By-and-by it opens, it is unrolled. Out flies a splendid butterfly! That is dying! "

Of the sensitiveness of genius he once said: " The songless domestic fowl will eat everything, but the nightingale's feeding is so choice that the fancier finds great difficulty in preserving either its song or its life. . . ."

Of the poetic spirit of modern America he had said in November, 1852: " Genius, so long delighting in rose

leaves and reveries, has sprung from the day dreams of its
youth, and gone forth to the substanial enterprises of its
manhood. Imagination hath itself become practical in
its energies. Poetry is not dead, for the word ' poet ' means
a creator, and its powers will cease only when a progressive
race has attained the loftiest height of its possible strivings.
Nor does poetry sleep even. Spite of all sentimental lamen-
tations over the homely utilitarianism of this age, it is,
after all, the most poetic and imaginative of all ages. But
then imagination hath become practical. The poet, the
creator of these later times, brings forth, not day dreams,
but realities. The steam engine is a mightier epic than
Paradise Lost. [This was before either Walt Whitman or
Emily Dickinson had written a poem on the locomotive.]
The magnetic telegraph is a lovelier and loftier creation of
true poetry than Spenser's *Faerie Queene* or Shakespeare's
Tempest. Genius hath flung the flowery garlands off,
and gone forth with a bronzed cheek and a hard hand,
to work for a race in the very van of advancing civilization. Whether in literature, or politics, or religion, the
man of dreaming speculations, and subtle metaphysical
theories, is at best a mummy of a bygone generation,
and ought to be secluded from the busy world in a
glass case, as a remarkable specimen, a monstrous
curiosity."

He may have revealed himself as a poet of peculiar
fellowship with the mind of Emily Dickinson by quoting
to her from his own poem delivered at the Union College
semi-centennial, July, 1845:

"And what is Death that I should fear to die?
I have communed with Nature as a friend,
And she hath taught me a philosophy
Starry as her own midnight, and doth bend
From the far heavens in glory to illume
With a strange light on the darkness of the tomb."

It was the stimulus of his mind and character that the distinguished preacher gave to Emily Dickinson. There is a strong probability that many of her poems on themes of death and eternity later were colored by the answers he gave to her eager questioning, and therein is our justification for a close scrutiny of his mind.

He was vigorous and fearless in his opinions, some of which provoked controversy in the newspapers of the time. He had a strong aversion to the bathos of anniversary harangues; to blusterers, sham-chivalry, swaggerers, quixotic politicians "who project interventions and invasions, as though the American eagle were only a game and gaffed fighting-fowl." He believed that the age needed men who had true and tried courage; who were not afraid to explode an old dogma, however popular it may have been for centuries, if it be a falsehood; nor to stand by an old custom against the world, if it be fundamentally true; who were not afraid "to tear the religious vizor from the face of a false reform, nor to turn the back on the old Sphinx of conservatism in the direction of a true progress."

He particularly disliked "those mongrel and monstrous good men" who considered slavery to be the only evil on

earth, and total abstinence from strong drink the only
virtue out of heaven. The age, in his opinion, needed
eminently the comprehensive man: the man whose mind
half an idea could not satisfy, in whose soul half a world
would leave a vacuum; whose religion was not breathed in
some sectarian shibboleth; whose patriotism could cross
a state line; whose morality did not " vapor everlastingly
about some one isolated cardinal virtue." He felt that the
age was in need of individuals who could be true to an
ideal; who were not victims of spasmodic feeling for attainment, whirlwinds on the sea, raising waterspouts, but
whose lives were inspired by a master passion, " like the
steady sweep of a trade wind, rousing the whole sluggish
ocean into billowy and resistless life."

It was said that a five-minute conversation with Dr.
Wadsworth had changed the course of many a life.
Friendship with him would serve to strengthen one whose
high purpose was already clearly defined.

" This one thing I do," seems to have been the inspiring
motto of his own life. To use his words concerning Paul,
" He was a man of one idea; one master passion moved
upon all his life-strings; one great object he cared for; one
great thing he did." He devoted all the resources of his
genius to his preaching. Dr. Charles Wadsworth had that
rich endowment of nature which Emily Dickinson herself well understood. It is said that he would go along
lonely streets, seemingly to avoid men. " He chose to walk
solitarily along the paths of life, in fellowship with Christ,
whose thoughts were his companions by the way."

He was a true aristocrat of the mind. He recognized power and genius in young Emily Dickinson. As one close to him has said, "If she were a poet, he would have identified her as such." His brilliant genius, his good sense, courage, and optimism became a portion of the human background from which she drew spiritual sustenance. Though he so often sounded notes of anguish in his preaching, his philosophy of life was essentially one of joy; and in this joyousness he drew nearer to her than did many of her other friends. Perhaps the fact that he was the senior by several years of all her other selected friends gave him a position of special trust as one of her " silver shelf."

In his own poetry Dr. Wadsworth sang of " life, with its triumphant harmony " (in his stanzas *On the Death of Mrs. Hemans*). He shared with Emily Dickinson the assurance that immortality is stronger than a hope. He said:

> " We are as those that on the main
> Have caught from far a landward strain."

And further:

> " The solemn voice of woods and streams,
> The song of evening's fading beams,
> And this fair chain of living things —
> This glittering cloud of insect wings —
> A strain of glory heard above,
> And heard below, a strain of love."

The qualities in him that she herself commented upon later were the delightful sense of fun with which he met her own engaging manner; and his ability to solace the thoughts that had disquieted her from childhood. " My friend . . . my great friend," she said of him.

In a paraphrased letter on page 46 of *The Life and Letters of Emily Dickinson* we are told that Emily and her sister were to visit in New York after Philadelphia. When she returned to her home in Amherst after an absence of about seven weeks, the hill region was blue and green and white. The cherry trees were in full bloom, and the peach blossoms were opening. . . .

*

Chapter Nine

THE LOVE STORY

*

SUPPOSE while one were examining in the British Museum a collection of manuscript sources of the Arthurian tales, from between two adhering pages there fluttered a small sheet — a sheet which proved to be a page from the private chronicle kept by the old servitor of Astolat, which read: " To-day Elaine, weeping, did speak to me of all her young life, and of Sir Lancelot's friend, the knight Mordivere of the King's Court, whose favor was to her the light of Heaven, and how his plumes did beckon in the clipping wind as the gate swung to. Of him only did she speak . . ." Or imagine the reader chancing upon a hitherto unbroken letter signed by the confidential Minister of Queen Elizabeth: — " but more than Raleigh or Essex or any gentleman of her Court the Queen secretly favored Sir Ronald Whiffen. Once, under stress, she told me how she and he talked together long and late with one mind, one heart; and the last time that he came through a secret portal into the castle . . ." Or, misplaced in the files, a note in the handwriting of Georgiana Keats: " Of all the women John ever saw, it was the lovely Phyllis R—— who held his thoughts these fifteen years. And when she said, . . . and how at parting . . ." Would the reader have any peace until he knew the whole from which such a fragment had fluttered?

So when an admirer of Emily Dickinson, reading in the Boston Public Library the manuscript letters and poems sent by her to Mr. Higginson, comes near the end, upon an unobtrusive letter from Mr. Higginson to his wife in which he says of his confidential talk with Miss Dickinson in 1870, "Major Hunt interested her more than any man she ever saw. She remembered. . . . And when he said he would come again in a year . . ." the mind of the reader leaps inquisitively. Who was Major Hunt? Why has this friendship been altogether omitted from her biography? What was his exact place in the pattern of her life? Could he, after all, have been the inspiration of Emily Dickinson's love poems, yes, even the impetuous lover of the family legend?

The love story of its poet is the richest heritage of a race. Emily Dickinson gave of her mind and of her heart joyously, unsparingly in a long " letter to the world." She shaped every thought, every heartbeat into beautiful songs though her own life went unsung. She wrote to the world about her love. She tells us that she had to keep her love a secret from those about her. Circumstances made her course necessary. Almost all her real life was something of a secret from them, anyhow. She once wrote that it was better to be afraid of a secret continually than of it and whom you told it to besides. That secret pushed triumphantly within her breast. The peril of it acted like a spur upon her soul. It seemed to her that she had never written but one or two poems, she said, when at the crisis of her "danger." But though she sang of her love unstintingly and in every aspect of its being, "her letter" was given to the world a few pages at a time, and spasmodically. Even now, according to an uncontradicted record, we have only about one-half [1] of "her letter," and the pages are shuffled. Her love story is consequently not as clear, perhaps, as she herself wrote it. We are, however, exceedingly grateful for the pages that we have.

For forty years no one attempted to pry into the factual side of Emily Dickinson's love story. It isn't the sort of thing one cares to pry into. It was tacitly accepted by a puzzled public that "her seclusion was due to no love disappointment," which was interpreted by the public to mean that there was no human background for these great love poems. Then came the story of Emily Dickinson's love for a clergyman, "all that concerns the public," a public that includes the family of the noted clergyman as well as the Dickinson family, a public to whom Emily Dickinson now belongs. It will seem to certain persons, perhaps, an impertinence to try to draw aside the veil that

---

[1] According to the *Book Buyer*, May, 1892, and also correspondence in the Galatea Collection, Boston Public Library, " besides the poems collected in the first volume [*Poems*, Series One] and in Series Two, at least 1200 poems were catalogued, and no one knows how many more." This would mean a total of at least 1600 poems, it would seem. Up to date, including *Further Poems*, only about 800 have been published.

keeps this poet's love story still something of a mystery. Such persons like to see all life through a veil. Emily Dickinson did not. It will seem to others, perhaps, something of an impropriety to raise a question where facts have been given by a member of the poet's family.

But while the ensuing study of Emily Dickinson's life, particularly her love story, may not yet have gotten at the whole truth, the presentation of such suggestions and the results of such research as may help to bring out the truth, is legitimate. Though it is doubtful if any single living person can give the whole story of Emily Dickinson's love affair, it is certain that several persons together can contribute facts which will clarify the situation. Such clarification is for the good of Emily Dickinson; it is for the good of American letters. Let us, then, consider the facts at hand in an effort to " carve away the mists " and let the figure of Emily Dickinson's lover show " his royal front."

There seems to be complete agreement that Emily fell in love upon this Washington-Philadelphia trip, and that her love was reciprocated. She met a great many brilliant men upon this trip, particularly in Washington. We do not know how many of these friendships may have been continued after her return to Amherst. Her father was continually entertaining in his home men notable in public life. Two friendships have so far been italicized; one formed in Washington, one in Philadelphia. Emily herself has eliminated one of these two new friends as a candidate for the possession of her heart in youth; for in a letter to Mr. Higginson in April, 1862, she says that after the death of her tutor she had formed one more friendship — only one — of great importance to her. Their happy relations had been altered because her friend wanted her to be more to him than his " scholar," and he had gone far away — away even from the land.

The biographer of Emily Dickinson has frankly stated that so far as the family were concerned, the secret of the poet's heart remained a secret to the end; that such confidences as may have been told to Mrs. Sue Dickinson, the biographer's mother, were never divulged to anyone. It would be natural for the family to draw their own conclusions and it would not be surprising if in the hundred years that have passed since the birth of the poet some confusion might now exist in the family recollections of what happened so long ago. Dr. Wadsworth is undeniably the subject of the Clark letters to whom attention is especially drawn in *The Life and Letters of Emily Dickinson,* but the facts of his life, as will become evident in the development of the narrative, leave a grave doubt as to his identification as the urgent lover with whom the public has become somewhat familiar. Indeed, we must certainly conclude that he could not have been " the lover," for his life does not accord with the story as it has lingered in the Dickinson family. Dr. Wadsworth cannot even have been the subject of Emily's important statement to Mr. Higginson in April, 1862, for the noted clergyman was still in Philadelphia when Emily was writing, but Lieutenant Hunt had literally left the land.

It has been suggested that Emily Dickinson's lover went west, the continent's full width. As a matter of fact, all of the men who were Emily's friends went west at one time or another. Three of them went to San Francisco: Lieutenant Hunt, in the fall of 1858; Dr. Wadsworth, in June, 1862; Mr. Bowles, in 1865. The first two named went on the business of their professions; the last, for travel. No one of them remained. Is it ever the west to which Emily's thoughts go? Ever the west of which she writes?

Emily Dickinson said that he went from the land. In 1857 Lieutenant Hunt was sent upon a long assignment which amounted practically to exile to a little island off the southern tip of Florida, a very hot, tropical island. Is it not, rather, the south, with its spices and tropical flora that colors her thoughts as she writes? We can go a step further. In an unpublished excerpt from a letter to Mr. Higginson in 1863 Emily Dickinson refers to that island, not by name, but by description.

Mr. Higginson says in his article in the *Atlantic Monthly* (October, 1891) that his Amherst friend made of him a confidant as well as a literary mentor. There is evidence of that in her published letters to him. A letter from her to him in 1863 and another with the published date of 1868 but which was, by internal evidence, 1866, contain sentences which strongly suggest that she was writing to Mr. Higginson about Major Hunt (as the latter was by that time designated). There were reasons why she might have mentioned Major Hunt to him. During the summer of 1863 Colonel Higginson was stationed not far from where she supposed her friend to be. In one of his reviews Mr. Higginson refers to Major Hunt's " quite unusual mental attainments." The *Atlantic* essayist first met Helen Hunt in 1866, and in the months of association that followed, Emily Dickinson's name was undoubtedly mentioned between them. He makes a published reference to the fact that these two women had been schoolgirl friends.

When Mr. Higginson went to Amherst in 1870 he went to meet the real Emily Dickinson. He had long wanted to do so. He had asked her relatives and friends about her wherever he had met them, but could get no satisfactory information. He had more than a literary interest in her. He felt something poignant in her case, and he had become truly her friend. Shortly after the death of Emily Dickinson he published in the *Atlantic,* and later in *Carlyle's Laugh and Other Surprises,* his impressions of that interview with his Amherst friend and some of Emily's remarks to him. All that he repeated has been accepted as a pulsating record of her mind. In the letter to his wife, written a few hours after his talk with Emily Dickinson, he gives more of the interview than he could publish in the 'nineties. There was no levity, no affectation in that conversation. The mood, the tone were so sincere that one cannot but take as the stripped truth everything that is given in that letter. He does not tell all of how Emily referred to Major Hunt, but she expressed herself in a manner that convinced Mr. Higginson of the supreme importance of the major's name to her, and he bequeathed that letter to posterity.

Until further letters are published which will throw more light upon that Washington experience we cannot know all that we should like to know about the love story of Emily Dickinson. Probably some of the story never will be fully known. One wishes that Emily might be permitted to speak for herself. One feels that she would wish to. It is inconceivable that anything ever was written by her or to her that could not be published. Emily herself once said that her life had been too devoid of incident and too unbending to cause embarrassment to anyone.

That she met the husband of Helen Hunt, that they became interested in one another, that he was calling upon Emily Dickinson in Amherst afterwards, and that when she was forty, and living upon a long memory, his was still the name of consequence to her, are matters of record. Was Lieutenant Hunt the one other, who was not satisfied she be his scholar? The internal evidence supports the suggestion that he was, as the narrative will show. When a forgotten picture fits a discarded frame, and that picture, metamorphosed into a jewel, fits the antique setting, it is more than coincidence. Nor are we made any happier to read that the letters from Emily Dickinson to Helen Hunt Jackson marked by Mrs. Jackson for publication after her death, disappeared; nor to find the only letter from Emily Dickinson to her friend which did manage to struggle through, split at the sentence that contains the word " forgiven " and republished in *The Life and Letters of Emily Dickinson* as two letters, with the second addressed " To ——," though the two are one letter to " H. H." on page 425 of the *Letters* edited by Mrs. Todd.

Even with the facts established, the influence of Edward Bissell Hunt upon two notable American women writers is important in literary history, so important that one is inclined to think we should erect a monument to him instead of trying to sink the spade a little deeper. I propose to continue the narrative of Emily Dickinson's friendship with Lieutenant Hunt as I believe it happened. I shall go beyond documentation only where there is a reason. Such reasons will be evident to those who will read and consider from this point of view all that has been written by and about Emily Dickinson, Helen Hunt, and Edward Bissell Hunt. Furthermore, there are persons living who have been in a position to know more about Emily Dickinson than has yet been given to the public, and memory tends to corroborate rather than to disprove the fact that Emily fell in love in Washington in the spring of 1854.

Emily Dickinson came from the capital in a dreamy state of mind. She had formed a romantic and violent attachment for a man, under impossible conditions. It would seem that every thought of him should be spiked with the sense of Helen: Helen's hands, Helen's kiss, and confidences, and childhood's games at growing up. On the contrary, Helen simply didn't exist for the time being, except as she intruded herself, and then she was a different

Helen. It was bewildering. For days Emily lived in the sensuous warmth of spring along the Potomac. Before she had time to shake herself thoroughly awake came the sermons and friendship of Dr. Wadsworth, seventeen years her senior, widely experienced in personal problems, and with a genius for deftly touching a life whose vane was a little unsteady. But even after she had heard him preach, it is the Washington scene that she is reliving, as she slips away from company to write to Mrs. Holland, and Minnie, and the doctor.

In certain respects Dr. Wadsworth resembled Dr. Holland, Emily's early poet friend, but the former was a much more brilliant and definite personality. Dr. Wadsworth and Lieutenant Hunt court a more interesting comparison. Both were comprehensive, creative. Each had a master passion as steady as the trade wind. One was a man primarily emotional, a poet, who wrote verses to express the mystical meaning of beauty as he saw it in all its outward aspects. The word was his medium of expression. The other was a man primarily intellectual, a mathematician, a " Euclid who looked on Beauty bare." With his eager hands he invented concrete expressions of the abstract with which he was continually preoccupied. The line, the curve were his medium of expression. One was devoting his life to the building of churches; the other was constitutionally so opposed to church forms that he preferred not to affiliate with the institution in any way. Dr. Wadsworth would have understood Lieutenant Hunt; no doubt would have sympathized with him to some extent. It is doubtful if Lieutenant Hunt could have sat through a sermon of even so brilliant a preacher as the famous Philadelphian, for the lieutenant hated the spilling over of emotion, and the mob reaction to it.

Emily Dickinson had something of each in her. She had made friends of both. Every one was an experiment to her if he had a body of seed within his mental husk. Both busy men of affairs, be it said to their distinction, sought her out in her village setting, encouraged her, made her one of their world. It is important that we know what influence each may have had on her mind and poetry. Their influence upon her personal life is particularly interesting, for there is indication that the drama of that southern journey was continued in Amherst to a certain extent almost to the time of her death. The man of heart had the greater influence upon her mind; the man of mind captured her heart.

Shortly after the visit of Emily Dickinson in Philadelphia Dr. Wadsworth was invited to preach at Amherst College, probably at the suggestion of Edward Dickinson, the college treasurer. The clergyman called at the Dickinson home. He may have been entertained there at tea, for Mr. and Mrs. Dickinson would be quick to extend such a courtesy. Emily talked with him again. She was always the questioner, eager, thoughtful, unprejudiced. As her letters show, she had strange and exquisite phrases for her thoughts. She compelled sympathy and affection. That their conversations were of an impersonal nature was commented upon by Emily herself near the close of her life when she wrote of Dr. Wadsworth to Mr. J. D. Clark, that the clergyman never talked with her of himself, nor did she attempt to penetrate his reserve. A conversation with him " toned her up," but it was not until much later in her life that she came to feel the full value of what the preacher had to give. She herself has said that it is opposites that most strongly attract one another. She was twenty-three and she was in love.

The year drew to its close. The snowflakes were falling, blotting out the footpaths, covering the wheel tracks, until the white stood up high against the houses and Amherst froze into the coldest winter in twenty years. But neither sleet nor frost could now penetrate to her heart, for she was wrapped in a hope that was warmer than her merino shawl — a hope for the perpetuation of that friendship which acquaintance with Lieutenant Hunt promised her. For it was he who aroused her into an expression of herself as no one else had ever done. Such self-expression was ecstasy.

Edward Hunt had chosen a career in the Engineering Department of the army, for the world demanded that a man earn his living, but he yearned to devote all his time to study, to a solution of those problems in physics and metaphysics which baffled and fascinated him. He could not help it. Put him to work on a problem of engineering in Boston harbor, and in three weeks he was absorbed in a new theory of gravitation and measurement of distances. Give him an assignment on charts for the Coast Survey, and within a month he was working overtime on a huge index of scientific subject matter. Order him to make repairs upon an old fort, and before the fort was one-third completed Lieutenant Hunt was sitting up all night working out an interpretation of Mariotte's Law. Not that he neglected his duty. "I know," once wrote his chief, Professor Bache, "that if you will undertake this work, it will be well done." But his mind was sleepless and without boundaries. His mind pushed to make room for itself. From childhood his whole being had been loyal to his brain. In those days there were so few in America who were devoting their lives to thought. One not only found almost no companions in such a life; one had to fight for the right to it. Shut oneself up for sheer study and the world would rap upon the walls, tease at the keyhole, and sometimes point a finger at "lack of initiative and ambition."

Until he was thirty he had lived in a man's world more or less. The free existence in the New York back counties, the seven years at West Point, had given him a habit of spending his surplus hours as he pleased. Then he met Helen Fiske, and fell in love with youth, vivacity, and sex-appeal. He was a man of strong physique and intense nature, a large, forceful man with the creative spirit. With marriage, women, all women had new meaning for him. But marriage and a growing family brought interruptions. It now became doubly hard to get time to be alone. He was proud of his wife, but, like the idealist, the sensitive thinker and man of mind, he regretted the turmoil of sex in life. He wished, unconsciously, perhaps, for a woman who, unlike Helen, would be all mind to him, wholly an inspiration without being likewise a distraction. For he was not long enough married in the spring of 1854 to find his wife much more than a charming distraction to him.

His transfer to Washington a year before his marriage had in one respect at least proved fortunate; for Professor Bache, who was himself a world-renowned scientist, took an interest in young Hunt and granted him time off for the annual meetings of the American Association for the Advancement of Science, where Lieutenant Hunt made friends and invariably distinguished himself. His army chief, however, was not so sympathetic with the extra-activities of the young physicist-engineer. Also, Lieutenant Hunt's fellow scientists found him impulsive, excitable, and, in their opinion, over-theoretical in the sectional discussions. In one of the earliest meetings which he had attended, back in 1849, he had been so insistent upon his theory that when his fellows had opposed him in the discussion, there was confusion, and the elder members had had to silence the eager young theorist.

In the spring of 1854 he met Emily Dickinson. She was the most brilliant woman he had ever known. She had an interesting face, a distinction of personality. After any conversation with her one kept on thinking about her, yet not so much about her as about something she had said. She left a stab in memory, not of pain, but as of a flower with all its color chaliced, straight upon its stem apart; or as that stop in memory which a haunting music will invariably find. He could talk with her as with a man; though she was personally pleasing, she did not obtrude her sex. She was a good listener. She would lift her fiery brown eyes to his in eager questioning. She could sit for hours and let him explain his ideas. In one respect she was better than his fellow scientists; she did not try to make him see the world in her way, but her one desire was to understand his conception of things. Furthermore, she could forego, wished to forego the round of gaieties that took so much of one's time from the real business of living — the projection of the mind into the unknown. She, too, was a patriot indigenous to intellect. When they talked it was as though they were huntsmen together in green and sovereign woods. Emily was not good at facts, but she " rived the dark with private ray." It seemed that in her he had found the ideal, the platonic affection. They became friends, in Washington. After her departure from the city there were letters which enkindled the minds of both. He began to talk with her about the subject matter of the papers which he was preparing. He turned to her more and more for inspiration and understanding.

Helen was not well so much of the time, and he, too, was ill and discouraged, for the Washington climate was proving to be injurious to them both. The first summer after their marriage they had remained in the capital, and the effect had been devastating. Lieutenant Hunt began to show symptoms of bilious dyspepsia, a family weakness from which one sister had died and a brother was near death; so in the summer of 1854 Lieutenant Hunt took his

family north, probably into New England. His ailing son
died in August and was buried in the West Point cemetery. In the following spring Lieutenant Hunt succeeded
in getting a transfer and was assigned to the Newport
neighborhood, for the construction of lighthouses.

There was only one occasion when he left his work, that
being the A. A. A. S., regularly in August, after 1854. For
the meeting in Providence in August of 1855 he prepared
one of his most provocative papers, and on his way home,
he stopped in Amherst to call upon Emily Dickinson.
There was a brilliant conversation. The lieutenant, fresh
from the stimulating discussions in Providence, was scin-
tillating. Emily, excited beyond her wont at the presence
of the uniform in her stiff New England parlor, was be-
witching. That Lieutenant Hunt talked with her of the
subject which was a part of the Providence discussion is
attested in the Higginson letter of fifteen years later, which
helps to date the visit, though we seem to be but following the manners of certain ladies of her day, in dogging
the poor young man's footsteps so closely and in trying
to peer into that cool, dim parlor. When Emily was but
twenty she had declared that she did not care for the body,
but the spirit was everything. She liked letters so well because they were one's thought without the enveloping
friendly body, she remarked later. We can, in general,
judge considerably even without the letters between them,
what some of their points of mental contact actually were,
for the records of the lieutenant's ideas are copious, and he
never wasted time in trivialities.

Into her closely bounded world the intellect of Lieutenant Hunt threw a brilliant, probing light, playing upon
and X-raying, analyzing and synthesizing. Sometimes they
looked at her world as through a microscope; again,
through a slowly revolving telescope. Upon the Pelham
hills was August haze, which might remind the lieutenant
of certain optical effects of which he had spoken only the
day before in Providence; lovely scenes from Crow's Nest
on the mountain just north of West Point; from Jones'
Hill in Sleepy Hollow; and from a sailboat in the harbor
of Newport or of Boston. He had a way of using illustrations close at hand. We know from Mr. Higginson's letter
that gravitation was one of the subjects of their conversation. Among other points, Hunt held that the sense of
gravitation depends on our sensibility in each part of the
body and limbs as an obscure physiological sensation of
weight and pressure in a particular direction throughout
the components of our bodily frame, a sensation which is
probably greatly dependent on the circulating fluids. As
they were talking together, Carlo lay on the floor near by,
his sober eyes filled with infinite wisdom. The dog showed
a particular liking for the young scientist. The lieutenant
turned from Emily, who was fascinated with his ideas and
was eagerly trying to understand, and he smilingly remarked, "Your dog understands gravitation." Indeed,
Carlo was a better logician than was his mistress.

Lieutenant Hunt tried to help Emily to see that energy
as well as beauty awakens in us a sense of the infinite. To
her he seemed to be serving Heaven, or trying to, when

he sought to approach a revelation of God through the reduction of all physical facts to mathematical abstractions. This was beyond her comprehension, but it was delightful to try to follow such conceptions under his guidance. Here was a man who could give her something entirely new. Her mind was untrained, but it was acquisitive. Her immediate world, even in its most commonplace aspects, became magical combinations of atoms and molecules in a great scheme. The whole world was mirrored in a dewdrop. She could sit for a lifetime in her garden or in her room, and in the playing of the daily changes of wind and rain and light and heat about her she had enough to think upon. Or so it seemed when he was with her or was writing to her. The world through his eyes took on aspects of an utterly fresh and magnificent poetry. How different from the science that she had once studied in school, the petty cataloguing of plants and of stars!

She could talk to him. She could tell him how the attempt to put her mind in contact with her mother's was like sinking it into a little feather bed, and he would not shrink, nor stiffen and coldly change the subject. She could speak every thought she ever had, and he would listen with gentleness and interest. For he believed that " it is not the method of true philosophy to belittle nature to our standards, but it is our duty to seek facts without bias or preconception." The singular beauty of his mind was its pristine freshness. Emily's mind had still some of the rag-tags of her New England heritage, but under his tutelage they were blowing away. . . . She might tell him of those five days of Amherst sleet and snow and windy rain after which all the houses in view of her corner window had been hung with soft fog that melted into a clear topaz day, and he would recall how he had studied from a train window a fog that hung over the houses and over the Hudson as he came down the river, and he could give a certain swift factual insight that did not take away any of the beauty, but only served to etch it in. " I think that the root of the wind is water," Emily begins in one poem, and in another, " The moon upon her fluent route," she packs into eight lines a large conception of evolution, culminating in the present dawn of humanity. She could hold up her end of a serious conversation with Lieutenant Hunt.

The hours must have seemed but one striking of the clock. It was a meeting that Emily Dickinson never forgot, — the peace, the flight, the violet afterglow. From the memory of such an occasion may have come the theme of her poem

> " I died for beauty, but was scarce
>   Adjusted in the tomb,
>   When one who died for truth was lain
>   In an adjoining room.

> " He questioned softly why I failed?
>   ' For beauty,' I replied.
>   ' And I for truth, — the two are one;
>   We brethren are,' he said.

"And so, as kinsmen met a night,
We talked between the rooms,
Until the moss had reached our lips,
And covered up our names."

When Lieutenant Hunt, at parting, told her that he would come again in a year, he added, "If I say a shorter time it will be longer."

For two such minds it was a difficult age in the history of our country. Said Mr. T. W. Higginson a little more than a decade after the conversations between Emily Dickinson and Lieutenant Hunt in Amherst: " One rarely sees in America, outside the professions, a man who gives any large portion of his life to study; and the professions themselves are with us mainly branches of practical activity, not intellectual pursuits. . . . The true great want is of an atmosphere of sympathy in intellectual aims. An artist can afford to be poor but not to be companionless. . . . What, then, is to save these virtuous and devout communities from deteriorating into comfort and good dinners? I know of nothing but that aim which is the climax and flower of all civilization, the pursuit of science and art. . . . It can scarcely be said that science and art have as yet any place in America; or if they have, it is by virtue of their prospective value, as with the bonds of a Pacific railway." [2]

There is no reason to believe that the lieutenant failed to keep his promise to Emily. Let us say, then, that he

[2] *The Atlantic Essays,* by T. W. Higginson: " A Plea for Culture," and " Literature as an Art."

stopped in Amherst again on his return from the meeting of the A. A. A. S. in Albany in August, 1856. These
friends probably recognized in the preceding summer that
parting was more painful than either had anticipated.
Now in the summer of 1856, after many more months of
probable correspondence, it would not be surprising if this
man of fine nature and such unusual mind were suddenly
quite overcome with a vision of what life with an Emily
Dickinson could mean. He had a little money, enough to
live on quietly, and he had found her who seemed perfectly to meet his need. It had come to the point where it
seemed that he could not write his papers unless he could
write them with the prospect of being with her. And she
needed him. He was a man of few words. Emily Dickinson, — in that stiff New England setting! To see her there
against that village background, to see her consigned forever to such a fate, was more than he could endure. He
must do something to rescue her. Everything was changing. Inspiration was turning into distraction. He was not
contented she be his scholar.

If he proposed a plan for their permanent happiness together, it was probably impulsive, not calculated. Emily
made the decision that sent him away, nor was it, perhaps,
an instant's decision. He was for her the only one whom
she had met, with the exception of her tutor, who accepted
her for what she was. Her tutor had said she had in her
the making of a poet. He had set something stirring in her
mind. Lieutenant Hunt roused her to the full development
of her whole being. Until one has loved, so she wrote to

Mr. Higginson years later, he does not become himself. "Love is God," said Emily.

When Helen Hunt saw that her husband was being distracted from her, as she could not help seeing, she had no choice but to hold him. He was physically that large, compelling masculine type that was fatal to her. When she was scarcely twenty she had fallen in love with him; a soldier "of noble presence," a dreamer, a man of quick consideration, tenderness, sweetness. She was very proud of his attainments. When she saw that he found an unusual attraction in her friend, she probably spoke first of Emily to him. She was too quick and shrewd not to see. The situation required clever handling. He was so impatient of pettiness, jealousy, suspicion. He was nine years older than she, and accustomed to giving orders. Twenty-four was young to have lost both parents, her first child, to have her husband slipping from her, and her second son born during the trouble that had come upon her.

What love meant to Emily, love meant also to Helen Hunt. Some one had to lose. One cannot expect less than that of life; for lifetime, as Emily Dickinson once remarked, seems to be for two. Even three become a committee. The preciousness of what the lieutenant gave to one he took from the other. He could not help it. No one could. Helen Hunt, too, was an idealist. She was not as highly specialized as were the other two, but she was sensitive, and she was deeply in love with her husband.

Emily had sinews of song to help her; Helen had her

good sense. Realizing, in time, that the crisis had passed, she either did not maintain her suspicions, or she tried to bury what her instinct told her was an unjust feeling toward two persons who had met heroically a situation for which no one was to blame. Her pride was hurt. There was a smoldering in her that showed some flame long afterward. She had suffered, so deeply, indeed, that twenty years later she had not forgotten nor wholly forgiven that suffering. *Mercy Philbrick's Choice* could scarcely have been written by a Helen unaware of Emily's love story. The book was the work of one stirred partly by an impulse to strike at Emily, though it showed a largeness of nature and a generous comprehension. There was enough jealousy in Helen, however, to cut noticeably into her generosity. One could not blame her. It had come out of such a clear sky. . . .

In the spring of 1857 a young engineer-physicist down in Newport, Rhode Island, was holding his head in his hands and muttering, " Stupid! " He was suffering so from the constitutional malady brought on him in Washington that he was totally incapacitated for work one-fourth of the time, so he reported to Professor Bache. It seemed that the New England climate had not benefited him much. He had a little office at six dollars a month in which he tried to keep up his work on the Index, but it was difficult to do under such conditions. Only the outdoor life afforded by his engineering duties in lighthouse construction made the confinement in his office endurable. He was restless, miserable, muddled. For mathematics had its surprises. He was confronted with a new formula. He was in love with two women, both of whom loved him. Actually, he had another love that had never loosened her hold upon him, who had linked arms with Emily, for the time, and had lifted a haughty eyebrow at Helen. With so much to choose from and an ever increasing conflict which necessitated an eliminating choice, he had been very nearly crazy during the last year or more. The mind had presumed to guide experience, but as Emily herself pointed out, experience is a road with angles that lure the mind from its sign-posts.

His was a mind which would be as impatient of marriage regarded purely as a social contract as of religion exemplified in church forms. A contract would, of course, have meaning for him; but " contract " and " marriage," as conceived by one of his sensitive and idealistic nature, would be cold bedfellows. Others might talk of marriage as some sort of Procrustean process of " character-building " necessary to the perpetuation of " society." He would see the whole problem through his sense of form, the mathematical-physicist's sense of form. It was a personal problem. He was the last man in the world to lock up his mind and twist himself under the standards set by other minds. His problem was not a simple two out of three. He was too good a mathematician not to know that. Of two things we may be certain: a man of his unusual intellect would have a very fine and original conception of every aspect of human relations; and a man of his capacity would be profoundly moved when he once fell wholly in love.

Another aspect of his case was that he was an army man. In one of his treatises he indicates clearly that he was a man who strove for and maintained self-discipline. His view was that no one can be really free until he has staked off his own domain and is able to maintain it.

Whether he had asked for a change in station we cannot say, but that there had been talk of a transfer is evident in the letter written by the lieutenant from Newport to Professor Bache on April 3rd of that spring:[3]

" DEAR SIR:

" I must either rent a house *for a year* during the coming fortnight or three weeks or give up housekeeping; for houses are only to be got here now for the season of four months from June to October 1, or by the year, one costing as much as the other. From this you will see how important it is for me to know whether I am to change my station. I must either take a $550 risk at once, or be houseless and if I am to be moved soon I shall lose roundly in case I rent, as I certainly should if I am to stay. If, therefore, you should be able to tell me anything reliable pretty soon it will help me particularly and pecuniarily. General Totten is habitually so close, that I must rely on more prompt *intimations*.

" Yours truly,

" E. B. HUNT."

[3] This letter and the ensuing ones in this chapter are in the *Alexander Bache Collection, Library of Congress.*

The " prompt intimations " that were forthcoming *via*
the Coast Survey office almost put the engineer in bed, for
the trend of the news was toward an assignment to Key
West. If the latitude of Washington had almost ruined
his health, what would life come to in that " tropical bird's
nest "! Key West! It would mean not only the loss of his
health, but total suspension of work on the Index, and
personal exile. To be taken bodily from the complex
situation in which he had become involved was something of a shock. He had a strong sense of responsibility
toward his wife. She had been " a good soldier " under the
vicissitudes of his career. On June 13th he wrote again to
his chief from Bristol, Rhode Island, where he and his
wife were spending the summer.

" DEAR SIR:
" I cannot answer your inquiry of the 11th to my own
or your satisfaction without a full statement of all the
bearings of the question on myself and others.
" First then it is entirely impossible for me to finish the
Index by November next. To be broken off then would be
extremely disastrous to the undertaking, and I should
never have heart to take it up again. I can do but little on
it when I am out of library range, and I see no way of
bringing the work to a satisfactory end without I am permitted to work straight forward. . . .
" This brings me to a point which I must in duty present to you fully. . . . The [Washington] climate developed in me a bilious dyspepsia, which has kept me ever

since more or less miserable and unfit for work. . . . I am almost certain that if I were now to go to a Southern station, I should forthwith have a fever. . . . I should expect to be used up with this infirmity.

"Another fact almost equally militates against my undertaking Southern duty. Mrs. Hunt is never well in warm weather and depends on the bracing effect of winter for renewing the wastes of summer. She is of delicate constitution, and could not rally her strength after being prostrated by a Southern climate. I should therefore not expect to take her to a Southern Station.

"Thus an order to the South is to me a virtual decree of divorce, and a consignment of myself to the tortures of bilious dyspepsia and fever. These are certainly very substantial reasons why I should not willingly go to the South. They are so substantial that were I ordered there, I should go as becomes a soldier, but I should *leave the service* on the first tolerable opportunity, which as I am not dependent wholly on my pay might occur very soon. I should indeed resign with great regret, but it would surely be mere folly for me not to resign when the alternative becomes that or solitary confinement with perpetual bilious miseries. I should shrink, moreover, from the professional responsibility of carrying on a heavy Southern work with my whole system in disorder. If I am . . . in this climate . . . as miserable and muddled as I was three days since, how could I carry on an important work at the South with that condition intensified and made chronic?

"I do not shrink from any amount of work that my health will permit me to do well. I am quite content to add to what I have. New Bedford or any other work *I can* attend to at the North. . . . I shall certainly do my best to bring the Index to a prompt conclusion but it is inevitably a work of time. Had I seen before beginning it that Dr. Schubarth was 30 years in preparing his work of less compass than mine I should probably never have touched it. But I have begun and have worked on it with 'all due diligence' I am sure, and I want to finish it. I know that in many ways the public service will be the gainer by my undertaking and I know too that no one would take it up if I were to drop it now. I think the reputation of my branch of the Service will gain something by such a labor, and I know that science will be duly grateful. . . .

"I need not say more. I can make the case no clearer. I have written with no fear of 'retiring Boards' before my eyes. I own myself in this bilious respect a poor stick, am sorry for it, but I really cannot help it, and I cannot persuade myself that it is a duty for me to stay in the Service till the characteristic influence of Southern residence shall fasten my old enemy upon me as firmly as Sinbad's Old Man of the Sea.

"I shall hope some arrangement of my station will be possible which will enable me . . . to stand by my colors. I am sure General Totten will do the best he can for these ends, and as he knows somewhat of my own and Mrs. Hunt's disqualifications for a Southern residence, I assume he will not send me there willingly. . . .

"I leave the matter in your hands, nor shall I write to General Totten on the subject, for he has a hard enough programme to arrange without any intervention on my part.

"Very truly yours,

"E. B. HUNT."

Almost with the drying of the ink upon his letter came a note from army headquarters. The lieutenant was greatly upset and took to his bed. On the 20th he wrote to his friend in Washington: "In spite of all the drawbacks on my undertaking Southern duty, General Totten finds it necessary to send me to Key West. The limits of time for service there of Nov. 1 to May 1 or 15 at farthest with orders each way will be the only means of making the duty tolerable, or of giving me a reasonable chance of being in working order after one season. I do not see my way to the end of the Index with any distinctness on this programme, but the sole *possibility* of my finishing it would be in the establishment of these limits. . . ."

With protracted spells of acute physical suffering, impelled by nature to crowd the work of thirty years into thirty months of driving toward the completion of his great Index, with thirteen lighthouse constructions to be disposed of during the season, and a good deal of petty detailed work at Fort Adams to be supervised, and off toward the equator, Key West lying like a St. Helena in a fiery mist, — life for the young lieutenant during the summer of 1857 was a hammered thing. . . . It was June. In August there would be the meeting of scientists, in Mon-

treal this year. The annual meeting of the A. A. A. S.
had been the flower of each year for him. But now he
hesitated. On June 26th he wrote to Professor Bache:

"I have just been turning over in my mind whether I
shall go to the Montreal meeting. By taking a reasonable
time for preparation I could prepare *there* communications of some interest. I suppose the labor of preparation
and the time of the meeting would subtract about a fortnight from my *Index* time. Although I should like very
well to go, I would not take this amount of time without your consent or even desire; for though it is doubtless well and desirable for me to maintain my place as a
scientific laborer from year to year at the Am. Assoc.
meetings, it is not a *duty,* which the *Index* now is. . . .
I shall surely not go without you say so, and may not even
should you advise it. . . . I am sorry to say that for over
a week past I have been too unwell to work with any good
results, but I am better now. I begrudge every day that I
lose at this crisis, & hope my stupidity has cleared off
for the season." Ten days later, " I shall take what comes
as well as I can. I think I will go to Montreal, though
work is very urgent here."

It is possible that Lieutenant Hunt went to see Emily
Dickinson once more in this August of 1857, and that the
meeting may have been the inspiration for her poem,
" There came a day at summer's full."

On September 12th his fate was settled, as he immediately informed Professor Bache: " I have just received a
note from General Totten in which he confirms the Key

West plan. . . . I am glad anyhow to be rid of Fort
Adams, which has been my greatest hindrance to Index
work. The lighthouses, I could manage without trouble,
& be all the better for something to give me outdoor work.

"General T. says, after various ' ifs' & ' &s ' — that
' he thinks I may be allowed to return to this coast in
the latter part of May next, to complete my unfinished
coast survey index, — retaining, however, the responsibility as to Ft. Taylor.' . . . I must stay at Key West as long
as his mercy or lack of it dictates, & he will be very
ready to find opportunities in the ' political cause for
pressing operations during the summer ' to which he alludes, for keeping me there the whole year. . . ."

Professor Bache promptly wrote kind views of the situation and certain suggestions, which seemed to cheer the
lieutenant somewhat. He made arrangements to keep his
little six dollars per month office through the winter, for
" he could not work without an office," put his Index notes
in a fire-proof safe, and turned his mind to the possibilities
for continuing in Key West the study and development of
his *Molecular Mechanics.* Already he was visualizing his
next large project to be undertaken upon completion of
the Index. He proposed to prepare for the Royal Geo-
graphical Society " a full account of the Coast Survey, its
history, progress, methods & results, in the hope of throwing some light into a dark corner."

Sometime in 1854 or 1855 he had had several talks with
a fellow scientist, Professor Henry, relative to the advis-
ability of the British Association undertaking some such

Index as Lieutenant Hunt had been pushing in America. Professor Henry sent a proposal to the British Association which led to their appointing a committee which reported in 1856. Young Hunt eagerly scanned the copy of the report which came to him. There was an allusion to Professor Henry, and the repetition of many of the ideas of Lieutenant Hunt's Providence paper, but, perhaps through some oversight, no credit was given to the lieutenant. The latter wrote to his friend for advice. " Would it be worth while to print a special edition of my Providence & Albany papers, with a preface, to circulate in England and elsewhere, for the sake of ' the truth of history '? I will cheerfully abide by your decision. The British Association Committee propose 8 quarto vols double columns and a large staff of laborers. I shall believe that if their plan is carried out its origin will truly date back to those un-ambitious pickings of which you were so well advised in the C. S. Office."

His heavy work of the summer had been practically compassed, his private plans arranged. One beautiful October day in 1857 a boat southward bound carried among its passengers a distinguished-looking and preoccupied soldier with engineering orders in his baggage, and combinations of atoms incessantly breaking and uniting in his brain.

Professor Bache made special reference to Lieutenant Hunt in his *Coast Survey Bulletin* for that year. The sounding apparatus proposed by E. B. Hunt was being tried out in New York Harbor. The lieutenant had worked out a system for the abbreviation of titles in connection with the great Index of Scientific References, for which he had examined eight thousand volumes and extracted over thirty-five thousand titles. He had persevered zealously with this work, though his chief time had been necessarily given to duties under the Engineering Department and the Lighthouse Board. His work on the Index . . . would be resumed in the next summer. It was a work requiring a peculiar combination of qualities to execute well.

In spite of the intense heat of Key West, Lieutenant Hunt began to get his bearings again. In the isolation of the little tropical island he was with his first love, and time went fast. Key West was a coral island seven miles long and not more than two miles broad. It was eleven feet above the sea. There were narrow little streets, scarcely more than alleyways between grass-roofed huts. The population was largely black.

He became especially interested in the origin, growth, substructure, and chronology of the island reefs, and the history and causes of the shipwrecks which were occurring at an average of about one a week. The stones of the Fort Taylor breakwater and foundations, the palmetto piles, the iron bars lost overboard, were becoming rapidly coated with solid, branching corals. He made a study of the reefs in an effort to calculate their age. There was half an inch growth of coral a year, as estimated from a narrow cross-section of the shore line, and from measurement of the average thickness and depth of the coral limestone formation of Florida, he calculated the age of the reefs " as certainly more than five million years, which makes the seemingly formidable chronology deduced by Professor Agassiz shrink into insignificance."

When he advanced his theory of the influence of the earth's rotation on the direction of the Coast Survey, even Professor Bache felt that his brilliant subordinate was a bit over-speculative, and he wrote a kind but frank letter to the scientist down in the tropics suggesting that this point be omitted from the paper which Hunt had sent him for special use. But Lieutenant Hunt held to his own. " I do not admit that what I say is a speculation, but it is a mechanical necessity. It is not different from the views generally accepted among scientific men, either, so far as I know. I could not therefore *consistently* allow that part to be omitted, if the paper is used at all." Are we not reminded of Emily's statement to Mr. Higginson that she would not let go a line because it was hers?

Far off in the New England snows Emily was writing, Helen was leading a gay social life. General Totten had been a better mathematician than was young Hunt in that summer of 1857. For Edward Hunt had been trying desperately to draw a triangle upon two points; the general peremptorily designated a third point, which gave a much better figure, with more room in the upper angles, particularly in the one projecting from Rhode Island.

With his increasing mental abstractions and the demands upon his time, the lieutenant probably let correspondence with Emily lag a little bit. After so many months of enforced exile the annual reunions with his family were particularly pleasurable, and there was the Index to be completed in those precious five months. His love for Emily did not permanently affect his marriage; after having had this interlude in Amherst he commanded the affections of his wife more surely. Either he told Helen about the affair in order to clear his conscience, or, if his conscience did not have the preconceptions which necessitated clearing, he saved Emily's letters and did not worry lest they fall into his wife's hands. Death, after all, seemed very far away.

In September, 1858, Lieutenant Hunt had been sent on a two months' engineering assignment to San Francisco, California, and to Galveston, Texas. In Key West the construction of Fort Taylor upon an artificial harbor was being pushed. General Totten had an eye upon the Secretary of War. In January, 1859, the lieutenant, writing to his Coast Survey chief, chanced to let his eyes rest for a moment on the map upon his wall. He frowned, and added another sentence. "I fear Jeff Davis . . . is going to *confuse* the Engineers & Topog . . ."

AFTERWORD

Emily Dickinson seems to connect the Key West assignment with her personal story, when she tells Mr. Higginson in April, 1862, of the catastrophe to her second important friendship. Lieutenant Hunt may have asked for a change in his location, or Emily may not have gotten the details of his transfer, or, as is most likely, she is using the word " so " in the sense of " and so " merely to introduce a statement of fact, when she says that he went away from the land. She was frequently careless in her grammar.

She kept the drama of that August afternoon as a photograph for the rest of her life. She knew that she had the love of the lieutenant, and for one brief moment she held the key to the situation in her hand. That Emily had handed him back to Helen was a barbed point in the drama as it affected the two women.

Emily Dickinson's nature was a special one. She was a creative artist first and last. Her tutor had recognized the literary temperament in her, cameo-like, years before even she had come to know herself. Her sensitive being ran to extremes of suffering and ecstasy, but she actually got more of rapture out of her experience in love, and the grief and pain which are reflected in her letters and in her poems were inextricably bound up with her life's condition.

From childhood she had dwelt intensely in anticipation. She was expecting love to be for her a dowry of future. It came, unexpectedly. The fact that her lover was already married had nothing to do with the case. One cannot bend and double back a flood and put it away in one's bureau drawer, as she later wrote. Afraid of life? said Emily. Why should she be afraid of that which had comprehended her? Just why she should have been given only a bowlful when the flood was so mighty was something of a mystery, but she made the most of what was given. It was like the opening and the slamming of a door on a cold night; it was landscape revealed to her by sheet lightning, so she said.

Her love did not make her a poet; it kept her from ceasing to be one. It kept her supplied with impulse and passion and suffering and joy essential to continued poetic creation. What might have stilled the voice of another, gave a powerful drive to her creative faculty. She now had a theme for real poems. Poetry and love were coeval in her life, she has told us.

Let us say, if we must, that fifty years ago there was an Emily Dickinson who lived shut up in a room in her father's house. Let us say, if we will, that sixty years ago there was an Emily Dickinson secluded in her garden. But let us not deny that seventy-five years ago there was an Emily Dickinson who was a vivid girl of flesh and blood. Nor fail to recognize the human background of her lovely lyric:

> " Of all the souls that stand create
> I have elected one.
> When sense from spirit files away,
> And subterfuge is done;
>
> " When that which is and that which was
> Apart, intrinsic, stand,
> And this brief tragedy of flesh
> Is shifted like a sand;

" When figures show their royal front
And mists are carved away, —
Behold the atom I preferred
To all the lists of clay! "

*

Chapter Ten

AMHERST AGAIN

*

EMILY was walking with Carlo across the garden and down toward the grove. They were talking things over together. It had been harder when the separation was so meshlike, she said. She could have tunnelled through a wall. She missed her lover more when a letter might have brought him within three hours, than now when oceans made him impossible. The pain caused by a furlong's separation is more fiery than that caused by the distance of a league. Carlo's eyes grew deeper, and he shortened his shaggy pace. There are several ways in which one may triumph, Emily added: when the finer mind holds its own in spite of the tugs upon it; when truth goes calmly forward, notwithstanding affronts; and the triumph of handing back a passport into heaven, because it came in the form of a bribe. But after all, said Emily, as the wind went in furrows through the sweet-grass toward the orchard, to be alive is spell enough.

She and Carlo looked up into the sky. God was supposed to be up there. But they could see no face. Only prairies of silence. The clouds were piled high in reckless revelry. People are all right, remarked Emily. The trouble is they are of such different shapes and sizes. When you've once known the big ones, the giants, with whom you can be everything that you are, nothing is the same afterward. With the smaller kind you become partial; perhaps it is not the prouder part that you are, with the smaller size, and the consciousness that you are incomplete makes you shy. The more incomplete one is with the lesser kind, the more shy he becomes.

There was a wind in the bushes and to Emily's sensitive ear the leaves were like bells ringing. Life *is* like a play, she said, thinking, perhaps, of her Shakespeare. But after all, there is no more vital expression of drama in human relationships than is to be found in any common day, especially a summer's day. Every sunrise is different. As soon as the flag is out in the east such a host of creatures large and small, visible and invisible, begin to creep and carry and breed and build and fly. Nor, as Lieutenant Hunt had pointed out, is Nature a member of the Peace Society. . . . No summer noon was ever long enough for the music that it gave, if one were still, by the pool. . . . And as for sunsets in an unobstructed sky! Sometimes, on late afternoons, the scarlet was handed swiftly from steeple to steeple until there was a great ball of it that dripped over the mountains. Then such a fire touched the tips of the grasses, there came such a gleam of diamonds and of gold that you knew you were about to have dinner with a duchess. . . . In the twilight where there had been the grove and the woods and Orient springs, there were domes of mystery, and the world began to nod. Until deep within the summer's night there sounded the horns of the bullfrogs and glimmered a subtle shimmering brightness that made one clap one's hands, for the curtain was going up again. . . .

The rose, said Emily to Carlo, is more logical than Cato. The rainbow carries more conviction than any system of philosophy we know. Henceforth, said Emily, with the wind in her hair, as she and Carlo looked up into that carnival in the sky, our lives are dedicated. We belong to the free-masonry of clouds.

Moving from Deacon Mack's house back into the brick house built by Samuel Fowler Dickinson had been something like the upheaval of the whale. "I cannot tell you how we moved," Emily had written afterward to Mrs. Holland, exasperated and laughing at herself. "I had rather not remember. I believe my ' effects' were brought in a bandbox, and the ' deathless me,' on foot, not many moments after. I took at the time a memorandum of my several senses, and also of my hat and coat and my best shoes — but it was lost in the *mêlée,* and I am out with lanterns, looking for myself. Such wits as I reserved are so badly shattered that repair is useless — and still I can't help laughing at my own catastrophe. I supposed we were going to make a ' transit,' as heavenly bodies did — but we came budget by budget, as our fellows do, till we fulfilled the pantomime contained in the word ' moved.' It is a kind of *gone-to-Kansas* feeling, and if I sat in a long wagon, with my family tied behind, I should suppose without doubt I was a party of emigrants! They say that 'home is where the heart is.' I think it is where the *house* is, and the adjacent buildings. . . . Mother has been an invalid since we came *home,* and Vinnie and I 'regulated,' and Vinnie and I 'got settled,' and still we keep our father's house, and mother lies upon the lounge, or sits in her easy-chair." [1]

One reason for the moving was that Edward Dickinson might be near his only son; for Austin was married to Emily's schoolgirl friend, Sue Gilbert, in July, 1856, and his father had built for the young couple a handsome house next door to the ancestral one. The advent meant not only one more intimate at hand; in Austin's home there were new books and new fashions and brilliant entertaining. Visitors of national reputation came to her father's house. On August 11, 1860, Governor Briggs of Massachusetts and his family were the guests of Mr. and Mrs. Edward Dickinson; and guests and hosts alike were thrown into a flurry of excitement by the arrival of a small and carefully sealed box sent by Mr. David Sears, of Boston, to the treasurer of Amherst College "with instructions that it not be opened for one hundred years, on pain of forfeiture of the gift which it contained." The shrewdest guess as to the contents of the mysterious box was that it held deeds of real estate in Boston, under lease for one hundred years, which in 1960 will become the property of Amherst College.

[1] *Letters of Emily Dickinson,* vol. i, p. 167.

But, philosophized Emily Dickinson, no matter how large nor how select an audience there may be, nor how many witnesses to one's effort, when one has dedicated oneself to the achievement of an ideal that is difficult, one finds that it becomes a solitary transaction. There must be unmistakable belief, and effort, and patience, especially patience with the forces that interfere.

Up in her room Emily kept her private wine-shelf — a row of little sealed jugs (books, Vinnie would have pronounced them, as she dusted). Whenever Emily felt like it she could pull out a silver stopper and take a long, refreshing draught from the mind of another who had dedicated himself. "Kinsmen," she called them. The labels were distinct — Sir Thomas Browne, the Brontës, George Eliot, Ruskin, John Keats, and two in which the silver stoppers were very loose, Elizabeth Barrett Browning, and Robert Browning, whose love story and family life in Florence were of absorbing interest to her.

It sometimes pleased Emily's fancy to give poet's names to the children of her friends. In 1860 she wrote to inquire as to the health of Mrs. Holland's " little Byron," who had injured his foot. When Mrs. Browning died, in June, 1861, leaving a grief-bowed husband who took flight from Florence with his only son, Emily's sympathy with the bereaved poet was intense. She wrote a poem to Mrs. Browning which concluded with the thought: if we who read her poems are suffering such grief, what must be the anguish of " the bridegroom " who had buried her in Italy. Emily's love for Elizabeth Barrett Browning was so well known among her close friends that three different ones sent portraits of the English poetess to her. Six months after the death of her favorite, Emily wrote to Mrs. Bowles, who had a new little son, asking if the mother would name the child Robert for that bravest of men with the motherless boy for whom everyone was weeping.[2] And she again mentioned the Brownings to Mr. and Mrs. Bowles three times in correspondence soon afterward. Her friends knew Emily too well to take her seriously in such matters. Mrs. Bowles named the child for Charles Allen, an intimate friend of Mr. Bowles; and Emily wrote as soon as she heard, " Could you leave ' Charlie ' long enough? Austin told us of Charlie. I send a rose for his small hands." For a time she alternately called the baby " Charlie " and " Robert."

With the sudden wash of a rough wave something cut across her reveries. The *Springfield Republican* carried words like shot. There were flags and drums and marching in the village streets. Amherst College boys were enlisting daily. The women were very busy weaving blankets and socks for the soldiers. Amherst professors were going

---

[2] There is an inference on pp. 47–48 in the *Life and Letters of Emily Dickinson* that the biographer believes Emily to be referring here to her own lover. Aside from the lack of identification of a " Robert " with any of Emily Dickinson's friends yet revealed to her public, can we quite agree that she would so far have spread the story of her heart among her friends in Springfield and Amherst that " all were weeping " ? The confusion in interpretation is a natural one; but when Emily Dickinson's allusion to " Robert " is considered in its full context, is it not obvious that she refers here to Robert Browning, as was first suggested by Mr. Frederick J. Pohl?

to war. The *Springfield Republican* sounded a pessimistic note that disheartened all its women readers. On August 23, 1861, Mr. T. W. Higginson wrote to his anxious mother, urging her not to " croon over " that *Springfield Republican* so much. . . .

Florida had been a charter member of the Confederacy. Of the eight Southern fortresses, six had been easily taken by the Confederates. Fort Pickens at Pensacola and Fort Taylor at Key West remained in Union hands. During the preceding months, President Buchanan, a states-rights man, had been urged by three members of his Cabinet to send troops to hold the forts in the South. Three other members of his Cabinet, all Southerners who believed in secession, had persuaded the President that to reinforce the Southern forts would alarm the South and precipitate a conflict. And now, the forts were being occupied by the secessionists. At Fort Sumter, Major Anderson with his eighty-four men showed such a spirited desire to protect the place that the sympathy of the North was aroused for the first time in many weeks of irresolution and delay. Fort Pickens was held by a garrison of forty-eight. Most important, strategically, because it guarded the entrance to the Gulf, around which lay the cotton states in a linked line, was Fort Taylor. Captain Hunt was placed in command of the fortifications and he directed the defense. He was hard pressed by the secessionist sympathisers on the little island, and a lesser brain than the captain's could scarcely have held the fort. The dangers of war-time in Southern waters were complicated by great storms that lashed the lower end of the Florida coast, and by sea fights with contraband runners and Confederate raiders. All the tropical warmth and the deep-sea mysteries — the "blue peninsula" fringed with coral — were turning into smoke and shot and flame. Letters came through intermittently, or ceased altogether. The Northern papers for August and September reported danger around Key West. Any issue, now, might bring the news of death in that area.

Is it not reasonable to find in the danger to Captain Hunt a cause for the terror and excitement into which Emily Dickinson was thrown at just this time? The peril of her lover seemed to bring him nearer to her. It was the general belief of her day — and of some people yet — that the grave would be a repeal of the marriage contract. It had been the theme of Dr. Hitchcock's conception of immortality which had so impressed her in childhood. After death she and her lover would be united forever. Her consciousness was heightened, her life dramatized, by a sense of impending crisis and the necessity for subterfuge. Fire seemed to ignite within her. Danger makes the sun itself a deeper one, she wrote. To most of us, she said in substance to a friend, death seems very far away; but to one it is as near as though it were a lady coming up the steps to ring the bell upon the door. On November 1st, Mr. Higginson wrote to his increasingly anxious mother that she would never be able to take a hopeful view of anything until she gave up "that unfortunate *Springfield Republican*."

Throughout the winter Emily Dickinson seemed to herself to be passing a long graveyard. She was alone. A tomb-stone stood up whitely ahead of her in the winter light. She put her hands in her pockets and began to whistle, lovelier tunes than she had ever whistled before. It seemed that a certain lyric quality, a fluency was released in her voice. Emily dated from September of 1861 the terror which she could confide to no one, and which caused her to do an unusual amount of writing in an effort to distract her mind from a fear that beset her. Her output was brilliant. Even she was surprised at the ease with which her poems had shaped themselves. There had been poems all along. The biographer of Emily Dickinson has dated eleven poems 1854–55. There was one to Mrs. Anthon in 1859, and in the summer of 1861 Emily sent to Mrs. Bowles that exquisite little lyric, " My river runs to thee." If there were these there were others, but with the exception of the last named her poems had seemed to have still something of mental effort in them.

Said Emily, twisting her fingers into Carlo's silky hair, power comes when extreme pain has been held deep down in one so forcibly through discipline that its scarlet hangs like weights at all four corners. The discipline can go, because the pain won't well up into one's throat any longer. Every day we feel more certainly what we may become. We have sued Mrs. Holland for a letter, and Mrs. Anthon for a visit, and father for some attention from his briefs, but we must not strut. Perhaps they're laughing at us. Perhaps the whole world is laughing at us. No matter. It is *our* business to sing.

During this winter two editors came to try to persuade her to write for their "journals," as Emily said. In spite of a slightly misleading plural, it is likely that the two were Mr. Bowles and Dr. Holland. "Why?" asked Emily Dickinson. "We want you to share your mind with the world," they replied. But the artist in Emily stood up. Was she ready for publication? After all, these were old friends, and their paper was the family paper. Were they overrating her? She had been completely happy to write in solitude, and she had very high standards for herself. She felt a sudden longing for literary criticism, an overwhelming necessity for a friend with whom she could talk.

Some one was running across the wide ground between the two houses. It was Austin, coming to tell of Frazier Stearns, his intimate friend and son of the president of Amherst College, killed at Newbern. The details were bitter: held up breathing for ten minutes in a soldier's arms — calling for water — murmuring, "My God!" — his heart shot away. Almost simultaneously Captain Hunt, to whose sagacity and leadership the saving of Fort Taylor was attributed, was ordered into the thick of the fighting in Virginia as chief engineer of the Department of the Shenandoah from March 29th to April 17th and promoted to the rank of major.

*

Chapter Eleven

A SCHOOLBOY AND A BEE

*

IN all literary history, no magazine has commanded more veneration and awe than did the *Atlantic Monthly* during its first half-century. To paraphrase an unsigned review: the *Atlantic* was not a channel for American literature — it *was* American literature; and anything not in the *Atlantic,* American though it might be, and perhaps interesting, even powerful, important, artistic, and enduring, was not and could not be literature. To its worshiping readers, the pages of the Boston periodical were a temple; its editor, high priest; and its contributors, deities.

The first number, dated November, 1857, was a distinguished issue. " Tritemius," by Whittier; " The Maple," a sonnet by Lowell, the editor-in-chief; the first installment of the " Autocrat "; an essay and four poems by Emerson; stories by Longfellow, Mrs. Stowe, Trowbridge — all made the number seem like a portion of a new Bible. Within a year these authors were joined by Thomas Wentworth Higginson with " Saints and Their Bodies," and he became the most frequent, if a slightly less famous, writer for the magazine. Succeeding numbers contained such work as: " The Battle Hymn of the Republic " (February, 1862), " The Man Without a Country " (December, 1863), " Prospice " (June, 1864); though there was a very nervous circulation for some time after Mrs. Stowe's " True Story of Lady Byron's Life " (September, 1869).

To become a contributor to the *Atlantic Monthly* meant not only that one was making literature; it meant also a personal acquaintance with these famous writers, for the editor brought the contributors together regularly at *Atlantic* dinners. Mr. Higginson wrote to his mother, in the summer of 1859, that as he sat at the table with Longfellow or Lowell or Emerson he was sometimes made very serious with the realization that these men and women of the *Atlantic Monthly* would doubtless one day be regarded as demi-gods, along with Milton or with Wordsworth. The number of feminine contributors was at first relatively small — Mrs. Howe, Mrs. Stowe, Miss Terry, Miss Spofford — and for a time, the ladies were not admitted to the dinners. When in July, 1850, prior to Mrs. Stowe's trip to Europe, a dinner was given at the Revere House, in honor of the lady, she accepted with a special stipulation that no wines were to be served. There were some wry faces among the gentlemen, but they contented themselves with " nipping at the water," passing *bon mots* upon Miss Prescott's story of a French winecellar, and gazing at Mrs. Stowe's elaborate head decoration, an artificial grape-leaf garland.

For several years the contributors to the *Atlantic* were

anonymous. Said Emerson, " The names of contributors
will be given out when the names are worth more than
the articles "; but the Boston correspondent of the *Springfield Republican* was able to send to his paper, immediately upon the appearance of the first number of the
Atlantic, the full list of contributors' names.

We can imagine, then, the flurry of excitement which
must have been occasioned among neophytes who cut the
pages of the April number in 1862 and read the title of
the leading article, " Letter to a Young Contributor: "

" My dear young gentleman or young lady — for many
are the Cecil Dreemes of literature who superscribe their
offered manuscripts with very masculine names in very
feminine handwriting — it seems wrong not to meet your
accumulated and urgent epistles with one comprehensive
reply, thus condensing many private letters into a printed
one. — And so large a proportion of *Atlantic* readers
either might, would, could, or should be *Atlantic* contributors also, that this epistle will be sure of perusal,
though Mrs. Stowe remain uncut and the " Autocrat " go
for an hour without readers. . . .

" In the treatment of every contribution the real interests of editor and writer are absolutely the same, and
any antagonism is merely traditional, like the supposed
hostility between France and England, or between England and Slavery. No editor can ever afford the rejection
of a good thing, and no author, the publication of a bad
one. — The only difficulty lies in drawing the line. . . .

Nor is there the slightest foundation for the supposed editorial prejudice against new or obscure contributors. On the contrary, every editor is always hungering and thirsting after novelties. To take the lead in bringing forward a new genius is as fascinating a privilege as that of the physician who boasted to Sir Henry Halford of having been the first man to discover the Asiatic cholera and to communicate it to the public. It is only stern necessity which compels the magazine to fall back so constantly on the regular old staff of contributors, whose average product has been gauged already. . . .

" An editor thus shows himself to be but human. . . . He is not a gloomy despot, but a bland and virtuous man, exceedingly anxious to secure plenty of good suscribers and contributors, and very ready to perform any acts of kindness not inconsistent with this grand design. Draw near him, therefore, with soft approaches and mild persuasions.

" . . . The defect of this [Dr. Channing's] standard is that it ends in utterly renouncing all the great traditions of literature, and ignoring the magnificent mystery of words. Human language may in itself become so saturated with warm life and delicious association that every sentence shall palpitate and thrill with the mere fascination of the syllables. The statue is not more surely included in the block of marble than is all conceivable splendor of utterance in *Worcester's Unabridged.* . . . There may be phrases which shall be palaces to dwell in, treasure-houses to explore; a single word may be a window from

which one may perceive all the kingdoms of the earth
and the glory of them. Oftentimes a word shall speak
what accumulated volumes have labored in vain to utter;
there may be years of crowded passion in a word, and half
a life in a sentence.

"Such being the majesty of the art you seek to practise,
you can at least take time and deliberation before dis-
honoring it. . . . Charge your style with life, and the
public will not ask for conundrums. . . . It is this un-
wearied literary patience that has enabled Emerson not
merely to introduce, but even to popularize, thoughts of
such a quality as never reached the popular mind before. . . . It is of no consequence whether one comes to
literature from a library, a machine-shop, or a forecastle,
provided he has learned to work with thoroughness the
soil he knows. . . .

"Be noble both in the affluence and the economy of
your diction; spare no wealth that you can put in, and
tolerate no superfluity that can be struck out. Remember
the Lacedemonian who was fined for saying that in three
words which might as well have been expressed in
two. . . . Roll your thought into one good English word.

"Have faith enough in your own individuality to keep
it resolutely down for a year or two. A man has not much
intellectual capital who cannot allow himself a brief in-
terval of modesty. . . . The age has out-grown . . .
[Carlyle] . . . and is approaching a mode of writing
which unites the smoothness of the eighteenth century
with the vital vigor of the seventeenth, so that Sir Thomas

Browne and Andrew Marvell seem quite as near to us as Pope or Addison — a style penetrated with the best spirit of Carlyle, without a trace of Carlylism. . . . Remember how many great writers have created the taste by which they were enjoyed, and do not be in a hurry. Inscribe above your desk the words of Rivarol, ' Genius is only great patience.' It takes less time to build an avenue of shingle palaces than to hide away unseen, block by block, the vast foundation stones of an observatory. Most by-gone literary fames have been very short-lived in America, because they have lasted no longer than they deserved. . . . To this day, some of our most gifted writers are being dwarfed by the unkind friendliness of too early praise. It was Keats, the most precocious of all great poets, who declared that 'nothing is finer for purposes of produc-tion than a very gradual ripening of the intellectual powers.' . . . Many fine geniuses have been long ne-glected; but what would have become of us if all the neglected were to turn out geniuses? . . . If, therefore, duty and opportunity call, count it a privilege to obtain your share in the new career; throw yourself into it as resolutely and joyously as if it were a summer campaign in the Adirondacks, but never fancy for a moment that you have discovered any grander or manlier life than you should have been leading at home.

" So few men in any age are born with a marked gift for literary expression, so few of this number have access to high culture, so few even of these have the personal nobleness to use their powers well, and this small band is finally so decimated by disease and manifold disaster, that it makes one shudder to observe how little of the embodied intellect of any age is left behind. Literature is attar of roses, one distilled drop from a million blossoms. . . . The difference between Shakespeare and his contemporaries is not that he is read twice, ten times, a hundred times as much as they: it is an absolute difference; he is read, and they are only printed.

" Yet, if our life be immortal, this temporary distinction is of little moment, and we may learn humility without learning despair, from earth's evanescent glories. Who cannot bear a few disappointments, if the vista be so wide that the mute inglorious Miltons of this sphere may in some other sing their Paradise as Found? War or peace, fame or forgetfulness, can bring no real injury to one who has formed the fixed purpose to live nobly day by day. I fancy that in some other realm of existence we may look back with some kind interest on this scene of our earlier life, and say to one another, ' Do you remember yonder planet, where once we went to school? ' And whether our elective study here lay chiefly in the fields of action or of thought will matter little to us then, when other schools shall have led us through other disciplines."

The " Letter to a Young Contributor " was written by Mr. Higginson. He was never an editor of the *Atlantic,* but he seems to have been in an unofficial capacity always quick to secure good things for the magazine, and often sent to Mr. Fields immediately papers which had been submitted to him for criticism. After this April essay his mail was unusually heavy with " wonderful effusions " sent him to read, with requests for advice which he found it hard to give, so he records in his *Journal*.

One morning, two weeks or more after his article appeared, Mr. Higginson took from the post office in Worcester, Massachusetts, where he was then living, a strangely phrased letter in which the writer asked him somewhat deprecatingly for an opinion of her verse and desired to exact from him in advance a pledge of secrecy. The letter was postmarked " Amherst," and the stamp had been put on so hastily that it was almost in the middle of the envelope, covering the word " Mr." The handwriting was unlike any that he had ever seen and reminded him, as he said later, " of the famous fossil bird-tracks in the college museum." The writing was, in his opinion, quaint rather than illiterate, and it was unique. There was little punctuation. The writer used chiefly dashes (which he had expressly warned against), and had a tendency to capitalize noun substantives. But what most startled him was the total absence of a signature. He reached into the envelope again and drew from it a smaller envelope. In this he found a card upon which was written, not in ink (as he had specifically advised), but in pencil, " Emily Dickinson." She had enclosed four poems: " Safe in their alabaster chambers," " I'll tell you how the sun rose," " The nearest dream recedes unrealized," and " We play at paste."

To say that Mr. Higginson was interested would be an

understatement. He was startled, intrigued, bewildered. Her letter indicated that the writer had individuality. She was evidently somewhat out of the current of modernity, she was alone in her writing, and she was very shy. He declared thirty years later that upon first reading of these four poems his mind received the distinct impression of a wholly new and original poetic genius. He had been arguing, searching for it; but when it suddenly stared up at him in the pile of papers on his own desk, the best he could do for the moment was to stare back. In subject matter there was freshness, but his ear was offended somewhat with " Bobolinks begun," and his brain was befuddled with the lines beginning, " Worlds scoop ——." True, there had been as great obscurity in some of Emerson's *Atlantic* contributions, but Emerson had arrived at the place where he was to be studied for his meaning. An unknown " Miss Dickinson " must be clear. Two names came to mind as he read these four strange poems: Walt Whitman, the most undisciplined poet of whom he could think; and Harriet Prescott, a young protégée of his whom he considered a most wonderful genius. He wrote promptly to his Amherst correspondent.

How eagerly Emily Dickinson must have sorted her poems to select the best, with an eye to variety of form as well as substance! For several days she awaited a reply in suspense. It came. Many a young poet of today, taking from an envelope the rejection slip across which is scrawled, " Send some more, please," will know how much heart even such words can give, when they come from one in a position of literary authority. Mr. Higginson wrote along with his criticism not only " Send me more," but he showed a very friendly personal interest in her. How old was she? What companions did she have? What books?

Though ill, Emily sent Mr. Higginson a second letter "from her pillow," April 26th. How she worked over these letters to impress the great man! Her story was a simple one: a brother, a sister, a mother more domestic than literary, a father absorbed in his legal concerns, who would bring home books for his talented daughter and be filled with terror at their power to unsettle the mind. All were religious except her. She likewise had had no " education," as Mr. Higginson would read the word, though she had, of course, gone to school. Her tutor, her lexicon, one friend more, who was not satisfied that she be his pupil; a terror since September which had driven her to singing as a boy does to stifle his fear as he is passing the graveyard. She spent most time with her dog, the hills, and the sundown. Her books? Emily named those on her shelf (all of whom had been approved in Mr. Higginson's article).

The freedom with which Emily Dickinson wrote of herself and her background to Mr. Higginson, a total stranger to her, is testimony to the stature which she attributed to him. She was as natural as a happy child. When Emily Dickinson was " complete," she put into her letters not only the brilliance of her mind but also the full charm of her irresistible femininity. She was, as he said of

Mr Higginson.

Are you
too deeply occupied to
say if my Verse is
alive?

The mind is so near
itself - it Cannot see,
distinctly - and I have
none to ask.

Should you think it
breathed and had you
the Leisure to tell me.
I should feel quick
gratitude -

Could you believe me
without -? I had no
portrait, now, but am
small, like the Wren.
And my Hair is bold,
like the Chestnut Bur
and my Eyes, like the
Sherry in the Glass,
that the Guest leaves.
Would this do just as
well?
It often Alarms Father -
He says Death might
occur, and he has
Molds of all the rest -

LETTER, JULY, 1862

the ensuing correspondence, like the bee before the schoolboy, "dipping, evading,"—finally bringing him to her
own front doorstep.

In his first reply to her Mr. Higginson had suggested the
names of two contemporary writers whom she should
know—Walt Whitman and Miss Prescott. Emily had
heard of "Leaves of Grass" as a very disgraceful affair,
but then she had also been told that Theodore Parker was
"poison," and had found that she liked "poison" very
well; but when it came to Miss Harriet Prescott there
were no two ways about it for Emily Dickinson. Her
brain curled at the recollection of the weird vision that
had crackled and moaned in her dimly lit room one late
spring night when she had first made the acquaintance of
Miss Prescott. Emily knew this writer by only one story,
"Circumstance," which had appeared in the *Atlantic
Monthly* in May, 1860. It is scarcely necessary to add that
this story was not typical of the *Atlantic* offerings even
for 1860. It is doubtful if any man could have passed the
editorial board with such a thing. But let a woman put
her pen to paper when she was a bit frowzy in her
thoughts, and her work was more apt than not to be regarded as a remarkable evidence of "feminine imagination." Even Poe, trenchant critic that he was in writing of
his contemporaries, was inclined to be a bit soft when
reviewing a book written by a woman. As an instance,
then, of what was, by chance, held up to Emily Dickinson
in 1862 as good work by a feminine writer, our reader
may be interested in a brief summary of "Circumstance,"

more or less in Miss Prescott's own words. It was a story
of the wilds of Maine.

A frontier wife had remained all day with a sick neighbor and had not observed the approaching night. Finally,
at sunset, she had donned cloak and hood, bade friends
farewell, and sallied forth — some three miles across a
copse, a meadow, and a piece of woods, the woods being
a fringe upon the skirts of the great forests that stretched
far away into the north. Her home was one of a dozen
log houses lying a few furlongs apart from each other,
with their half-cleared demesnes separating them at the
rear from a wilderness untrodden save by stealthy native,
or deadly panther tribes.

She was depressed and walked slowly. As she began to
cross the meadowland, walking more rapidly, she distinctly saw in the air before her what was not there a moment ago — a winding-sheet, cold, white, ghastly, waved
by the likeness of four wan hands, that rose with a long
inflation, and fell in rigid folds, while a voice, shaping
itself from the hollowness above, spectral and melancholy, sighed: " The Lord have mercy on the people!
The Lord have mercy on the people! " Three times the
sheet with its corpse-covering outline waved beneath the
pale hands, and the voice, awful in its solemn and mysterious depth, sighed, " The Lord have mercy on the people! " Then all was gone. She looked about her, shook
her shoulders decidedly, and, pulling up her hood, went
forward once more.

She entered the woods and went along, biting a bit of spicy birch. Suddenly a swift shadow writhed through the air before her, and she felt herself instantly seized and borne aloft. It was that wild beast known by hunters as the Indian devil, and he held her in his clutches on the broad floor of a swinging fir bough. He caught his claws in her clothing and then began to lick her bare arm with his rasping tongue and to pour over her the wide streams of his hot, fœtid breath. She was not of the screaming kind, but as the monster crouched, his white tusks whetting and gnashing, his eyes glaring through the darkness like balls of red fire, a shriek tore through her lips. The beast left the arm, once white, now crimson, and looked up alertly.

She did not think at this instant to call upon God. She called upon her husband. Again the cry, loud, clear, prolonged. The beast, about to gnaw, stopped to listen, for the echoes were most musical, most resonant, dying with long sighs of sweet sound. Quick-wittedly, she recalled that music charmed wild beasts, and she opened her lips a third time — for singing. First a cradle-song, but that brought to mind the tender picture of the hearth scene, baby on the settee, father cleaning his gun, the merry firelight, etc., and she ceased.

Immediately the long red tongue thrust forth again. Before it touched, a second song sprang to her lips, a wild sea song. Her voice rose on long swells and subtle cadences, now and then like belfry bells. The monster flared his fiery eyeballs upon her. She ended; he snapped his jaws together, and tore away the fettered member with a snarl. She burst into the gayest reel that ever answered a fiddle-bow. As she sent her voice trilling up and down, the creature uncurled his paw and scratched the bark from the bough. She must vary the spell, and her voice spun leaping along the projecting points of time of a hornpipe. She felt herself twisted about with a low growl and a lifting of the red lips from the glittering teeth; she broke the hornpipe's thread and commenced unraveling a lighter, livelier thing, an Irish jig. Up and down and round about her voice flew; the beast threw back his head so that the diabolical face fronted hers, and the torrent of his breath prepared her for his feast. Frantically she darted from tune to tune; his restless movements followed her. She tired herself with dancing and vivid national airs, growing feverish and singing spasmodically as she felt her horrid tomb growing wider. The beast lay his paw across her with heavy satisfaction. She did not dare to pause; through the clear, cold air, she sang. Alas once more her thoughts wandered to the hearth-fire scene, and her voice faded. Suddenly the dagger teeth penetrated her flesh. The beast stood up, bristled, foamed, hissed, and withdrew a pace. She was free; she measured the distance and rose to drop herself down. Instantly the creature bounded forward with a yell and caught her. She flung up her voice again, and he settled himself comfortably upon the bough. God! If her voice should fail! If the damp and cold should give her any fatal hoarseness! The beast whined, fawned, scored her cheek with his tongue. She asked herself, as she sang, what sins she had committed, and sought eagerly for some reason why her husband was not up and abroad to find her. He had failed her! And she turned to God! She now began to sing grand and sweet Methodist hymns, with all the involutions of tune to suit that ecstatic worship. Out of this strange music, peculiar to one character of faith, her voice soared into glorified chants of churches. " Though He slay me, yet will I trust in Him," and she began to sing the Bible through. Was she not in God's hands? Did not the world swing at his will? And she thought tenderly of her first communion, and she chanted on and on. Night passed. The cock crew. There was a crashing of brushwood, and her husband, bearing the baby and the gun, at last drew near. Far up in the wind-rocked branches he heard a voice. He looked up and saw his wife, — but, great God in heaven! how? He raised his gun. His wife looked down, rigid, blood-stained, but she never once ceased chanting. The husband was afraid to fire lest he miss the mark. She shuddered; all calm forsook her. Her face contracted, grew small and pinched. Her voice was hoarse and sharp. One gasp, and silence! She had lost her voice and the beast made a movement. The man raised his gun. The animal seized his prey. There was a rifle crack — a yell — and both fell to the ground, the beast under her.

" I think," said the author, " that the moment following must have been too sacred for us." — They continued through the woods, husband in advance. Suddenly, the wife stooped to examine a singular footprint in the snow, and looked up with a hurried word. She sprang to the side of her husband, who stood alone on the hill, his arms folded across the babe, his gun fallen. He had a fixed stare. There was no longer any home there. Log house, barns, fences, blotted out in one smoking ruin. Tomahawk and scalping-knife had been at their work and had left one subtle footprint in the snow.

For the rest, the world was all before them, where to choose.

" 'Circumstance' tagged me in the dark," said Emily, in substance, in reply to Mr. Higginson's query; "I shall have to avoid her."

In her second letter to her new literary friend, she inclosed "Your riches taught me poverty" and "A bird came down the walk." In her third, she sent him "There came a day at summer's full" and "Of all the sounds despatched abroad." It is interesting to note the nice sense of balance with which Emily Dickinson made her selection each time; never two poems of a kind in the same mail.

The essence of Mr. Higginson's criticism was that she was a poet of great promise, but that she was uneven and not always clear. She did not yet, in his opinion, have perfect control of her medium. She needed criticism. It seemed to him that her thoughts were dark, though how one could have grown breathless over "Circumstance," and have had a shadow cast over him by any one of those remarkable poems by Emily Dickinson, is inexplicable to

Courtesy of Mrs. T. W. Higginson

COL. T. W. HIGGINSON

us now. Mr. Higginson wrote Emily further that she had flashes of deep insight into life, brilliant, incisive expressions that were unusual in one who had never written but " one or two" before. He suggested that she delay publication for a time until she could express herself more clearly and until her form was better disciplined. So much we can assuredly read between the lines of what she says in her replies to him.

Emily met him brilliantly point by point. She had been told before that she was a poet, and the first intoxication of such praise could never be repeated. She could judge what was good and what was not good in selection of material for a poem. She could catch the poem in embryo intuitively. She could *feel* the poem from the prose. She knew the quick from the dead as thoughts lay in her mind. But in the process of putting these thoughts into arrangements of words, the warmth and passion and fragrance seemed to ebb. As she read her poems over to herself they all sounded alike to her and " numb." She was too close to them for perspective. She was being urged to publish, and had written to Mr. Higginson for advice because she had liked his *Atlantic* essays.

She wished true criticism because she was sincere. His praise was good because it helped to strengthen her belief in herself; it confirmed what less authoritative friends had told her. But though Mr. Higginson might have found so much wrong as to make her poems appear to be but foolish work, Emily Dickinson informed him that she would not stop. A chestnut tree in blossom, a cloud of light deep in the orchard, a whimsical wind filled her with an ecstasy that only the verses could relieve. If her verses were but foolish matter, if, instead of being a poet, she were but a jester, let the cap and bells remain; for the jingling that accompanied the shaping of self-expression was cooling as she walked in beauty.

As to form, continued Emily Dickinson, if she seemed to Mr. Higginson to be uneven and " spasmodic," it was perhaps because she was in " danger " still, in June, 1862. Form is but the expression of oneself. She could not set rules for herself, could not appoint a form and try to pour herself into it. She had never known such constriction in any aspect of her life. When, after a walk through the woods in summer, or the rising of love within her, she sat down and tried to compress herself into a poem, the idea exploded, and words were on the paper like scattered fire. When one catches his breath in the heart of the green-sweet woods it is not himself that does it, but the divine working through him.

She would like to have a compass. If Mr. Higginson would be that friend whom he suggested that she needed to guide her, she would be grateful to him. Perhaps he was, after all, somewhat amused at her. No matter. Her business had been to love, and then to sing, and now, since her province was all circumference, there was need for all the knowledge she could acquire. She felt a need also for grace. Sometimes when she threw open her shutters in the dawn, or felt the colors from the low sun streaming upon her, she felt as awkward as a little kangaroo. She would like to acquire such shapeliness that self would not obtrude, that beauty would pass unobstructed into words. Though every poem had its inception in truth, no one was to be taken as an intimate revelation of personal experience. The more personal the inception, the more universal the finished product. Emily agreed with Mr. Higginson that rewriting was well worth while. Twenty-four hours of distance from it would often make clear the imperfections in a poem.

As for her fancies being darkly colored, had not Mr. Higginson's essays indicated that he shared with her a kinship with the butterfly, the orchis, and the lizard in the sun? People were continually missing her meaning, saying " what? " to her until she had come to the conclusion that it was but a habit of carelessness with them. Surely it could not be, as Mr. Higginson said, that her thoughts were sometimes of a special nature?

His suggestion that she delay to publish she accepted not because he said so, but because she agreed with him. She recognized that her growth as a poet had been slow. She was ambitious. She had had encouragement, but she felt a need for sympathy of aim. There can be little question but that Emily Dickinson, like every other poet, had to have her audience. She had created one, of a sort. To the young people, to Dr. and Mrs. Holland, to Mr. and Mrs. Bowles, to Mrs. Anthon, and to others she had been sending her poems from her girlhood. Was her talent large enough? If so, she knew her course. Mr. Higginson's advice was temperamentally congenial to her. We cannot but feel that if he had sent those first poems of Emily Dickinson's to the *Atlantic Monthly,* she would have been shyly gratified. It was not publication but perfection in attainment that was her goal, however. Let not a little jeweled fish warming its fins in sunny waters aim to leap and swim among starry clouds. If, by perseverance, in the end her work were good enough, it would find its audience.

Emily assured her trusted adviser that she would give heed to his criticism faithfully, though some of it was inexplicable to her. It is interesting to note what revision she made in these eight poems that she had first submitted to him. We are not permitted to give a reprint of the original manuscripts now in the Galatea Collection in the Boston Public Library, but the reader who has the *Complete Poems* will note the following changes: " Safe in their alabaster chambers " was sent to Mr. Higginson in 1862 as a two-stanza poem, the stanzas being the first and last in the three-stanza version given in the *Complete Poems of Emily Dickinson;* the only change that the poet made later in " I'll tell you how the sun rose " was to substitute " which " for " that " in the third stanza. There are no asterisks between stanzas two and three in the original manuscript. She made no changes in " We play at paste " or in " The nearest dream recedes unrealized." " Your riches taught me poverty " and " A bird came down the walk " also are in the original manuscripts exactly as published in the *Complete Poems.* Emily Dickinson, or her editors, later made four changes in " There came a day at summer's full "; the facsimile that appears in *Poems:* Sec-

Your Riches. taught
me. poverty -
Myself a Millionaire
In little wealths - as
Girls could boast.
Till broad as Buenos-
Ayre -
Ere drifted our Do-
minions
A different Peru -
And I esteemed all
poverty -
For Life's Estate, with you -
Of mines, I little know.

Success . is Counted
sweetest
By those who ne'er
succeed -
To Comprehend a Nectar.
Requires soorest need.
Not one of all the
Purple Host
Who took the Flag . Today.
Can tell the Definition
so clear. of Victory
As he - Defeated - dying .
On whose forbidden ear.
the distant strains of

POEM, WRITTEN IN 1863-64. EARLY MIDDLE PERIOD

ond Series, is as the manuscript was sent to Mr. Higginson in 1862. For the benefit of the reader who may not have the facsimile at hand be it noted that "Where revelations" in the first stanza (see *Complete Poems*) was originally "When resurrections"; "sail" in the second stanza was originally "soul"; "symbol" in the third stanza was "falling"; and "failed" in the sixth stanza was "leaked." The 1862 version of "Of all the sounds despatched abroad" was very different from the one familiar to the public: there are three additional stanzas in the original version which have never been published; in the fourth stanza of the published version (*Complete Poems*), "He" was originally "Who" and "in" was originally "on"; in the last stanza "on" was originally "off," "broken" was "parted," and "passed" was "swept," as Emily Dickinson sent the poem to Mr. Higginson. It will be observed that the first six poems that Emily sent to him were regarded by her as finished work, and that, regardless of his criticisms, she laid them away, with two negligible exceptions, exactly as she had submitted them to him.

In her second letter to Mr. Higginson, Emily Dickinson had slipped into the signature, "Your friend"; in the third she became, "Your scholar." The figure of life being but a school was a much-used one. Mr. Higginson had referred to the planet "where once we went to school" in his "Letter to a Young Contributor." Emily Dickinson's terms, "Preceptor-Scholar," "Master-Pupil," were not unusual ones. May we not believe, too, that she got a good deal of fun out of the correspondence and the relationship? Emily had always had a beautiful sense of values when it came to acquiring an " education." She had from the beginning had a very good time in school. To criticize her signatures to Mr. Higginson, to accuse her of affectation, of stiltedness, is to take her too seriously and to take her out of her setting.

That she had now a friend with whom she could let herself play freely, some one with whom she could talk as well as think, brought the tears into her throat. She told him long afterward that without realizing it he had been the means of preserving her life; and Mr. Higginson gave the full meaning to her words when he said many years later that she made of him not only a literary mentor, but a confidant. At first, so he later declared, he had tried to lead her a little way toward the conventional in poetic form, but he soon gave it up and became more interested in her " unregenerate condition." Her delightful coquetry, that description of herself which she gave him in lieu of a photograph, those " startling " allusions to " drunkenness " and " rum," " that extraordinary signature, ' your Gnome,' " as he says, led him to make eager inquiry in Worcester about her, for there was a Mr. Dickinson living in that town; but Emily's uncle could tell the literary man very little about his Amherst niece.

In June, 1862, Emily Dickinson was still " in danger," so she wrote Mr. Higginson. Far off there were cannon, and dungeons, and hearts being torn away by big " minie balls," and men were lying in blood in the dark of the sun.

But it was summer in Amherst, and war seemed unreal and oblique.

Late in that summer of 1862 Mr. Higginson recruited a company for nine months. He was captain, and by November had received orders to go to Newbern, North Carolina. The plans were changed by a proposal from General Saxton's headquarters that Captain Higginson should take command of a regiment of freed South Carolina slaves. Throughout the winter of 1862–63, he was stationed at Camp Saxton, Beaufort, South Carolina. One day late in February, 1863, so he recorded in his *Journal,* his drum major, an old Belgian temporarily detailed from the Nineteenth New York, then at Key West, came to him in great anxiety, to plead for his discharge, that he might not have to return to Key West, because of the epidemic of yellow fever there. In Jacksonville, to which Mr. Higginson was ordered for a short time in March, he saw more men from Key West, a regiment of negroes who were a problem to their commander, because of their blistered feet. The seven miles by two allotted on the little island was the longest distance these negroes had ever walked in their lives. In April, Colonel Higginson was ordered up to Port Royal Ferry, South Carolina. He took with him from Jacksonville a little sailboat which he kept near by at Seabrook, and he would take the boat and cross to an island for recreation. He wrote Emily Dickinson late in the spring or in the early summer of 1863, and evidently told her something of his environment, particularly of his little island retreat. There had come down into his neighborhood General Lander's widow, the former actress, Miss Davenport, who hoped to become head nurse. He thought her "off the stage what she was on it, simple . . . high-minded, sensible." One May day she and Colonel Higginson got up a picnic on the island in honor of General Saxton's guest, a young Mr. Hay, President Lincoln's private secretary, " a nice young fellow who looked about seventeen and was oppressed with the necessity of behaving like seventy." It was a beautiful place — old trees, a view across the river to the rebel shore, a scarlet-lined coat here and there, black sentinels in the background, a band, officers and young ladies, and a great sailcloth laid down to dance on. For refreshments, there were blackberries and milk, and then all galloped home through the wood paths in the moonlight.

Emily Dickinson wrote in reply to him soon afterward (summer of 1863), that she also had an island in her consciousness to which she could go for recreation and retreat from all the " realities " of the day. There the air was heavy with roses and magnolia blossoms which she had never seen, and there were black people living there who were but an enticing prospect to her. . . . Evidently she had not heard of the major's transfer.

*

Chapter Twelve

86 AUSTIN STREET

*

ON Wednesday, September 30, 1863, there was unusual activity at Red Hook Point, Brooklyn. An experiment was to be made with the submarine rocket, the " Sea Miner," upon which Major Hunt had been working for many months. The success of his invention would render his country's navy impregnable to the attacks of foreign navies. To the major it would mean much personally. It would justify him for having remained so long out of the field of battle and apparently idle, a point on which he was somewhat sensitive, the more especially since, as a brother of Washington Hunt, ex-Governor of New York State, his course was certain to be publicly scrutinized. Ordered into Virginia as chief engineer of the Department of the Shenandoah on March 29, 1862, he had in less than three weeks been transferred to Connecticut as superintending engineer to complete an eight-gun battery at Fort Trumbull, to construct temporary works at Dutch Island for the defense of the west passage into Narragansett Bay, and to erect temporary defenses at New Haven Harbor. For several months now he had been on special duty under the Navy Department at the Brooklyn Navy Yard, constructing his projected " Sea Miner " for firing under water.

He was whole-mindedly devoted to the winning of the war for the Union. Now, as always, he lived in his brain, for he felt that through his mind he could make his greatest contribution to his country. In August, 1860, he had read a strong paper on " Modern Warfare: Its Science and Art," before the scientists assembled in Newport, and his paper had appeared in *The New Englander* three months later. In September, 1862, he had written with a scientific approach a brilliant treatise, " Union Foundations " (" Truth is King: Cotton and Corn are Subjects "), which was read before a prominent group in New York and published in January, 1863. His article made an impression. *Harper's* gave a condensed recasting of it in " The Editor's Study." The *Atlantic Monthly* asked him to review important new foreign books on engineering. There lay before him a distinguished future. His career meant everything to him. But it is not easy during the shot and shell of war to convince everyone that the badge of courage is not necessarily red.

It was a bright, clear autumn day. The major stepped alertly — always a commanding figure — absorbed in his invention. He set to work at once in experimentation. One rocket was discharged. Eager to investigate, he climbed down a ladder into the hold of the caisson. An instant later, something terrible was happening. One said that a shell exploded. Another, that by inadvertence the outer slide was not drawn up and the rocket could not get out of the gun. There was a gunpowder discharge and the hold was filled with gas. Major Hunt reached blindly for the ladder, climbed unsteadily almost to the top, but was overcome and fell, striking his head so sharply that there was concussion of the brain. Instantly a man went down with a rope to try to draw up the body, but the rescuer fell insensible. A third went down, with the same result. By pouring in water, they purified the air so that the fourth man was able to adjust the rope, and Major Hunt and one of the men were drawn out. The other two were able to help themselves. All recovered quickly but the major, who was taken to the Brooklyn Naval Hospital, where he lay insensible, with no hope of his surviving. He died there at one o'clock on October 2nd, at the age of forty-one.

All of the leading newspapers of the country carried notices of the event. The *New York World,* in nearly half a column of obituary account, said, " He died, although not on the battle-field, yet in harness, devoted, with all his power of soul, mind, and heart to the service of his country." The *New York Times* eulogized his character and attainments, and spoke especially of the affection felt for him by his wide circle of friends in both army and civilian life. The *Springfield Republican* on October 3rd gave as its first general news item a brief story of the accidental death of Major Hunt.

On October 5th the major was given a military funeral and was buried at West Point. For thirty days thereafter the officers of the Corps of Engineers and of the Military Academy wore the badge of mourning by direction of the Engineering Department in Washington. Major Hunt's grave lay close to the north wall of the old cemetery, overlooking the Hudson River. On one corner of his tombstone was carved a flag draped in folds which fell over an edge of a laurel wreath in the center of which was a turreted castle and the word " Essayons." Under the personal inscription, Helen Hunt had placed the words, " Blessed are the pure in heart."

Must we not feel it more than coincidence that Emily was stricken at just this time? In April, 1864, her illness of the past seven months was causing her family great concern. She was getting no better, and so her father took her to Boston, placed her under the care of a physician, and left her with her cousins, Louisa and Fannie Norcross, in Cambridgeport. Thirteen years had elapsed since Emily Dickinson's last visit in Boston. The Irish influx had set in; the population was increasing, but it was still " half the Boston of 'The Autocrat.'" The ways were mostly graveled ones. As for the famous suburb, Emily remarked that living in Cambridge seemed to her like living in Westminster Abbey. It was as incredible and as sanctified. She had visited Fannie and Louisa while they were living at the Hotel Berkeley. Changes had come in these thirteen years; the " little cousins " were now orphans. Emily was driven through the shady streets of Cambridge, past neat suburban gardens into Austin

Street, where the driver stopped before a large frame house with a luxuriant open garden on one side of it. Out onto the front steps came Fannie and Louisa in tight little waists and ballooning skirts; in the doorway stood the ample Mrs. Barnabas Bangs, keeper of the lodgings. Austin had visited his cousins two years before, and had reported them to be looking very well indeed, and living in a particularly fine lodging-house. Emily wondered if the house had been transported from Carrara, so elegant was its marble interior.

She had a quiet room. Mrs. Bangs and Miss Bangs were attentive to her every wish; there were servants at her bidding. Emily thought of Elijah and the ravens as she sat in her strange surroundings and saw people go in and out of her room, with a pair of her stockings in a mending-basket and fresh water for her flowers. She remained for months, " a Bedouin guest " among the company, May, June, July, and a sizzling August. Every night came Barnabas Bangs to his home across the Charles River, far from the rattle of the Boston business house in which he was a bookkeeper, and pottered among his flowers, clipping leaves and sprinkling. Sometimes he and the lodgers exchanged wisps of ideas on the current of affairs. In the summer before there had been the terrible draft riots in New York, one thousand persons killed or wounded, and private property worth a million and a half destroyed. In March, 1864, a Thirteenth Amendment had been introduced into Congress; it had passed the Senate, but had failed of the necessary two-thirds majority in the

House. Public discussion had not yet crystallized opinion in its favor. On June 7th, the Republican Convention had renominated Mr. Lincoln. The summer of 1864 was a gloomy one politically in the North. In August, the Democrats nominated McClellan in Chicago. On September 3rd, Sherman entered Atlanta.

Directly across the street was a belfry under a steeple, and people were thronging the steps that led to war-time prayers and services. Another side of 86 Austin Street was neighbor to an animated livery-stable, half hidden from view by a huge pear tree out of which many a small boy was daily shaken, that there might be preserves for the livery-keeper's wife. Behind the house, across an alley, was a long row of squeezed block houses, an orange stripe of city in an otherwise coolly sprigged section of rural green. The Cambridge sky was beautiful, the trees were thick and flowering, but to a Connecticut Valley stranger there was a peculiar flatness everywhere. One learns that there are physical levels to existence.

At first, the doctor may have come to Austin Street, for Emily was very ill. Her eyes were causing her serious trouble and she seemed to be suffering from nervousness and depression. "No more writing for a time," said the doctor, and he took her pen away from her. She wrote a faint note in pencil to her friend, Mr. Higginson, for she heard in Cambridge that he had been wounded, and she inclosed her address cut from a letter. She told him that she had been ill since September, 1863, and had come to Boston in April for a physician's care. The physician insisted that she remain for some time; she was, therefore, making poems for companions in place of Carlo and the mountains. She longed now more than ever to see her kind literary friend. She told Mr. Higginson that Heaven seemed to be flashing bulletins as rapidly as did the news boards of the great cities.

Just how Emily Dickinson first learned of the death of Major Hunt we do not know. The news came quickly to Amherst. It is said that Emily's brother and sister-in-law both knew of her deep attachment to Helen Hunt and to the major; and if so, one of them may have kept from her the October 3rd *Springfield Republican*. The news may have come by telegraph. It is strongly suggested that Emily refers to this crisis in her poem, " If he were living — dare I ask? " (*Further Poems of Emily Dickinson*); and in the poem, " I read my sentence steadily " (*The Complete Poems of Emily Dickinson*).

Boston friends came to call and brought flowers to Emily; she knitted and wrote poems and was able to go to the doctor's office in Arlington Street by the end of the summer. Is it not reasonable to accept her sojourn in Cambridgeport as the background for her poem:

> " Bereaved of all, I went abroad,
>   No less bereaved to be
> Upon a new peninsula, —
>   The grave preceded me,

> " Obtained my lodgings ere myself,
>   And when I sought my bed,
> The grave it was, reposed upon
>   The pillow for my head.

"I waked, to find it first awake,
　　I rose, — it followed me;
　I tried to drop it in the crowd,
　　To lose it in the sea,

"In cups of artificial drowse
　　To sleep its shape away, —
　The grave was finished, but the spade
　　Remained in memory." [1]

The physician said she would certainly get well, but Emily wrote to Lavinia that so accustomed had she now grown to confinement that an invitation to liberty would be an indifferent matter. But she wanted to get well. The ecstasies of mere existence in so beautiful a world were overpowering still. To her cousins she later remarked that after all, health and heart are very closely allied. The change, and the companionship of Louisa and Fannie, their cheerfulness, did more for her than the doctor could. Years afterward she wrote to them that their sunshiny parlor with its books and its quiet brought a Wordsworthian calm to her in retrospect. Much improved in health, Emily returned to Amherst in the fall. Is it not possible that her poem, " 'Twas just this time last year I died " (*The Complete Poems of Emily Dickinson*), was written during the fall of 1864?

For the first few weeks Emily spent most of her time

---

[1] This poem from *The Complete Poems of Emily Dickinson* was titled by Mr. Higginson and Mrs. Todd, " Trying to Forget."

with her exotic flowers in the conservatory, and tried to take her place as usual in the domestic routine. But she was no better than a year ago, and she was losing weight. She could not stifle the mood of many months, the mood, may we not say, that is clearly defined in her poem, " I felt a funeral in my brain" (*The Complete Poems of Emily Dickinson*) ?

In acknowledgement of a letter from Louisa in the winter of 1864-65 faintly suggestive of some romantic happening, Emily replied with an interesting short poem, " This was in the white of the year " (now in *The Complete Poems*). It was from Cambridgeport that Emily sent to Dr. and Mrs. Holland the poem, " Away from home are some and I " (*The Life and Letters of Emily Dickinson*). In February, 1865, Emily wrote to Louisa Norcross, " I chop the chicken centers when we have roast fowl. . . . Then I make the yellow to the pies, and bang the spice for the cake, and knit the soles to the stockings I knit the bodies to last June. They say I am a ' help ' . . . Mother and Margaret are so kind, father as gentle as he knows how, and Vinnie good to me, but ' cannot see why I don't get well.' This makes me think I am long sick, and this takes the ache to my eyes. I shall try to stay with them a few weeks more before going to Boston, though what it would be to see you and have the doctor's care — that cannot be told. . . . I have so much to tell I can tell nothing, except a sand of love. When I dare I shall ask if I may go, but that will not be now. Give my love to my lamp and spoon, and the small lantana. Kindest remem-

brance for all the house." ² Louisa had suggested that if
Emily would come at once to Boston she would postpone
her prospective visit to Eliza, who was now married to
a Reverend Mr. Dudley of Middletown; but Emily urged
her cousin to make the heart-warming visit: " Go. . . .
Write next from M——." We cannot hold the reins on
life, added Emily in substance, for life is too fleet.

In the late spring of 1865 Emily Dickinson returned to
the lodgings in Austin Street. Her cousins gaily declared
that as soon as she appeared their pink lily put out five
new flowers. The three women sewed together on a fashionable hood that Emily was going to take back with her
to Amherst, but in Cambridgeport and Boston persons
were wearing no bonnets, as Emily noted with interest.
Fannie had a fashionable narrow straw hat with ribbon
under the chin. The Norcross sisters bought books at the
quaint little shops around the corner and over in Boston,
and they joked, and hummed new airs. Literature in this
decade was producing nothing original, however; the war
was too close. The intellectual sway of the New England-
ers and the Victorians was still dominant.

There was great excitement in the lodgings when news
came that the President of the Confederacy had been
taken. Louisa thought it might be fun to send to Austin
a picture of Mr. Davis dressed up in a skirt and wearing
spurs, and she wished that Edward Dickinson might drop
in upon them with his inimitable version of the affair. No

² *Letters of Emily Dickinson*, vol. ii, p. 255.

one else could give the story quite the Dickinson turn of speech. So the time went — August, September, October, November — in the city. Shortly before Thanksgiving, and two weeks before her contemplated return to Amherst, everything seemed to become dull and hopeless and leaden again. She did not even love her flowers as she once had, so it seemed to her. She wrote to Vinnie that Amherst would be like a strange country to her now. All life seemed to have gone out of the world. The drums were still beating, beating, for a man who could not hear them, — with this thought she concludes her letter to her sister. This thought may have personal meaning; on the other hand, she may have been referring to some continued public memorial to Abraham Lincoln or to a prominent man who had died more recently.

Mrs. Todd — editor of the *Letters* (1894), co-editor with Mr. Higginson of the *Poems,* First and Second Series, and editor of the *Poems,* Third Series — divides Emily's handwriting into three distinct periods: the early style of about 1853 to 1863 (*Letters of Emily Dickinson,* Vol. I, page 155); the early middle period, from about 1863 to 1870 (*Letters,* Vol. I, page 217); and her later years. Though Mrs. Todd has not in these volumes dated the last period exactly, we note that the final change came near in time to the death of Emily's father. We may say, with assurance, that each change in her handwriting came at about the time of the death of some one of major importance to Emily Dickinson. Mrs. Todd says further, in

her Preface to *Poems,* Second Series, page 5: " The handwriting was at first somewhat like the delicate, running
Italian hand of our elder gentlewomen; but as she advanced in breadth of thought, it grew bolder and more
abrupt, until in her latest years each letter stood distinct
and separate from its fellows. In most of her poems, particularly the later ones, everything by way of punctuation
was disregarded, except numerous dashes; and all important words began with capitals. . . . There is nowhere
a date." The manuscript letters and poems in the Galatea
Collection in the Boston Public Library are all of the
middle and later periods (1862–85) and afford a very interesting study. The writing of the latest period, when
each letter was distinct and separate, is noticeably smaller
than that of the " large, bold " middle period. In this
Higginson collection we see the change by about 1868 or
1870, as Mrs. Todd has stated. The handwriting is still
fairly large, but the tendency to a separation of the letters
is very noticeable.

In addition to a change in her handwriting, 1862–63,
Emily Dickinson seems to have begun to wear white exclusively from about this time, and to have withdrawn
almost entirely from general social gatherings, with the
exception of the annual reception given during Commencement by her father, as treasurer of the college, in
honor of the trustees. Of this event Emily wrote lightly to
the Norcross cousins in May, 1862: " My little girls have
alarmed me so that notwithstanding the comfort of
Austin's assurance that ' they will come,' I am still hope-

less and scared, and regard Commencement as some an-
thropic bear, ordained to eat me up. . . . Didn't they
know Cousin Aspen couldn't stand alone? . . . Commencement would be a dreary spot without my double
flower, that sows itself and just comes up, when Emily
seeks it most." [3]

As these receptions become the occasion for Emily's
annual public appearance in Amherst from 1866 to 1874,
descriptions of her under the circumstance are particularly
interesting. Her niece, Mrs. Bianchi, gives a very charming brief description of Emily Dickinson upon these
occasions in *The Life and Letters of Emily Dickinson,*
page 42. Mr. Higginson in his Preface to *Poems,* First
Series, also comments upon these annual receptions when
Emily Dickinson acted the part of hostess " as though it
were a daily occurrence." In a lecture on the Amherst
poet, Mrs. Todd speaks of how Mr. Edward Dickinson,
gravely receiving his guests, would be asked, " But where
is Emily? " " In the library," he would reply, with a grand
gesture; and there in the dimly lit library was Emily,
dainty and an object of attraction. A graduate of Amherst
College, who was introduced into the home of Edward
Dickinson in the autumn of 1864, by Emily's cousin, Mr.
Cowan, when both young men were students in the college, writes: " She would sweep in at one door of the
double parlor, clad in pure white, an angelic appearance,
make her bow to each of the guests, rarely touching the
hand of anyone, and sweep out again at the other door

[3] *Letters of Emily Dickinson,* vol. ii, p. 245.

and disappear entirely for the evening. Even Mr. Cowan told me that he knew but very little of his cousin and did not feel privileged to call upon her without an invitation. She seemed to be always in profound thought and living in another world." [4]

If we find in Emily Dickinson's reputed custom, after the early 'sixties, of always wearing white, an analogy with Mrs. Whitman who is said to have sat much in her room in a half-shadow, wearing white to perpetuate the tradition of a poet's love, it is a coincidence rather than an imitation, apparently; for Emily did not read until 1879 Mr. Higginson's *Short Studies of American Authors,* in which he gives this account of Mrs. Whitman. Emily wrote, apropos of the book, that she knew practically nothing of Poe, and she made no further reference to that chapter. One wonders if the idea of perpetual white may not have been somewhat exaggerated. That she wore white at an annual tea-party in the summer-time would, of course, prove nothing. Mr. Higginson records particularly that her costume was white and blue when he saw her in August, 1870.

Had Major Hunt lived, he would have been, at the age of fifty-five or sixty, one of the conspicuous personalities in American public life. With the experience he was getting, the travel, his brilliant mind, his personable qualities, his initiative in the field upon which he had chosen to expend the better part of his genius, his character, he would

[4] Reminiscence of Professor John Burgess.

have left such a record as could be found on every library shelf. Nothing in life could have stopped him. We must certainly feel that Emily Dickinson was deeply affected by his death. Had he lived twenty years longer he might not have had the influence upon her that his tragic and premature death evidently did have.

There are suggestions that the bulk of Emily Dickinson's love poems were written between 1855 and 1870. For evidence, we have factual history, the psychology of the situation, illuminating passages in the letters (published and unpublished), the handwriting of the poems sent to Mr. Higginson, and also the handwriting of the *Further Poems* as described by the editor on page 1 of her Introduction to those poems. Mrs. Todd has indicated that a chronological arrangement of the manuscripts by handwriting could be made. Perhaps the heir to the manuscripts will, in time, permit such an arrangement, which might settle many a disputed point.

It is not improbable that some of the poems included with those labeled by the editors as poems of " Love " do not belong in that group; some that are placed in the divisions called " Life " and " Time and Eternity " might be included with the body of the love poetry. The " Love Poems " fall easily into two groups: a very small one, of verses inspired by the poet's affection for any one of several friends; the larger body of poems inspired by the love for one person. The latter poems may be very easily subdivided into two groups — those written before the death of the lover and those written after his death. It is not the purpose of the writer to try to prove a case from these love poems. The prohibition placed upon the quotation of even a single line from within the poems makes an attempted analysis here unsatisfactory, if not impossible. But it is interesting and worth while to consider the love poems with an eye to the direction in which the weight of the evidence tends to fall. There is confusion, but on the whole Emily Dickinson does certainly have some very definite things to say about her lover.

Is there, in these remarkable poems, internal evidence that they were inspired by a clergyman? In her Introduction to *Further Poems of Emily Dickinson,* the editor of those poems and biographer of the poet believes that she has found in " As the eyes accost and sunder " factual evidence that the romance was a case of love at first sight during a church service in Philadelphia. The description of Dr. Wadsworth in the pulpit testified to by many people who knew him — his last minute appearance, his instant and complete absorption in his sermon to the extent that he was totally unaware of his audience as individuals, his faulty vision, are details. Is not the idea of the poem in itself a usual one in poetry? Walt Whitman wrote: " Out of the rolling ocean, the crowd . . . I have travel'd a long way merely to look on you "; " To you, whoever you are, a look "; " Passing stranger! You do not know how longingly I look upon you." The poem, " He fumbles at your spirit " (*The Complete Poems of Emily Dickinson*), entitled by the first editors, " The Master," might be construed to be a description of a sermon by Dr. Wadsworth, but not necessarily so.

In the love poems Emily uses biblical terminology in many instances. What is the source of this influence upon her writing? She tells us four times, if we need to be told, what one of her strongest prose influences is — that mystical book of *Revelation,* one of the three prose favorites on her bookshelf, so she tells Mr. Higginson; from this source she draws her figures of the heavenly marriage. In the poem, " There came a day at summer's full," she further compares the lover and his beloved to two churches, doors and windows tightly sealed. Why? In her poem, " When I hoped I feared " (*Complete Poems*), she gives the full figure. The week-day New England church, spare and sealed, white and solitary, in bloom or in snow, is the symbol of loneliness to her — an excellent figure. Consider her poem, " I cannot live with you " (*Complete Poems*). It is written to one who has died. The poet wonders how she and her lover are going to be judged. After all, she says in substance, he had served Heaven — or at least he had tried to. She weighs the possibility of his being lost or his being saved. Is the poet's thought compatible with her kindly references to the clergyman who had died at the age of sixty-eight, after more than forty years of service in church work, whom she calls one of the aborigines of heaven? Can we feel that the poet whose lover's face was a " delirious charter," as she indicates many times, would refer to him as a man whose countenance was " mysterious," as in her final letter to Mr. C. H. Clark?

Theological terms were a part of Emily Dickinson's heritage and background. In her later years especially, her

letters to her friends are colored with such terms. She
has a poem criticizing a preacher (the narrow-minded
preacher), and a poem or two criticizing the scientist (the
narrow-minded scientist). These have nothing to do with
her love poems, however. What definite suggestions may
one find in the latter?

Emily Dickinson writes of having lost by death two
who were of very great moment to her: "I never lost as
much but twice," "My life closed twice before its close,"
"Going to Heaven!" (*The Complete Poems*). In the last-
named poem she says that the two died in the autumn. Is
it not reasonable to believe that these were the two of
whom she wrote to Mr. Higginson in April, 1862, both
of whom did die in the autumn — if we accept Major
Hunt as the second to whom she alludes? By way of paren-
thesis it is helpful to note that her father died in June, and
the noted clergyman in April. The tutor is a special case.
The body of her love poems indicates that Emily Dickinson was preoccupied with one love, a love for a man who
commanded her entire and permanent devotion, and almost humble admiration for his knowledge and prestige.
His mind was a new dominion utterly different from her
own. He was a man who traveled by land and by sea, and
he lived at some time in a very hot climate. Their meetings in Amherst occurred in August. Circumstances were
such that she could not speak of him freely before others.
They corresponded. There is influence upon her thought
of a career stopped midway, as in, "Success is counted
sweetest" (Helen Hunt's favorite). She indicates that

there was something tragic and bitter in connection with his death. The reader will analyze the poems and judge for himself.

Assuming for the sake of study that Major Hunt was the man whom Emily Dickinson loved, what influence did he have upon her poetry? He undoubtedly influenced her to hold steadily to her course. He may have helped to develop her ability to think, though he did not really affect her ideas so much as discipline in expression. There must be no mushiness in her poetry. It must pass the laboratory test. But the chief influence which he had upon her love poetry, apart from the basic fact that he may have been the inspiration of the poems, is to be found in her vocabulary. Whether we accept Major Hunt as the lover or not, we must concede that he had a noticeable influence upon the vocabulary of Emily Dickinson's poetry.

Her lover was to her " the sea." Peninsula, island, are recurring words. One notes her fondness for the figures of the military, the shore, the harbor. The Civil War could be taken as sufficient reason for her use of military figures, were it not that her poems and letters indicate an individual more than a general influence. Nor can the death of Frazer Stearns, Austin's friend, be interpreted as sufficient human background for particular uses of these figures. Why try to substitute another soldier when we have Major Hunt, "who interested Emily Dickinson more than any man she ever saw "? One notes recurring throughout the vocabulary of Emily's poetry such words as: " promoted — escape — dungeon — fortress — drums (a favorite figure and employed in an unusual connection in the poem, ' I dreaded that first robin so ') — marksman — target — shot — skirmish — salute — battle — swords — bullets — cannon — soldiers — trench (an unusual figure in ' If he were living — dare I ask? ') (*Further Poems*) — epauletted brother — epauletted white — mathematics — science — atom — ratio — Finite Infinity — harbors — fathoms — divers — tides — frigates — sands — fictitious shores — reefs — gales — shipwrecks — charts — blue havens — isles of spice — latitudes (many times) — coral," etc. One notes how her mind dwells upon hot and far southern places when she thinks of him she loves: "India — Peru — Buenos Aires — Brazil — Italy," etc. One can double this list in a very short time.

Emily Dickinson made events out of incidents, it is true. She who could dream of bees fighting for pond-lily stamens, when a fly buzzed upon her windowpane; could see London nights in the flare of a village fire at midnight; and could send the poem, " Just once! Oh, least request! " to Mr. Bowles apropos of his acceptance of a barrel of apples — was one who could get an overpowering flood of love from one kiss. Whatever her experience in love had been, it was enough for her singing. She knew real love, requited love. Emily Dickinson was no pervert, no sickly little spinster shaping as love poems mere wish fulfillments out of a fantastic brain. Upon that point we must agree heartily with her biographer.

*

Chapter Thirteen

BEHIND THE HEDGE

*

ONE summer morning, a five-year-old boy in search of
his little Dickinson playmates, came through the gate of
"The Mansion" and started toward the barn behind the
house. It was to him a somewhat terrifying prospect. The
hemlock and pine which greenly darkened the house and
grounds; the courtly proprietor with his stern face and
kindly smile and lofty bearing; the mysterious lady who
so seldom appeared, yet who loved dogs and flowers and
children — these made the place an awe-inspiring one.
As he passed the corner of the house some one called to
him. He saw his friend. She was standing on a rug which
had been spread for her on the grass, while all about her
were potted plants among which she was busy. To the
child she was a beautiful woman, with soft, fiery brown
eyes, and youth upon her auburn hair; with her voice,
clear, low-toned, sweet, she talked to the child as to any
intimate, of this flower and that, touching a favorite, grieving lest the weather might have injured them. The child
knew how she could make things grow; could make wonderful things come true. Beyond were the old-fashioned
flowers of her summer garden: the nasturtiums, the holly-

hocks, and sweet-peas, the scarlet hawthorn, and especially the grass and the clover blossoms; but the child
knew that she loved best of all those strange ferns, and the
cape jasmines, and the *Daphne laureola* in the little glass
house just off the dining-room, which made summer for
her all the year. She cut a few buds and gave them to the
boy to take, with her love, to his mother, Mrs. Jenkins.
He ran home directly in great excitement. The day was a
momentous one. He had seen " Miss Emily."

He saw her many times. He and his sister and Emily's
nephews and niece were never denied by her. Whether
she were talking with them about the butterfly that had
just burst its bonds of chrysalis and was floating in the
sunshine among her exotic plants, or dangling baskets of
gingerbread and cookies and cakes to the gypsy marauders
who pitched their tents beneath her windows, or sending
to them the most entrancing messages that ever went from
the mind of a poet to the mind of a child " panting with
secrets " — she cast a spell upon them which the niece,
who lived to become her aunt's official biographer, never
threw off. No one can have an adequate picture of Emily
Dickinson until he has read Mrs. Martha Dickinson
Bianchi's chapter, *A Hedge Away,* which gives so in-
imitably Emily's relations with her brother's children.

Mr. Samuel Bowles would come, driving up through
the beautiful mountain gap, to spend the day with Austin.
He was on familiar terms with the Dickinson household,
and was " Uncle Sam " to the children, in later years.

Sometimes he would arrive unannounced; again he would telegraph ahead with a request for some favorite dish. He would sometimes be accompanied by Mrs. Bowles. He found a lazy enjoyment in these visits, talking on every subject except his newspaper, picking up the latest book, or lying on the lounge. Frequently he would write back, on his return home, "You gave me too rich food; the talk was too stimulating." Once, lying on Austin's piazza, with apple blossoms blowing over him, and his large dark eyes upon the distant range, he said, "This, I guess, is as near heaven as we shall ever get in this life."

He was only a little more than four years Emily's senior, and he and she became great friends. He was the never-failing news-bringer, a man who had inherited from his father and built up a paper which was not only the best of the New England papers, but one of the four best of the country. He went everywhere, as reporter of the Know-Nothing Council in Philadelphia in 1855; of the Republican Convention in Chicago in 1860; he went to Boston, Washington, New York, on countless business trips, and met the leading political and literary people of his generation. He loved to travel. Restless, suffering much from insomnia, change of scene and of personalities was better for him than idleness. He had tried to start a newspaper in Boston and had lived in that city from April to October of 1857, but "Sam Bowles and Boston did not suit one another" and the experience was an unhappy one. Cambridge, New Haven, New York, and Washington were, he thought, the most attractive residences in America for cultivated people. Maine, the White Mountains, Europe (April to October, 1862, 1870, and 1874); his famous trip in May, 1865, across the continent with Schuyler Colfax, speaker of the House, Lieutenant-Governor Bross of Illinois, Albert D. Richardson, war correspondent of the *New York Tribune,* and George K. Otis — two thousand miles in stages; Colorado in 1868; the next year with his wife and a party of friends on a western trip; Cincinnati, 1872; California with Mrs. Bowles in 1873; the spring of 1877 in Virginia and Kentucky and Chicago with Henry Watterson and Murat Halstead — such was his life.

He brought to Emily Dickinson the objective world as perhaps no one else of her acquaintance did. He was, moreover, keenly alive to current literature, though never in any sense a literary man. He wrote travel letters for his paper, and a travel book. *Across the Continent,* in December, 1865, will give some idea of his original points of view toward people and places. He was, of course, more interested in politics than in any other subject, yet he enjoyed conversations of a speculative nature — on religion and metaphysics. His closest intimacies were with women of a characteristic New England type, described by Mr. Bowles' biographer as women who " inherit a fine intellect, an unsparing conscience, and a sensitive nervous organization; whose minds have a natural bent toward the problems of the soul and the universe; whose energies, lacking the outlet which business and public affairs give

to their brothers, are constantly turned back upon the
interior life, and who are at once stimulated and limited
by a social environment which is serious, virtuous, and
deficient in gaiety and amusement. There is naturally developed in them high mental power and almost morbid
conscientiousness; while, especially in the many cases
where they remain unmarried, the fervor and charm of
womanhood are refined and sublimated from personal
objects and devoted to abstractions and ideals: platonic in
their attachments, speculative in their religion; intense,
stimulating."

Mr. Bowles was as free a spirit as wandered into Emily's
circle; almost a heretic in the eyes of the conformists.
Whether roasting oysters for breakfast in his open fireplace, or taking his house guest on an impulsive midnight
stroll through the moonlight down to his little office in
the *Springfield Republican,* or acting as host to weekly
Saturday night suppers, he was as delightful a man as
one would encounter. He was a man who stirred deep
affection in others. Dr. Holland was soothing, graceful,
and gently encouraging at a time when Emily was in need
of just that friend; Mr. Bowles was stimulating, brilliant
in his field, and with him Emily's mind traveled far and
wide. In 1866 he was made a trustee of Amherst College,
though not without some fear on the part of the authorities that he was too iconoclastic for their meetings.
Edward Dickinson wanted him, however. Thereafter, he
came annually to Commencement and to the Dickinson
tea party, to smile with Emily " at the gravities." He dis-

liked Mr. Higginson greatly. "Parker came, Higginson
stays to abolish Christ — conceited upstarts," he declared
in May, 1870.

On February 14, 1866, Emily Dickinson's poem, "The
Snake," was printed in the *Springfield Republican*. It
seems to have created some excitement in the family, for
Mrs. Austin Dickinson had given the poem to Mr. Bowles
without Emily's knowledge, and it was very uncertain as
to how the author might react. Here is the poem as it
appeared:

"A narrow fellow in the grass
Occasionally rides;
You may have seen him, did you not?
His notice instant [1] is.
The grass divides as with a comb,
A spotted shaft is seen;
And then it closes at your feet
And opens further on.

He likes a boggy acre,
A floor too cool for corn.
Yet when a boy,[2] and barefoot,
I more than once, at noon,[3]
Have passed, I thought, a whip-lash
Unbraiding in the sun, —
When, stooping to secure it,
It wrinkled, and was gone.

[1] "instant" later changed to "sudden."
[2] "boy" later changed to "child."
[3] "Noon" later changed to "morn."

Amherst
Dear friend
Whom
My Dog understood
Could not Clad to
Others.
I should be glad
to see you, but
think it an
Apparitional pleasure.
not to be fulfilled.
I am uncertain of
Boston.
I had promised
to visit my Physician

FACSIMILE OF LETTER FROM EMILY DICKINSON TO COL. T. W. HIGGINSON, WRITTEN
IN 1866. MIDDLE PERIOD

in a few days in
May, but Father
objects because he
is in the habit
of it.
Is it more far
to Amherst?
You would find
a Minute Host -
but a Spacious,
Welcome.
Last say meant
my Snake and
suppose I discuss
it was dossed
of me - defeated

too of the third line
by the punctuation
The third and
fourth were one.
I had told you
I did not mean —
I feared you might
think me ostensible
If I still entreat
you to teach m
Are you much
displeased?
I will be patient.
Constant, never
reject your knowledge
and should my

My Sternness goad

Sue saw them before
Myself that
Except the smaller
size

No tires are round
these hums to a
sphere

And show and end
The Argen - stones
grow

And later hang
the Summers of
Hesperides
Are long.

Dickinson

" Several of nature's people
I know, and they know me;
I feel for them a transport
Of cordiality;
But never met this fellow,
Attended or alone,
Without a tighter breathing,
And zero at the bone."

Mrs. Bianchi has given Emily's reaction to the manner of publication. In her correspondence with Mr. Higginson we have an interesting evidence of her reaction to the matter of the printing of her poem. The artist in her was annoyed that any change in the form was made by the editor, and she was fearful lest Mr. Higginson question her sincerity. She wrote to him [4] that if he should meet her snake and think her deceptive (since she had told him she did not publish), the poem was used without her knowledge, and also with her intention in the third line balked by the printed punctuation. The third and fourth lines should not have been separated.

Though her correspondence with Mr. Higginson had been throughout the war a very slender one, his interest in her had not relaxed. He took her at her word when she first told him that she did not wish to publish, and apparently he advised against it even when she seemed twice to desire it. The poems that she sent to him

[4] The passage, omitted from the letter printed in *Life and Letters*, page 268, is in the original manuscript postmarked June 9, in the Boston Public Library.

after 1862 were seldom her best, if we may judge from
the collection in the Boston Public Library. Sometimes her
grammar was like a tack in his mind. Her sudden lapse
of rhyme, her involved thoughts, her ellipses, were in his
opinion serious defects from which she must free her
writing before any publication, in justice to herself. His
whole policy was one of delay, slow growth, taking plenty
of time, where genius was at work. The experience, the
fate of Hawthorne and Thoreau he held to be impressive.
He felt, and said, that the greatest triumph of Hawthorne's
genius was that he was unembarrassed by his own ideas
and went ahead quietly, steadily, with a general public
so indifferent and an audience so small. " There is no
fame more permanent than that which begins its real
growth after the death of an author." Emily Dickinson
accepted his philosophy the more easily that the circumstances of her life, particularly her father's character and
advancing years, made it difficult for her to get away from
Amherst.

Mr. Higginson took her at her word in 1862 and he declared in his preface to her first posthumous volume of
poems that she wrote with absolutely no thought of
publication. There are suggestions to the contrary in her
writings. Twice she wrote Mr. Higginson himself — in
1876 and in 1880. In the first instance, Mrs. Jackson had so
far persuaded Emily that had Mr. Higginson been equally
encouraging perhaps Emily might have published. In the
second instance, she had promised three poems to a charity,
had chosen her poems, and was proposing to make spe-

cially prepared copies for her preceptor (who had complained of her handwriting). Whatever Mr. Higginson said was more than a personal matter to Emily Dickinson. He was a symbol. He represented *belles lettres* to Emily as he did to many writers of his generation. He had power.

There were other factors in her situation which might have had some influence upon her apparent disinclination to print her poems. When one writes in secret because there is something hopelessly unsympathetic in his immediate environment and sends his poems to persons at a distance, it is as if he were living on an island and communicating with friends on shore. The communications may be direct and perfect, but there is something, always will be something, between. May it not be possible also that the situation in regard to Major Hunt had its influence? Emily was writing her life's story in her poems. So long as she did not publish she could do this freely, happily. Part of her story was unknown to her family and friends. Helen Hunt began to write and was instantly successful. Her poems also were straight from her heart, were revelations of suffering, always expressed with reticence. It is true that Emily Dickinson wrote a great many poems which had no connection at all with her love story, but who can say how far the complications of that story may have had their psychological influence in tending to keep her poems in her portfolio. Furthermore, her development had been slow. She refers to that fact many times. Upon her bleak, small acre Emily Dickinson very late produced literary results which *she* thought were vital — wine and bread to the reader. Eagerness for publication is stronger in youth. As one grows older he cares less to make a start because the world cares less. Critics discourage late beginnings. In Emily Dickinson's own day much was made of the age of a writer. Mr. Higginson's advice was to a " young contributor." He wanted to know at once how old she was. The *Springfield Republican* more than once headed its column of " Gleanings and Gossip " with such an item as, " Jean Ingelow is 28, unmarried, and homely."

The lack of recognition of her work did not affect Emily's spirit. Into what seems to have been her deliberate delay of publication there may have been woven a bit of compensation for disappointment by reckoning the disadvantages of notoriety and how impossible it would be for her to continue to shape her own life were she once known as a successful poet. She noted that fame is fickle, that men seldom survive the evils attendant thereon. She cared for life as an emotion rather than as a science of climbing.

Her preference for obscurity was no mere diffident shrinking from applause. She craved readers, but she felt that the human spirit ought not to be displayed for vulgar sale. She hated the commercializing of one's art, the putting of one's mind up at auction which publication seemed to entail. She observed that the achievement of one who receives acclaim bursts upon public notice thunderously. Thereafter the one who has won recognition, struggling

to maintain his prominence, finds himself forced to call
to the fickle crowd as insistently as a drum, as solicitously
as bells used by hawkers, until descent to so cheap a stim-
ulant as rum. Notoriety that flaunts itself in periodicals
and newspapers welcomes even a trip to jail for its advertising value. She frequently refers to herself as a beggar.
In one poem Emily Dickinson speaks of the beggar here
and there who is working for Immortality, a gold which
is slow but everlasting. Though he who buys and sells
poetry in the manner of a broker may not have perceived
the worth of one in barefoot rank, now and then a beggar
has enough insight to carry him forward, though it be
with bleeding feet. It is interesting to note also Emily's
sympathy and affection for neglected, despised, and fur-
tive fellow creatures — the spider, the rat, the bat.

All of these contributory factors and thoughts of her
own kept the poetry of Emily Dickinson behind the hedge.
There she labored in the dark until she was thoroughly
ready, perfecting her art, aware of her extraordinary
power, and conscious also of her limitations. She held that
each should write whereof he knows: the queen, of her
court; Emily Dickinson, of her own world. Whatever
Emily's whim of flower, bird, tree, or snow was true art
if expressed as she saw it. If each poet will but interpret
the familiar his reader will wonder in amazement why
he has not written that poem. Emily Dickinson had pre-
science that her work would be so received posthumously
by discerning readers. There is reference after reference
to suggest this.

She who was "Nobody" took "vaster attitudes" when
the "bronze and blaze" of a sunset painted "her simple
spirit with tints of majesty." At such moments, "disdain-
ing men" she exclaimed:

> "My splendors . . .
> Will entertain the centuries
> When I am, long ago,
> An island in dishonored grass,
> Whom none but daisies know."

She wrote to Mr. Higginson that often, when tempted
by entreaties to publish, his paragraph in his "Letter to
a Young Contributor" had saved her. She quoted the
sentence: "Such being the majesty of the art you presume
to practice, you can at least take time before dishonor-
ing it."

The writings of Mr. Higginson were especially pleasing to her. "The Procession of the Flowers" in the
Atlantic for December, 1862, eight months after her correspondence with him began, might have been composed expressly for her, so congenial to her was his
thought:

"There are moments when the atmosphere is so sur-
charged with luxury that every pore of the body becomes an ample gate for sensation to flow in, and one has
simply to sit still and be filled. In after years, the
memory of books seems barren or vanishing, compared
with the immortal bequest of hours like these. Other

sources of illumination seem cisterns only; these are foundations. No man can measure what a single hour with nature may have contributed to the molding of his mind.

" The soul is like a musical instrument; it is not enough that it be framed for the most delicate vibration, but it must vibrate long and often before the fibres grow mellow to the finest waves of sympathy. I perceive that in the veery's caroling, the clover's scent, the glistening of the water, the waving wings of butterflies, the sunset tints, the floating clouds, there are attainable infinitely more subtle modulations of delight, than I can yet reach the sensibility to discriminate, much less describe. If in the simple process of writing, one could physically impart to this page the fragrance of this spray of azalea beside me, what a wonder would it seem! — and yet one ought to be able, by the mere use of language, to supply to every reader the total of that white, honeyed, trailing sweetness, which summer insects haunt and the Spirit of the Universe loves. The defect is not in language, but in men. There is no conceivable beauty of blossom so beautiful as words, none so graceful, none so perfumed. It is possible to dream of combinations of syllables so delicious that all the dawning and decay of summer cannot rival their perfection, nor winter's stainless white and azure match their purity and charm. To write them, were it possible, would be to take rank with nature; nor is there any other method, even by music, for human art to reach so high." [5]

[5] " The Procession of the Flowers," *Atlantic Monthly,* December, 1862.

She never forgot the thrill of her first reading of a book by Mr. Higginson. As late as 1876 she recalled the pleasure of that initial discovery; it was like an entrance into Paradise. She had often heard of a certain rare flower that grew in the woods, but when she first found a blossom and took the stem into her hands, the ecstasy was like that which his book had given. His writing was both truth and romance to her, and also revelation.

She agreed with him that in writing, the most fundamental facts of life cannot be put into words; that candor calls for less than complete frankness. In the Prelude to *Malbone,* 1869, he expressed the view that in most vital matters reticence is compulsory. " One learns, in growing older, that no fiction can be so strange nor appear so improbable as would the simple truth. . . . For no man of middle age can dare trust himself to portray life in its full intensity, as he has studied or shared it; he must resolutely set aside as indescribable, the things most worth describing, and must expect to be charged with exaggeration, even when he tells the rest." It was the recognition in his writings, of truths which she had accepted, that drew Emily toward Mr. Higginson. She tells us that she read every book he wrote. We do not know to what extent her brilliant and original mind may have influenced his thought. Similarly, a passage like the following, the thought of which can be found paralleled in a number of her poems (such as " A wife at daybreak I shall be " and several poems on death), may have had a greater influence upon her than we can prove. " Is this life so long? May it not be better to wait until its little day is done, and the summer night of old age has yielded to a new morning, before attaining to that acme of joy? Are there enough successive grades of bliss for all eternity, if so much be consummated here? Must all novels end with an earthly marriage, and nothing be left for heaven? Perhaps for such as hope, this life is given to show what happiness might be, and they wait some other sphere for its fulfill-ment. The greater part of the human race live out their mortal years without attaining more than a far-off glimpse of the very highest joy. Were this life all, its very happi-ness were sadness. If, as I doubt not, there be another sphere, then that which is unfulfilled in this must yet find completion, nothing omitted, nothing denied. And though a thousand oracles should pronounce this thought an idle dream, neither Hope nor I would believe them."

Privately, Emily Dickinson had been accepted by Mr. Higginson as an author. He read her poems to his wife, to his sisters, and to his friends. Apropos, apparently, of such an event, Emily wrote to him (1876) that she was glad to have been of joy to his friend, and was avaricious to possess further so sweet a privilege. There is evidence in the letters that he sent her some of his own poems, and that they sent each other books. That he continually encouraged her writing is also evident. Every influence brought to bear upon her mind and art had tended to confirm her in a belief in herself. Certain similar ideas were running through the study of her young tutor, through the minds of Major Hunt and of Dr. Wadsworth, through the philosophy of Emerson, through the essays and literary doctrine of Mr. Higginson. Be yourself. Life is sturdy; write of the things about you, life as it is. Take time, the world has always been indifferent to genius. Emerson in "Experience" and "The Poet" was supported by Mr. Higginson in *Americanism in Literature*. Mr. Higginson's quarrel with American poetry in 1870 was that it was too placid, too literary. Emerson had set free the poetic intuition of America; Hawthorne, its imagination; but in Mr. Higginson's opinion, there was no American poet of passion. The heart of the poet must unlock its secrets, must interpret life, must sound the depths of all human emotions, must give us great love songs. There must be ardor, energy, depth of feeling or of thought, and a vast amount of oxygen in one's style, but a fine execution aids these positive qualities. And it was this fine execution that Mr. Higginson felt that Emily Dickinson on the whole yet lacked. He wanted more grammars and dictionaries in making a literature. Emily's own question as to her writing was, "Does it have life? Is it breathing?"

The phase of Emily Dickinson's case which most troubled her friend was her being so much alone. Yet he understood the reason. Her life was one such as Emerson and Thoreau proposed as the kind of life a great soul should live. She put into practice, unconsciously, perhaps, the precepts advanced in "Experience" and "The Poet." She did not miss a step. But while the philosophers might

approve, the world in general has criticized. The Emily
Dickinson who for years did not cross her father's ground
to visit any other, has been variously assailed as a recluse who was too self-centered, too consciously superior,
too selfish to do any good in the world; a charming poet,
doubtless, but a failure as a woman; a peculiar being
whose chosen manner of living was a misguided one, the
result either of miseducation or of a love-disappointment
for which alone she is deserving of personal sympathy;
a high-minded soul, but a victim of her own inflexible
standards; a woman whose poetry is to be adored, but
whose way of life is by no means to be held up for emula-
tion by modern American girlhood. The public has not
reflected with what justice a comparison might be drawn
between an Emily Dickinson who gave the precious whole
of every day to living her poetry (for it is out of living
that poems come), and a Thomas Alva Edison who gave
sixteen hours a day to his laboratory with complete absorption every waking moment in his experiments. But, we
fancy some one saying — but Edison's achievement was
for the good of mankind, while Emily Dickinson's work
had another aim. We answer that life is not too rich to
spurn any contribution. The time may come in America
when men will see in another direction as far by the illumination of poetry as they now see by the light of the incandescent bulb. If we are pleased to accept Emily's poetry,
we must equally accept her life. The one could not have
been without the other. The Dickinson house and grounds
were Emily's laboratory. There she labored, self-immured,

creating her poems, impatient of trespass, holding herself to the largest pattern, with no time for smaller designs. She was even among poets one who was singularly devoted to her art. She avoided men and women who had no appreciation or reverence for beauty, who were petty and partial and chattering. Intercourse with them brought cross currents, interference. It was a waste of time.

One day between 1865 and 1868, Mr. Higginson received a two-word note that informed him that Carlo had died; there was a five-word postscript that poignantly inquired whether he would instruct her now. He felt for her sympathy and affection. He was earning his living by his writing and lecturing and was too busy to go to see her, but he tried to bring her into contact with literary people in Boston. From relatives and friends of hers whom he met in Worcester and in Newport he made inquiry, but no one could explain, even describe, Emily Dickinson clearly to him. In the absence of all letters from him we have an impression of coldness and indifference on his part which did not exist. The long letter published in large part in Mrs. Bianchi's *Life and Letters of Emily Dickinson,* page 72, gives a warmer impression of the situation.[6] In 1866 Mr. Higginson wrote suggesting that Emily Dickinson come to Boston to meet some of his friends. Emily was again having trouble with her eyes, and her physician in Boston had exacted from her a promise that she would come for an examination in May of that year, but her father could see no necessity for it and objected.

[6] See Appendix.

Mr. Higginson wrote again late in the spring of 1868, urging that she come to Boston, for he felt that if he could talk with her and widen her acquaintance with literary people, he might be better able to penetrate that fiery mist with which she seemed to enshroud herself. He made partial arrangements for her entertainment by one of his friends, and the prospect was so attractive that she seems to have taken up the matter with her father again, but her plan was negatived. She requested Mr. Higginson to thank the lady who proffered her hospitality, but her father would not let her come. He liked to have her with him when he traveled, but objected to any separation. She invited Mr. Higginson to be her guest at the Amherst Inn, for she was eager to talk with him and have more of his criticism and advice. She was grieving for Carlo, but had the hill behind the house for remedy. Immortality was the subject which burst all dikes. Infinite beauty, like death, was too near for seeking. Paradise was a matter of choice. Anyone who would might dwell in Eden in spite of the curse on Adam. Like a Cabinet Minister making a report, she signed herself only by the family name. Then she dreamed of Paradise, of meeting Tennyson at Ticknor and Fields, of having Mrs. Higginson for a friend; and one morning in August, her golden month, after a night of such dreaming, she received a note saying that Mr. Higginson would call upon her in Amherst on the 15th.

At two o'clock on the appointed day, Mr. Thomas Wentworth Higginson arrived in Amherst. It was apparently his first glimpse of the college town, and he found

it to be " a lovely place, at least the views." He went, by
direction, to the home of Edward Dickinson, "a large,
country lawyer's house, brown brick, with great trees,
and a garden." He sent up his card and waited for his
hostess in the cool, dark parlor. In the little delay which
followed he noted a few books and engravings and an
open piano, Malbone and O. D. Papers. There was a
pattering step in the entry and Emily Dickinson came in.
She was very nervous. She walked up to him in a childlike way and placed in his hand the two lilies which she
carried for introduction. She admitted to him at once
that she had lost a little of her self-possession for the moment because she so very seldom talked with strangers.
As she seated herself, she regained her poise and began to
converse. He sat at one end of the room, a kindly gentleman in his late forties, with a scholarly face, sideburns
according to the fashion of the time, and mild gray eyes
which bent upon her with curiosity and deep interest. She
was in white piqué and a blue worsted shawl. She sat
timidly facing him with her great dark eyes upon him in
perfect confidence. The hour had come at last when she
could talk, such an hour as she had not had in fifteen years.
There were certain points that he wanted to settle in her
case: her age, her personality, her background, her attachments, her occupations. Her brief biography in April,
1862, was in his mind: asterisks; a tutor; a friend who
was not satisfied to be but her teacher; a father, a mother,
brother, and sister who got down on their knees every
morning to address a God unknown to her; some fear

A View from the East of the Dickinson Home as It Appears Today; the Boxed Garden Is Where the Orchard Was in Emily's Day

which she was trying to forget through absorption in her writing. Deftly, he encouraged her to talk, while he sat and listened most of the time.

The first thing that he scrutinized was her hair; not bold like the chestnut burr, but " in smooth bands of reddish brown." Her eyes, however, were, as she had told him, like dregs of sherry. He thought her plain, without good features except her remarkable eyes. She talked continuously, deferentially, brilliantly. Her conversation reminded him of no one so much as Bronson Alcott, he said afterward, but better than Alcott, more simple and direct. It seemed to him that she talked for her own relief. Led on by him, she told much of her early life in which her father was the conspicuous figure — a man not severe, but remote. She told Mr. Higginson that she had never known that close maternal relationship which is reputed to be the essence of home life; that she had never had anyone to whom she could go when in trouble. Many of her unusual remarks were later given by Mr. Higginson in *Carlyle's Laugh and Other Surprises:* her amazement that many people had the courage to try to go through life, apparently, without any thoughts; her definition of poetry, which was dynamite in her brain; the utter impossibility of her ever being lonesome in any length of future time. She told her friend that it was delightful to talk to him truthfully because she so rarely had the opportunity. She spoke of Major Hunt. She had written to Mr. Higginson, four years earlier, that she could not fail to understand one whom her dog had comprehended. Sometimes she paused

and begged him to talk instead, but readily recommenced
at his suggestion. She was kept busy with household tasks,
she told him. She made all the bread to please her father,
and " one must have puddings " (timidly, " as if they were
meteors or comets "). When he said, at parting, that he
would come again sometime, she replied: " Say in a long
time. That will be nearer. Sometime is nothing. . . .
Gratitude is the only secret that can't reveal itself."

The next morning he visited the college museum to see
the world-famous ichnological collection. He met President Stearns, who was also taking the morning train, and
so they traveled in the cars together. From the window
were glimpses of cool mountains, but the river was low
and all was dry and burnt. At noon, as he was stopping
for dinner at White River Junction, he mailed an account
of his visit to his wife:

" If you had read Mrs. Stoddard's novels you could understand a house where each member runs his or her own
[illegible]. Yet I saw only her. . . . I saw Mr. Dickinson
this morning, — a little thin, dry, and speechless. I saw
what her life has been. Dr. Stearns says her sister is proud
of her. . . . Major Hunt interested her more than any man
she ever saw. . . . I never was with anyone who drained
my nerve power so much. Without touching her, she drew
from me. I am glad not to live near her. She often thought
me tired and seemed very thoughtful of others. . . . This
picture of Mrs. Browning's tomb is from Emily Dickinson.
Timothy Titcomb gave it to her."

*

Chapter Fourteen

"A NEW ENGLAND CHEVALIER BAYARD"

*

I⊤ had been Emily's habit ever since her 'teens to read and write late into the night. Hers was usually the last lamplight to go out. Then came sleep, and dreaming as the early sunlight sifted through her shutters: dreams of gathering roses with the Hollands, gathering with all their might to fill a basket that was never full; of standing by a pond of water-lilies darkened with bees; of breaking the seal of a letter from Austin whose very scrawl was drollery —— there came her father's knock upon the door. The sound of his " Emily! " punctuating the rap of his knuckles upon that door had broken some dream for many years.

He was a lonely man in whose circumference she seemed to have no part. Yet she understood him perfectly. Father and daughter had the same auburn hair, the same eyes of burning brown. A shy reserve was to her the foundation of sweetness. He had his dreams, no doubt; perhaps his secret, too, locked in that stern heart.

In Samuel Fowler Dickinson's home of straight-faced geniality such impulses and fiery instincts as the boy Edward may have had were painstakingly molded into a pattern of dark and simple hue. He must be sound in health, careful in expenditure, upright and honorable in deportment, and have a purpose in life. If he cared for literature and science, look to it that they did not lead him from religion and a moral life, lest he thereby lose his soul. Samuel Fowler Dickinson had impressed upon his children that no one of them could be a neuter. One's actions, concepts, motives, all pointed toward heaven or hell. There was no mean. Except for the Bible there were no books in his father's library, only dissertations and treatises.

He had seen his father grow poor for a cause. He had known his father to pour all of his passionate spirit into that cause, the building of a college in Amherst, the home of his choice. His father's life was a stinging plus. Edward was the sixth of his direct line to be born within sound of the old meeting-house bell. His father had been compelled by circumstances to uproot himself, and to break new sod in a far-away place; had died in that distant home in Hudson, Ohio, still serving a college, and (so far as there is evidence) without Edward at his bedside. The son had not seen his father in those five years before his death. He owed his father much.

Samuel Fowler Dickinson had put the wilderness between them; Austin should not. Edward Dickinson's only son, named for one of their positive religious ancestors, should stay within the sound of that unforgettable meeting-house bell. And so, when Austin, with much of his grandfather's exuberance of feeling and healthy restlessness, but with imagination and laughter strange to the ears of his father, seemed to like Boston over well and showed tendencies of remaining, the father was alarmed. Once the father had come home from a visit to his son, so grim and speechless that the women had not dared ask him about his journey. And when Austin, with his lawyer's diploma in hand, had come bounding into the house with the news of an opening in the West and his intention of accepting a legal partnership in Detroit which had been offered to him, so Emily Dickinson's biographer tells us, Edward Dickinson had been unable to face the separation and had offered to build his son a fine house next door if he would stay. He asked nothing more than that. The son chose the style of the house and of his living. Whether there had been a conflict of wills we cannot say. Austin was the pride of the women as well. More probably Edward Dickinson conquered by his stern-lipped veto.

For he had never been known to speak an angry word to any member of his family. He was more terrible than that. His was frozen disapproval. The very space from which he had silently withdrawn was potent. And still worse, there were the family prayers. He was a hollow iron sphere filled with explosive, that never went off in his home life because his family knew where the fuse was hidden; but in politics, his other life, he was frequently in the midst of sparks and flames which caused an explosion. In the absence of his published correspondence,

we turn to his printed political speeches for some slant
on the man, and are surprised to find how quickly he
comes to life. In his letters to local papers, in his speeches
before the legislature and before the House of Representatives, he has something to say; he says it clearly and with
variety in style; he has humor, wit, occasionally, and —
most amazing! — we find him quoting poetry to his fellow Congressmen after Emily's visit to Washington.

On July 13, 1854, he made a long speech in the House
of Representatives in support of the minority report of
the select Committee on Superintendence of the Armories,
of which he was a member. The proposition was to change
the superintendency of the government establishments
from military to civil. Mr. Dickinson had been unable
to go to Harper's Ferry, but he had visited the Springfield Armory to get the facts, and he argued that the
military should remain. It had been a subject upon
which Lieutenant Hunt might have talked with him
interestingly.

"I believe they [members of the committee] are all
colonels but myself," said Congressman Dickinson to his
respectful audience, "and I am nothing but a major. I
was afraid to go a grade higher, lest I get too strong a
thirst for military glory. . . . It is said that the military
system discourages enterprise, paralyses inventive genius,
is an insult to the mechanics of the country, and weakens
their attachment to our republican institutions. . . . If I
believed the charge to be true, I would be among the foremost in my efforts to put an end to a system which pro-

duces such results. Not believing the charge to be true, the obvious answer to it is that while our mechanics as a body are superior to those of any other country in intelligence, skill, and mental power, and while the instances are numerous of those who have made the most brilliant discoveries and signalized themselves by the highest scientific and literary attainments and been conscious that no circumstances could control or diminish the power of the 'divinity that stirs within them'—while we are proud as American citizens of the honor they have earned for us as a nation, . . . they need not the feeble aid which we can render them in placing them in responsible positions —they need not our praise to make them conscious of their own deserts. . . . [They] will ever look above all distinctions of class or caste, . . . and cordially adopt the noble sentiment of the poet:

> "'Honor and shame from no condition rise,
> Act well your part, there all the honor lies.'"

Edward Dickinson's independence in not joining the church at the customary age is the more to be appreciated in days when church membership carried with it social standing in the community as well as the sure sign that one was destined for heaven rather than for hell. When he did join the church it was with a seven-word statement that no one who heard him ever forgot.

When Mr. Kimberley's barn took fire and a gale of wind swept across the dry roofs and Mr. Palmer's house was charred and his barn caught fire, and Deacon Leland's also, Mr. Dickinson was one of two in charge of the situation, and after the fire was put out he ordered the workers to march to Howe's for refreshments as his guests. Their three cheers for Edward Dickinson preceded their cheers for the insurance company. When the new railroad was opened for the first regular trip from Palmer to Amherst in May, 1853, Edward Dickinson wrote to his son, " We have no railroad jubilee till we see whether all moves right, then we shall glorify becomingly." [1] The celebration did occur. His was the justice of an emotionless legal decision, yet we can believe that it was sometimes tempered with mercy, since we are told that his eyes would fill with tears at the sight of the sufferings of a wounded animal or of a bruised heart. At the cattle show Edward Dickinson was in the chair, with the president of the college on one side and the preacher on the other. At the dedication of the new church, Mr. Dickinson read a speech " in which he humourously remarked. . . ."

His love letters were " kindly," and his ideal of marriage as expressed to his *fiancée* was for a life of happiness governed by reason. He did not expect or wish for a life of pleasure. His ideal of reasonable happiness did not include the little dancing parties (which Emily and Austin invited to their home in his absence), nor the notes of a Jenny Lind, nor the training of the South Sea rose before breakfast, nor the " *Rev-e-ries* " *of a Bachelor,* which he thought the limit of the ridiculous. There was

[1] *Letters of Emily Dickinson,* vol. i, p. 115.

but one thing that he could not face — separation from any member of his family.

He traveled only as his profession or the necessity of public affairs dictated; to Boston, where he could combine business with a family visit; to Springfield, Baltimore, Washington, New York, and Philadelphia. Emily traveled as far as her father ever did and saw the same New England towns.

She was from the first his companion spirit in that household. He liked to sit in the dim parlor and listen to her playing the piano; he preferred her bread and prune whips. When she was a little girl he guarded her health jealously. It was he who took her driving with him that she might be out in the fresh air as much as possible in her babyhood; he who mixed the doses of medicine. Emily was not meekly quiescent before him. Where he had but one way of expressing disapproval she had two — she could withdraw to her room, or she could go out behind the house and smash something.

From those days when her father had knit gloomy brows at Santa Claus and all such midnight prowlers, Emily had studied him. She and Austin had their little jokes about him beneath his spectacles. She wrote to her brother that in his absence their father was like a trout in the desert, whereupon Austin would slip a fantastic paragraph or two into his bulky letters to be-addle their father's fifty years of " reality." She respected Edward Dickinson's reserves. He " did not take all the clothes off his soul." And from his silences there sometimes flew golden sparks. He

wanted to own the fastest horse in town; he rang the
village bell to call attention to a magnificent sunset; he
fed the birds and hid from them shyly.

She found delicious humor in watching him. She liked
to hear him call, " Tim-o-thy," to the new man in the
barn. It sounded for all the world as if he were reading
the text for a sermon. She loved that step of a Prime
Minister with which he went for kindling. Her father
sat through the " monkey-business " of Jenny Lind with
a rising anger that had a twinkle in it, too. He was certain to pull a dry joke about it all afterward, but he had
sat like one of the patriarchs throughout the applause.
"Father says our steelyard was fraudulent, exceeding
by an ounce the rates of honest men. He had been
selling oats. — So scrupulous was he! I cannot stop
smiling." [2]

To Mr. Higginson Mr. Dickinson was " speechless." But
Emily did not choose her friends for their interest in her
specialty. She chose those who were superiors each in his
own field and from whom she could learn something —
a famous preacher, an unusually promising young scientist,
one of the leading newspaper editors of the country, a
widely acclaimed woman poet, the most representative
literary man in the *Atlantic Monthly* group — and her
father was fully qualified to take his place among her
selected ones as a first-class representative of the science
of politics in his day. It was that she might not disgrace
her father that she continued to appear at his Commence-

[2] *Letters of Emily Dickinson*, vol. ii, p. 176.

ment tea-parties long after she had discontinued calling and general social participation; and to play her part as a hostess when Major Dickinson, once a member of the Governor's staff, lifted his glass of sherry in honor of the Governor of Massachusetts, his house guest. Her father built for her a winter garden of glass, and in the days of her long illness he broke a new pathway in one of the groves where she could go with her sewing or with a poem and not be seen.

It was the absence in him of an expressive, a caressive affection that was hurtful to her. Too busy with his work, she once complained. She wrote to Mr. Bowles that she thought her parents cared for him. To her cousins, in the year that her father died, Emily said that affection is so common an emotion that no one even notices it until he is without it, — long without it, and starving for it. Then his attention is centered on it. It becomes the refrain to his singing, and the subject of his painting; while below his window run ragged little waifs who have more of it on their poor doorsteps than their hearts can hold.

As he grew older — sixty, sixty-five, sixty-seven — Emily no longer opposed his wish, though she laughed a little to the end. When his lantern's glow was thrown upon the snow on winter nights she made a mocking gesture, but went home with him from her brother's house at once. When he asked her to do so, she gave up the proposed trips to Boston in the late 'sixties. This was not domination of one over the other; it was sympathy, deep-rooted in comprehension. At the same time, may

not Emily's intense interest in the English poetess suggest
that she saw a certain comparison of Edward Dickinson
with Edward Barrett?

When he was seventy, Emily saw that he was breaking, that summer was slipping into autumn. He had
never played, and like every straight piece of machinery
he had his leaning hour. There came a Sunday afternoon
early in June, 1874, when Mr. Dickinson, very weary, ill,
and seventy-three, wandered aimlessly and unhappily
about the house. Vinnie was upstairs asleep. Emily had
been neglecting her father somewhat lately. Now she
flitted in to the darkened living-room and saw his need.
Mrs. Dickinson was sent away on some pretext or other
and his daughter remained. Her companionship was such
that as the sun dropped lower behind the great blue-green
pines he said quietly that he wished the afternoon were
without end. Emily was embarrassed at this unwonted display of feeling. Austin happened to come in, and so Emily
suggested that father and son take a walk together. In
Emily's room stood an unopened box of books that her
father had brought her from Boston the day before, *The
Life of Theodore Parker,* and the *Poems* of George Eliot,
his daughter's choice.

The next morning Emily woke him for the train. That
evening, an unusually hot one, came Austin's footsteps
while the women were at supper. He brought a message,
and his face was very white. Tim ran to the stable to get
the horses, but almost immediately came the final word
that the Honorable Edward Dickinson had died suddenly

LETTER TO COL. T. W. HIGGINSON, AUGUST, 1870. LATE MIDDLE PERIOD

LETTER, JULY, 1874. BEGINNING OF LATE PERIOD

in the Hotel Tremont of a stroke which had come upon him while he was delivering a speech in the legislature at noon. In the distinguished group that attended his funeral, including a delegation from the legislature; in the resolutions passed by that body and the long obituary in the *Springfield Republican* on " this New England Chevalier Bayard " who was to be honored especially for his nonconformity and the courage of his convictions — Edward Dickinson had realized his ideal of a life of rational happiness.

When word came that their father was dead, the children had feared to tell their mother. She learned of it from a friend and crumbled completely. On the first anniversary of her husband's death Mrs. Dickinson was paralyzed, and the two daughters devoted themselves to the care of her, as she was helpless. Most of the unpublished letters from Emily Dickinson to Mr. Higginson in the Galatea Collection in the Boston Public Library were written during these years when Emily was confined to the house more closely because of her mother's condition. Emily wrote to Mr. Higginson that while her father had lived she had not been able to travel much because her father had come to depend so upon her as he grew older. After his death she was freer and might have gone (so we may infer from her letter), but her mother's utter helplessness confined her further. In a letter to her cousins Emily writes that she is kept so busy with physical attentions to the invalid that she has scarcely finished " Good-morning," to her mother, before she finds herself saying " Good-night." For a time her mother had begged Emily to sit up through the night lest her father come walking across the threshold and there be no member of the family downstairs to meet him.

Not long after her partial paralysis Mrs. Dickinson broke her hip and was thereafter unable to lift her head even for a glass of water, so Emily writes. The mother lingered for eight years after her husband's death. Austin succeeded his father as treasurer of Amherst College, and now had probably additional professional and business responsibilities as a result of the death of his father. Every day he ran in to see his sisters and his mother. In Edward Dickinson's bereft household, Maggie, the servant, must have had her hands full with her end of the work in that large house; Lavinia had all the personal and social contacts to meet; so we must believe that to Emily fell much of the duty of constant attendance upon the prostrated woman.

Emily had suffered from the lack of physical expression of affection in her father; with her mother she felt the lack of intimacy. Mrs. Dickinson kept one eye open during a funeral prayer that she might not miss a little drama of the dead woman's chickens trying to fly in at the window. She took food and clothing to the cottage of one of the workingmen and was followed to the door by the poor mother of the pale brood. She sometimes kept some childish misdemeanor from Mr. Dickinson's attention. The young people eventually won her over to their side. But she was not a mother to whom Emily could talk. The

Dear friend.
Mother
was very
ill, but is
now easier,
and the
Doctor thinks
that I'm
more hope-
ful. She was
partly imbecile.
She was
ignorant at

LETTER TO COL. T. W. HIGGINSON, JUNE, 1875, ALTHOUGH THE HANDWRITING IS
THAT OF 1870–74

Dear friend.

Are you
willing to tell me
what is right?
Mrs Jackson
of Colorado
was with me a
few moments this
week, and wished

LETTER, 1876. NOTE THE CHANGE TWO YEARS AFTER HER FATHER'S DEATH modern scientific approach to an understanding of human relationships is exploding many a shibboleth, not the least of which is the strength of the filial tie. In Emily Dickinson's day, boys and girls were taught that one of the Commandments of God is to love and honor as well as to obey their parents. We read in the *Springfield Republican* even during Emily's earlier years of the occasional suicide of a young boy; but on the whole, sons and daughters followed the dictates of their parents without question.

Anyone who believes that *The way of all flesh,* and such a contemporary expression of the same essential theme as *Andy Brandt's Ark,* are the products of a special point of view, should read the essays on the subject, "My Father's Philosophy," that are handed in annually by large classes of seventeen- and eighteen-year-old boys to a teacher in one of our Brooklyn high schools. Emily Dickinson was more sweet-natured, thoughtful, and dutiful toward her parent than the majority of these twentieth-century youths, but like them her honest mind told her that "honor" is something that cannot be commanded. Her feeling on the subject at forty was no different from that at thirty. Her mother made no effort whatsoever to enter into Emily's mental processes. She probably could not. Her maturing elder daughter was strange to her.

In those final eight years Emily grew closer to her mother than in all the forty-eight years of earlier association. The mother who went rambling after a spring rainfall and came in with a burr on her shawl had a place in the heart of the daughter who once brought home fields of daisies. Emily wrote to the cousins that they would scarcely have recognized their aunt, so much had she developed in character and spirit and mind in these stricken years. But in view of Mrs. Dickinson's condition may it not have been, rather, that Emily was seeing there something of the reflection of what she was giving, as expressed in this poem by the daughter?

> " I showed her heights she never saw —
> ' Wouldst climb? ' I said,
> She said ' Not so ' —
> ' With me? ' I said, ' With me? '
> I showed her secrets
> Morning's nest,
> The rope that Nights were put across —
> And *now*, ' Wouldst have me for a guest? '
> She could not find her yes —
> And then, I brake my life, and Lo!
> A light for her, did solemn glow,
> The larger, as her face withdrew —
> And could she, further, ' No? ' "

Emily Dickinson influenced every member of her family far more than they influenced her.

It was a night in March during the late 'seventies. Emily's light was burning very late as she sat in her room writing to Mr. Higginson. She had also been exchanging letters with Mrs. Higginson during the last five years or so. The rain was falling. The eaves were dripping with a lush sound that gave to her thinking a soft vermilion hue, so she wrote. The house was warm and still. She was answering a letter received perhaps a month earlier. Mr. Higginson had asked her if she were seeing anyone now, if she still wrote poetry, if she liked the February cold.

Emily replied that Judge Lord had been their guest for a week in October, and that she had talked with the family clergyman, Mr. Jenkins, and with Mr. Bowles. She was so busy with many little acts, by the way, that only at night, after the others had gone to sleep, did she find time, now, for reading; and her poetry was still her only recreation. Her eye fell upon Tennyson's " Harold," which she had intended for a present to her friend. After reading it Emily had put it aside, so she wrote to him now. The Tennyson whose " Princess " had pleased her thirty years ago was beginning to wane, like that Browning, once her favorite. . . .

*

Chapter Fifteen

HELEN HUNT

*

In the spring of 1865, in Cambridgeport, Emily Dickinson, ill and despondent, worked upon her poems and made company for herself; in West Roxbury, Helen Hunt had been secluded in her room for months, seeing no one. The physician who attended Mrs. Hunt feared she might literally die of grief.

Since the burial of Major Hunt his wife had devoted her life to two objects — the perfection of the Sea Miner and the development of her only child, a beautiful and precocious boy eight years old at the death of his father. She was assisted in the matter of the submarine rocket by Professor Twining of New Haven, and Mr. Trowbridge of the Engineer Agency, both of well-known scientific ability who were sanguine of the success of Major Hunt's invention and who felt that with an appropriation from the Navy Department to enable experiments for purposes of adjustment, the Sea Miner would be established as of great importance to the government. On March 19, 1864, Mrs. Hunt, still living in New Haven, had read in the *Journal* an attack on submarine warfare, with a reference

to Major Hunt which impelled her to write a long letter [1]
to the editor. She corrected a false impression as to the
accident by which her husband had lost his life; spoke of
the superior simplicity and reliability of the Sea Miner to
all other submarine inventions; reminded readers of her
husband's eminent position in the field of science; spoke
of her own more personal feeling in regard to the perpetuation of the principle of the Sea Miner. " I feel,"
she wrote, " that after Major Hunt has sacrificed his life
to it, it will be a cruel injustice to his reputation and a
poor return for his devotion if the government refuses to
afford every facility for the completion of the invention.
The personal sacrifice that he made in remaining so long
out of the field, and apparently idle, no one but myself
could ever appreciate. But he felt that the value of this
submarine defense to the country was so immense that it
would be wrong for him to allow considerations of more
personal advancement to weigh against it. And I never
knew him to waver for a moment except in one instance,
when a high rank with staff and engineer duty was offered
to him — the very position in the whole field which he
would have best liked; — for a few hours then the struggle
was very great and he felt that in refusing to take it, he
had practically laid aside his only chance for a satisfactory
promotion and advance during the war." But in the absence of a special appropriation, the question of expense
was an insurmountable one to the Department, and no
action seemed to be forthcoming from that source.

[1] Letter in the New York Public Library.

Her absorption in her son, Warren Horsford, known among their friends affectionately as " Rennie," was touching. He was an unusually promising boy who had inherited the remarkable mental characteristics of Major Hunt together with the winning charm and beauty of his mother. She devoted every thought and purpose to him. He was the quintessence of all the beauty she had known in life. . . . Her life was flowing over the rockbed of her mind: early, ardent, and adventurous Amherst years when she had gone skipping " from road to field, and field to road again " with heart of thistledown and eyes that held visions of Bagdad; her frail and lovely mother, from whose rich and exuberant imagination came better stories for children than the books could supply; her scholarly father, preoccupied with philosophy and theology, but never indifferent toward his family; the burial of her mother in the February snows; confused years of the two girls with an aunt away from Amherst; visits from their affectionate father, who was now living alone in Amherst; his parting from them when she was seventeen; letters from the ship and from the eastern Mediterranean where he sought rest and health; word of his death and burial in the Holy Land so soon afterward. There were a few years in the Ipswich Female Seminary and in Reverend Abbot's school in New York City; and she had been married, a week and a day after her twenty-first birthday, very happily married. The impulsive, intensely emotional, vivacious, witty, and beautiful girl offset and complemented well her serious, disciplined, self-contained, and intellectually distinguished husband.

Helen Hunt Jackson's Birthplace, Amherst

Friendships had always come easily. She was accustomed to popularity. She had enjoyed life in its full prismatic values. She loved the æsthetic pleasures, beautiful clothes, and social gatherings. They had gone to live in Washington. . . . She had had enough of Washington and did not care ever again to reside there. She had been happier in New England — Newport, Boston, New Haven, Providence, and especially Bristol.

She had accepted easily the orthodox religion of her Amherst father, who had delivered sermons as well as lectures at the college. Yet she understood and was sympathetic toward her husband, who was unorthodox, a non-churchman, concentrating his whole being upon a life of the mind, impatient of any interruption to his long hours of study and invention. She proudly accompanied him, when possible, to the scientific gatherings where he was in demand. For a brief time there had been her son Murray. To the deep and quiet pools of her husband's absorption with his mental processes, she had brought lights and shadows of loveliness, and eddying emotional currents that gave variety to his life. The nomadic career of an army man was interesting to her and she reacted easily to the vicissitudes and difficulties presented in such a life: the five winters during his location at Key West; the rasping anxiety of the war months of 1861–62; his permanent return to New England in good health; his overseeing of a hundred workmen in the New Haven fort; the building of the Sea Miner in which his whole future was bound up. It had been exactly as he had remarked: " All the balls, shells, rockets to which gun-

powder gives wings proceed on their death-dealing
courses in trajectories strictly conformed to the physical
laws expounded. . . . Were the lives of states pending,
the fatal missile, once sped, would not turn a hair's-
breadth . . . ruled by the same forces which rule celestial
spheres and falling raindrops." Truth, which he had followed so undeviatingly, had suddenly curved back upon
him. From the tortured recollections she had composed
her elegy, "A Funeral March." It is a poem of stately
beauty. She describes the slow funeral procession, the
pomp:

> " The air is full of shapes
>   We do not see, but feel;
>   Ghosts which no death escapes,
>   No sepulchre can seal;
>   Ghosts of forgotten things of joy and grief;
>   And ghosts of things which never were,
>   But promised him to be: they may defer
>   Their pledges now; his unbelief
>   Is justified. . . ."

The grave is filled. Swift winged seeds of autumn drift
down upon it noiselessly. She thinks of her lover, of the
father united with his child.

At thirty-two her life was yet before her and she had
Rennie. She made a confidant of the child and talked with
him freely of death. In the spring of 1865 in West Roxbury where they were then staying, Rennie, not yet ten
years old, was suddenly stricken and at the close of a brief

illness he knew that he was going to die. Helen Hunt was desperate. She exacted from the child a promise that if it were possible he would communicate with her after death. So wild was her grief that the nine-year-old boy is said to have exacted a promise from her that she would not kill herself. He died on the 13th of April. She had taken Murray in an August and her husband in an October to the West Point cemetery. Now in April she buried Rennie beside his father and brother, and then shut herself up in her room for months. There is a tradition that the fact that she received no communication from the child was responsible for her later skepticism, but her writings scarcely support this idea.

One summer day her door opened and she came out, pale but smiling, and resumed her activities in a manner that held much of her old vivacity. She placed pictures of her husband and her son where she could always see them, and talked of both freely. Whatever had been the hidden complexities of her suffering, she had mastered herself. The chapters of her life as Helen Hunt were ended, and the life of " H. H." was to begin.

> " Blindfolded and alone I stand
> With unknown thresholds on each hand. . . .
> Blindfolded and alone I wait;
> Loss seems too bitter, gain too late. . . ."

In October, 1865, Mr. Godwin of the *New York Evening Post* received a letter from Mrs. Hunt of Hingham,

Massachusetts, whose verses he had printed: "Dear Sir —
Will you give me a frank and a patient [answer], if the
inquiry seem presumptuous — to the question, whether
such odds and ends of verses as I have sent you and as two
or three similar things you may have chanced to see in the
Nation, are worth any money? — This is the only kind of
digging for which I discover in me any sort of capacity,
and if it can be made of any amount I shall be glad. I
know very little about such matters beyond a vague impression that everybody writes a great deal, and that it is
not worth an editor's while to pay anybody." [2] And a few
days later: "Will you say honestly if you would judge it
worth while for me to make a serious attempt at anything of the kind? I have no confidence in the urgings
and flatteries of partial friends: I would have more confidence in your unbiased criticisms than in that of any
other man in the country; the worst you honestly might
say would only corroborate my own estimate and misgivings; the best you could say would not go very far
towards allaying them." [2]

With the encouragement of Mr. Godwin, who engaged
her to write " pleasant and gossipy letters on the very un-
pleasant subject of Boston," and who did, apparently,
think her verses worth remuneration, Helen Hunt determined upon the profession of writing. And with Helen
Hunt, thought and action were one.

Early in 1866, Colonel Higginson, then residing in the
select boarding-house of Mrs. Dame in Newport, recorded

[2] Letters in the New York Public Library.

in his *Journal* that there was a new boarder at Mrs.
Dame's, with two dainty rooms upstairs which she had
arranged. She was Mrs. (Major) Hunt, a young widow.
She was in deep mourning for husband and child. He
thought her very bright and sociable, and prophesied that
she would be an accession.

Mrs. Hunt proved to be a lively person whose amusing
opinions, ready sympathy, and social talents made her a
leader in the household. She had a fine mental heritage,
a good education, and a first-hand knowledge of life. She
was from the beginning in daily conversation with Mr.
Higginson, under whose influence she rapidly developed
her taste for the literary. But though Newport was her
home, she continued to be something of a bird of passage. She sent flowers to Mr. and Mrs. Higginson from
many different places: from Brattleboro, gentians and a
mammoth basket of moss and climbing fern and leaves
and vines with all the dampness of the woods upon them;
from New York, a strange lilac and orange South American orchid; from Nice, ten varieties of wild flowers. The
philosophy of life with which she had come out from
behind a closed door (for her, an unnaturally closed door)
was expressed in her poem " Solitude," the concluding
lines of which are:

> " In anger, then, at last I cried, ' Betray
> Whomever thou canst cheat, O Solitude,
> With promise of thy subtler, rarer good!
> I seek my joy henceforth in haunts of men,
> Forgetting thee, where thou hast never been! '

When lo! that instant sounded close and sweet,
Above the rushing of the city street,
The voice of Solitude herself, to say,
' Ha, loving comrade, met at last! Which way? ' "

In an unsigned review in the *Nation* for August 20,
1885, which is by index attributed to Mr. Higginson, the
opinion was expressed that it was the Newport influence
which so rapidly developed a literary talent in her who
had given absolutely no signs of it before her residence
there in 1866. Helen Hunt had published some poems
before she went to Newport, but her association with Mr.
Higginson and his Newport friends did have a very stimulating effect upon her, and her residence there was, as he
said, a distinct epoch in her life.

Helen Hunt, now "H. H." in the literary world,
worked fast. With her unbounded vitality, initiative, genuine ability, and great capacity, it is small wonder that
she had a quick success. Emily Dickinson, sipping
imaginatively a nectar, then soaring skyward, in more
corporeal moments sent Mr. Higginson a book; but Helen
moved right in with " the Master," left her charming impress with wit and smile and flowers when she was away,
and in less than two years was included in his column and
a half on the female poets of America — Mrs. Howe,
Mrs. Aken, Alice Cary, Rose Terry, and " H. H." What
must have been Emily's feelings when she opened the
Atlantic Monthly for February, 1869, to read another installment of Mr. Higginson's " Malbone," and found

Helen Jackson

therein a poem by Helen! Here was her girlhood friend from her own home town, who had shown no symptoms of the literary, suddenly writing verses which the *Atlantic* took, and living in almost daily association with the Great Worthy himself, while Emily's verses, pride of the girlhood crowd, were only in the *Springfield Republican,* and grist for a correspondence course. One year more, and Mrs. Hunt, who had found time to do a great deal of traveling, even in Europe, and to write papers on domestic subjects for the *Independent* and other periodicals, had brought out a booklet of her collected poems, at her own expense, *Verses by " H. H.,"* published in 1870 by Fields, Osgood & Company, and had become the leading woman poet of America. On the heels of that, she had Mr. Higginson's pronouncement that she had made Christina Rossetti and Jean Ingelow look like second-raters and that she was a close rival to Mrs. Browning; Emerson was cutting her poems out of newspapers and magazines and carrying them about in his pocketbook; and Charlotte Cushman was reading " A Funeral March " from public platforms, with intense feeling and prolonged applause. Emily may have taken the major's heart; Helen took the literary honors and Mr. Higginson.

Helen Hunt did not forget her childhood friend. She was not one to do that. She loved Emily Dickinson and felt that Emily had genius, a truer genius, perhaps, than her own; though none of Emily's friends, it seems, ever saw the best of her poems during her lifetime. Time had removed the cause for a break in their friendship, if there had been a break. With her new interest in life as a writer, Helen Hunt was further broadened. She returned frequently to Amherst to visit her sister and to see her friends there. We are told in the *Life and Letters of Emily Dickinson* how Helen would come driving into Amherst dramatically and would have her horses walked up and down before the Dickinson hedge while she and Emily talked in secret with all doors closed. No member of the family dared go in, according to the biographer, who tells us further that Helen Hunt often tried to persuade Emily to meet some of her own new literary friends.

There must have been conversations over Emily Dickinson between Helen Hunt and Mr. Higginson. One speculates inevitably on how much Helen might have accomplished in Emily's behalf through her influence with Mr. Higginson, yet such speculations are scarcely fair.

After *Verses* of 1870, " H. H.'s " writings were in demand, and in 1873 Roberts Brothers published an enlarged edition. Together with these poems let us consider also her sonnets and lyrics (1873–85), which were collected and published posthumously. Her subjects are various: poems based upon myths and legends, allegories; poems inspired by her visits in interesting foreign places; poems on death — the death of a husband — the death of a child; poems written to prominent persons (Emerson, Charlotte Cushman) and to personal friends; religious poems; philosophical poems; genre poems; love poems; and nature poems.

One of the earliest, perhaps the first published poem, was a translation from Victor Hugo, in the *Nation*. Then came "Burnt Ships" and "Ariadne's Farewell," also in the *Nation*; "Coronation" (February, 1869), "The Way to Sing," "July," "August," "September," "October," in the *Atlantic*. These were among her best known. For years every school child in the land knew "October's Bright Blue Weather" and "September." "H. H." was a true poet. Her success was merited. Her poems are well worth the reading today. The philosophical, genre, love, and nature poems of the woman who best suited the taste of her own age, in comparison with the poetry of her friend who was to be accepted, though slowly, by a later age, present a fascinating study. Helen used a bow, Emily a pistol, in those years when archery was still the favored method by which people liked to have poetic ideas presented to them. Some impression of the difference between the personalities of these two unusual women who spent their childhood days together in the Amherst hills and woods can be gained by reading in immediate succession Helen Hunt's calendar of sonnets and the following suggested nature calendar by Emily Dickinson. The first lines of the twelve poems by Emily Dickinson are these:

For January — "It sifts from leaden sieves — "
For February — "There's a certain slant of light"
For March — "Dear March, come in!" (and also)
       "We like March, his shoes are purple — "
For April — "An altered look about the hills — "

For May — " Pink, small, and punctual — "
For June — " One of the ones that Midas touched — "
For July — " From cocoon forth a butterfly — "
For August — " Farther in summer than the birds — "
For September — " The gentian weaves her fringes — "
For October — " These are the days when birds come
        back " (and also)
    " The morns are meeker than they were — "
For November — " The sky is low, the clouds are
        mean — "
For December — " Like brooks of steel — "

Helen Hunt's religious poems were filled with a strong
faith and hope. Her philosophic, moral poems were
moody, yet ending on an optimistic note. A favorite figure
was of the blind singer, the blind spinner; or ships, shores,
tides, and lighthouses. She had traveled widely, had lived
in many cities, had married and had children, had won
and lost all that life held best; yet her poems, touching
upon broad lines of common human experience, seemed
not usually to touch the experience of the common human.
In the last analysis, her poems expressed more often the
mind and heart and mood and perception of rare and
sensitive spirits. This noticeable tendency is particularly
evident in her genre and love poems. The fact that she
was a New Englander by birth does not seem sufficient
reason why she should have turned invariably to the type
of character to which she chose to give expression, and
which impresses one as being personal in its inception

rather than a composite. For example, there is the poem
"Found Frozen," which concludes:

> "And yet
> 'Twas in the place she called her home, she died;
> And they who loved her with the all of love
> Their wintry natures had to give, stood by
> And wept some tears, and wrote above her grave
> Some common record which they thought was true;
> But I, who loved her last and best — *I* knew."

Personal, also, seems the poem, "In Time of Famine,"
ending with the words:

> " 'That woman's life I know
> Has been all famine. Mock now if ye dare,
> To hear her brave sad laughter in the air.' "

Helen Hunt's love poems are sincere, simple, lyrical.
Her theme usually is love distracted from one by
another interest; another love of the heart or of the
mind. In several poems she is specific. The heart of the
poet is a troubled one; hers is a great and powerful love,
but a love that has met a disillusionment. There is her
poem, "Two Loves." Two women love the same man.
One woman is a singer in the sun; the other a singer in the
shade. The singer in the sun loves her love because of his
high kingly head, his trailing glory, his beauty, his goodli-
ness, the promise of his triumph, and his fame. She has
pride in him. She binds him surely to her with her beauty.
She expresses her love in giving him "every swift bliss"

which men may know. The singer in the shade loves her love because of the patience with which he treads hard paths not of his choosing, his self-sacrifice, his ability to smile in his grief. She has tenderness for his failures, his mistakes. She has faith in him. She loves him so much that she makes a personal sacrifice for him. She is not so young nor so fair as the other woman. She knows that her love will miss in her what thè other only can give.

> " So fearing lest I may not feed
> Always his utmost want and need,
> In trust for her who can succeed
> Where I must fail, his love's estate
> I solemn hold. Its rightful heir,
> A woman younger and more fair,
> Loving my love, I bide and wait. . . .
>
> " ' O Love! ' I said, ' which loveth best?
> O Love, dear Love! which wins thy rest? '
> But Love was gone; and in the west,
>   The sun, which gave one woman sun,
> And gave the other woman shade,
> Sank down; on each the cold night laid
> Its silence, and each song was done."

Poems that will repay the reading are: " Avalanches "; " Dropped Dead "; " Appeal "; " Two "; " Exile "; " The gods said Love is blind "; " Forgiven "; " At Last." There is the poem " Tides," in which the poet says that the heart must be like a lonely, patient shore from whom the restless sea looses his strong arms and turns away to another shore that seems more sweet. The patient, forsaken shore must have trust even when the sea, compelled to fold the shore to his heart, is cold, and has no kiss, no smile. The shore waits, knowing that there will come a season when the high, warm waves will leap and the sea will return caressingly.

> " O sweet wise shore to be so satisfied!
> O heart, learn from the shore! Love has a tide! "

A beautiful short lyric is " Two Truths." Love came with tears in his eyes, penitent for having hurt her. He would not deliberately have hurt her for the world, but — he forgot. . . . With her own face stained with tears, " selfish tears," she forgave. She understood.

> " But all the same, deep in her heart
> Rankled this thought, and rankles yet, —
> ' When love is at its best, one loves
> So much that he cannot forget.' "

In her fiction, this same tendency was very clear cut. Her two novels, *Hetty's Strange History* and *Mercy Philbrick's Choice,* harp upon that same theme: a sharply etched New England girl, tied down by responsibility and her devotion to a parent, and falling in love with a man upon whom another woman has a strong and jealous claim.

" H. H." published *Bits of Travel* (1872), *Bits of Talk about Home Matters* (1873), *Bits of Talk for Young Folks*

(1876), *Bits of Travel at Home* (1878), pleasant sketches which might have been written by any intelligent woman of equal cultivation and experience. In her work between 1873 and 1878 she exhibited what some of her critics called " the idiosyncrasies of her genius." There appeared in certain well-known monthlies, notably *Scribner's,* a succession of stories signed " Saxe Holm." They were interesting narratives of New England characters, and attracted considerable attention. At once there was speculation as to the authorship. Persons came forward to claim the honor. There is in the New York Public Library some correspondence between the editors of a leading New York newspaper and Mrs. Hunt (apropos of a claimant to the authorship), which is a Chinese puzzle of cryptic queries and replies in shorthand. The astute literary critic of the *Springfield Republican* pointed out convincingly that Helen Hunt was the mysterious " Saxe Holm." There was general controversy over the matter and Mrs. Hunt finally denied the authorship, thus leaving it, even at her death, a mystery. The *Journals* of Richard Watson Gilder and Thomas Wentworth Higginson, who were the only ones in on the secret, leave indisputable evidence that Helen Hunt was " Saxe Holm." She readily admitted her authorship of the two novels in the " No Name Series " published by Roberts Brothers, and got a great deal of fun out of the whole adventure in mystery. The love of it was born in her. In 1876 she tried to induce Emily Dickinson to enter the great guessing game — went to see Emily about it, wrote to her — until Emily, more than

half persuaded, put the question up to Mr. Higginson,
who promptly negatived it.

Mrs. Hunt had been subject to severe attacks of perni-
cious throat trouble, and in 1873 it was deemed advisable
for her to try another climate. She went to Colorado
Springs, where her sister, Mrs. Banfield, was then living.
Two years later, she married Mr. W. S. Jackson, a
banker and a gentleman of very congenial tastes. In Colorado Springs, Helen Hunt Jackson filled her beautiful
home with objects of art: carpets from Cashmere, tilpahs
from Taos and other Indian pueblos, silk portières from
Bellagio, Egyptian bowls, Madras wicker work, Belgian
and Swiss brasses, Indian wallets, Chinese and African
carving, and a notable collection of water-jars from all
over the world. The house was built with its back to the
mountains, but Mrs. Jackson cleverly rearranged it and
converted the back porch into an open living room from
which she could have the mountain view. She lived very
largely in the open, and once entertained a party of Eastern friends at a luncheon for which she had gathered, as
a table decoration, twenty varieties of Colorado wild
flowers. Flowers had for her a conscious existence. *The
Procession of the Flowers in Colorado* was one of her
best-known expressions of this passionate hunger for natural beauty. She was not only a lover of nature, but of
natural people. She had a marked aversion for conventional and rigidly conforming minds; she preferred the
shriveled carpet-weaver, the toll-keeper of a certain moun-

tain road, the Indian basket woman at her gate, the car-
penter who stared at her Lucca della Robbia above the
fireplace, and exclaimed, "Well, ma'am, isn't that young
fellow just a-singin' hisself loose!" She had the artist's
love of types and local color.

She took as her literary model Mr. Higginson's *Outdoor Papers,* which she regarded as one of the most perfect specimens of literary composition in the English language. "I go to it as to a text-book, and have actually
spent hours at a time, taking one sentence after another,
and experimenting upon them, trying to see if I could
take out a word, or transpose a clause, and not destroy
their perfection." She was one of the painstaking writers
of her generation. "Form," in a poem of that name, she
called the "hidden secret of all things. Beauty than
beauty's self more fair," and possibly reminiscent of
Major Hunt's conception of the mathematical basis of
matter, she wrote,

> "No man dared say to curve, to line,
> 'Be beautiful, by word of mine!'
> Before all men the line, the curve — "

Young writers, poets particularly, sent to her and
brought to her their work, and she was their friend. "I
would give anything if I had written that!" she would
say of a poem written by an unknown girl. And to the
editor of a monthly, "Now I know you don't want another manuscript, but you simply *must* listen to this."
Once when there had been returned to her a sketch by

another which she had eagerly sent to a publisher, she replied, laughing at his criticism that it lacked genius, " How often do they bring *that* to sell! " She advised writers against the obscure phrase and the unusual word, and it is likely that she agreed with Mr. Higginson in some of his criticism of Emily's poems. With such a varied and impetuous and outspoken nature as hers, it was inevitable that she antagonized as well as magnetized, and that she was sometimes unjust, though she was quick to apologize to anyone whom she had wronged.

Helen Jackson continued to travel back and forth across the continent as frequently as though it were only a day's journey, and her intense activities made it difficult for her to make and maintain many friendships in the Colorado region. It was said that her participation in Indian affairs in the Southwest made her unpopular in certain localities there, and that when she lived in California, toward the close of her life, she was for a time unacclaimed by " the literary crowd." She thought California writers to be without standards and slovenly, and said so. She was very happy in the West and would have paid little attention to counter-currents had she been aware of them; such were to be expected when one was sincerely working for the righting of wrongs. Mrs. Jackson was too experienced a woman to bear enmity.

The Western epoch in her life brought not only a great personal happiness with her remarriage, but it marked a new period in her literary work. With her contributions to the " No Name Series " she began to get away somewhat from her love for a veiled form of writing and to exhibit strong moral interests. In Boston, she had heard the Indians, " Bright Eyes " and " Standing Bear," lecture on the wrongs of the Poncas. She met the two Indians in New York City at the home of a friend and was so moved by their story that she dedicated her life to their cause. After three months of research in the Astor Library, Mrs. Jackson published *A Century of Dishonor* (1881), and sent a copy, at her own expense, to every member of Congress. But in spite of her careful study in the libraries, which almost broke her health, and in spite of the assistance and counsel of army officers who had had experience in Indian affairs, her book did not have the effect that she hoped. Civilian critics, Theodore Roosevelt among them, set it aside as feminine sentimentalism. The Commissioner of Indian Affairs did, however, appoint Mrs. Jackson, with Coates Kinney, Esq., to prepare a report on the condition and need of the mission Indians of California, which was published in 1882. Since her historical work had impressed people with its fictional properties, Mrs. Jackson now cleverly hit upon the scheme of writing a piece of fiction that should be accepted for its historical value. In California, she saw the old Mexican life intermixed with just enough of the Indian to give her the background and local color that she needed.

Though something of her childhood love of mystery was disappearing in the more serious concern to which she was now devoting herself, Helen Jackson kept to the end her childlike intensity of grief and joy in her dreams.

She declared that she often obtained her stories from dreams. One morning in October, 1883, she rushed into her husband's room and told him that in less than five minutes, just before she had awakened from a dream, the whole plot for a novel about the Indians had flashed into her mind. In December she went east, and at the Berkeley Hotel in New York City she wrote *Ramona*. She told a friend in this winter of 1883–84, that in her *Century of Dishonor* she " had tried to attack the people's conscience directly and they would not listen. Now I have sugared my pill, and it remains to be seen if it will go down." *Ramona* appeared first in the *Christian Union,* a weekly, because Mrs. Jackson could not wait for monthly installments, and it was published in book form in 1884. In this novel Helen Jackson, as she now signed herself, found an unusually happy field for the blending of her varied talents. Poetry, fiction, characterization, history, purpose, sympathy, — all combined to make the book the most famous of her works. The *North American Review* in September, 1886, said that *Ramona* was " unquestionably the best novel yet produced by an American woman." It was ranked with *Uncle Tom's Cabin* as one of the two great ethical novels of the century, and it placed Mrs. Jackson second only to Mrs. Stowe in fame and breadth of audience.

Throughout her residence in the West, Helen Jackson kept up her friendship with Emily Dickinson. When Mr. Jackson accompanied his wife on her first return to New England after her marriage, one of the first things she did was to take him with her to Amherst to call upon Emily. Although Emily had declined to contribute to the " No Name Series " in 1876, Helen Jackson took the initiative in another venture. *A Masque of the Poets* was being prepared for publication by Roberts Brothers, and Mrs. Jackson, who was to contribute a poem, looked through the verse that Emily Dickinson had sent her from time to time, and chose a poem which was a favorite with both women, one which might easily have been inspired by the death of Major Hunt. In 1878 the volume came from the press. It is now out of print and not readily obtainable even in the libraries, but to those who are interested in the literary history of Emily Dickinson, this little book, the only book in which one of her poems was published during her lifetime, is worth examining. It was a famous company, among whom she appeared as the last in Part One, just preceding *Guy Vernon,* a novelette in verse. No names were signed. Emily's lyric, " Success is counted sweetest," was printed as a twelve-line poem without a break in stanza form, and differing in two words from the version in the *Complete Poems.* The eighth line was, in the *Masque of the Poets,* " So plain of victory "; and the last line, " Break, agonizing clear." In still another version which Emily sent to Mr. Higginson, she had written the poem as we know it in the *Complete Poems,* except for the last line, in which she wrote "burst" for " break."

One of the reviewers of the book was permitted to give to the public the names of the poets included, and we find that among the comparatively small and selected group were Lord Houghton, E. C. Stedman, Miss Alcott, Thoreau, Lowell, Bayard Taylor, G. H. Boker, Miss Rossetti, " H. H.," W. E. Channing, Aubrey de Vere, Bronson Alcott, Mrs. Annie Fields, R. R. Bowker, Celia Thaxter, and Sidney Lanier (with no less than " The Marshes of Glynn "). Whether the name of Emily Dickinson was omitted through lack of interest in " Success," or at the request of Helen Jackson in view of the circumstances of publication, we do not know. But we do know that Mr. Thomas Niles of the literary department of Roberts Brothers — the same Mr. Niles who had said to a Miss Louisa Alcott, visiting his office from Concord, " Why don't you write a story for girls? " — became interested in the new poet, wrote her, became one of her friends, and tried to induce her to publish some of the unusual verses which she sent to him privately.

Emily's persistent disinclination to publish met with Helen's disapproval. In September, 1884, Mrs. Jackson charged her friend with wronging her generation in not publishing those poems with which her portfolio must be full. Helen Jackson asked that she might be made Emily's literary legatee and executor in case she should outlive Emily Dickinson.[3]

Helen Jackson had become a reformer, and " work — work — work " was her slogan. She conceived that in heaven one would certainly continue working; that any other eternity was unthinkable. She had grown impatient

[3] Letter in Preface to *Poems: Second Series.*

with Emily's concealment of her work from the public.
She was, by nature, too socially active to feel that Emily's
life was other than narrowing. Emily, upon whom fell
hard the line of habit, seemed content to continue in the
grooved existence which she had always known. Helen,
who grew by contacts with the world, retained to the end
a flexibility of reaction toward changing environment.
Even though her actions at one time may have been mo-
tivated by depths of pride, they later received their impulsion from a will to large and unselfish service. Out of
her own agony, through varied experiences, Helen Hunt
became a woman of heroic mold, in magnanimity and
forgiveness as complete as in understanding and affection.
Her spirit soared above the mundane.

*

Chapter Sixteen

"MERCY PHILBRICK'S CHOICE"

*

WHEN copies of *Mercy Philbrick's Choice* were put into circulation, there was excitement among the readers in Amherst. The novel was published anonymously, and the authorship was attributed to Emily Dickinson. So impressive was the evidence that a member of Emily's own family, presumably Sister Sue, asked her point-blank whether she had written that book, and the charge was repudiated in a glance. Ten years later, Mrs. Sue Dickinson, writing an obituary of Emily for the *Springfield Republican,* considered it necessary again to deny the authorship, " unwilling though a large part of the literary public were to believe that she had no part in it."

The novel was interspersed with a dozen or so poems, and the assumption has been that the authorship was attributed to Emily Dickinson because of a certain mystery surrounding her seclusion, coupled with the knowledge that she wrote brilliant poetry which she never published. Perhaps Emily's family connected her so readily with this anonymous novel of the " No Name Series " because they knew that Helen Hunt Jackson had called upon Emily early in 1876 to try to persuade her to write for that series, which Mrs. Jackson's own publishers, Roberts Brothers, were producing. It seems surprising that those who were familiar with Emily's verse should ever have taken the question of *Mercy Philbrick's Choice* seriously, for her poems are quite unlike those in the novel, both in form and in content. They are Helen Hunt's poems and it was Helen Hunt's novel. The idea so interesting to readers in the Amherst region was not that Emily Dickinson was the author of the book, but that she seemed to be the heroine of the story. The Penfield of the novel was Amherst, described to the last detail. Mercy Philbrick might have been Emily Dickinson except for the heroine's lack of a sense of humor. The plot was fictional, but Helen Hunt Jackson, encouraged, doubtless, by anonymity, had verged dangerously near to fact more than once. Only Helen Hunt could have done it, and her frank character portrayal, her own opinions and judgment, are of special interest in absence of almost all correspondence between these two brilliantly gifted women whose lives touched at so many points.

This little book is of special interest not only for the author's revelation of the character and life of Mercy Philbrick in this particular setting, but also for the author's own reaction to her experience in life as herein reflected. The date must be emphasized, — 1876, when Mrs. Jackson was happily remarried and at the height of her literary career, trying her hand at her first novel, a novel which is a sign-post; a blending of the love of mystery which so colored her Saxe Holm stories of the preceding years, and the moral tendency which was to appear more fully in her succeeding work, at the turn of the decade. It was also the 1876 of Emily Dickinson. The passing of twenty years, a busy and successful literary career, residence in the invigorating far West, remarriage, had given Helen Hunt Jackson a vantage-point from which she could now look back upon the events of her early married life and view them as interesting drama, subject for literary material. Mrs. Jackson's approach to her subject in its various aspects is interesting.

She put her love for Amherst into that description of Penfield; — the impressive outlook and offlook from the town, the view of the fertile meadow country, the bold, sharp-cut range of mountains heavily wooded to their summits, the winding river which separated the westernmost peak from the rest — all in all, the fairest, goodliest country in New England. The poet's sensitiveness to seasonal beauties went into her pictures of autumn, winter, and spring in that valley region. Her detail, in both general and particular setting, will leave no question in the mind of those readers of *Mercy Philbrick's Choice* who know Amherst that Helen Hunt Jackson was giving her natal background. A hotel from which the ground fell away slowly to the east and south, a poorly kept, oblong-shaped " common," " the incoherent bit of architecture " known as " Brick Row," several times burned down in spots, a medley of odd signs, was Penfield.

Mrs. Jackson's treatment of Mercy Philbrick is sympathetic. She feels tenderness for Mercy, she defends and explains much that others were misunderstanding, she shows a special knowledge of the influence that the creative faculty can have upon one's actions and one's moods. She describes Mercy as of slight frame, gentle, laughing, attractive, but not pretty; with small hands and feet, brown eyes and hair, a sweet mouth with short upper lip and a full lower lip. It was Mercy's eyes upon which people commented when she was animated and blown by a keen wind, after one of those rambles through the countryside of which she was passionately fond.

Mercy was a combination of the realist and the idealist; she had some of the traits of an impulsive nature combined with those of an unimpulsive one. She would say things, do things, feel things with the quickness and intensity of a poet; afterward the realist in her would weigh and judge those thoughts and deeds and feelings, — often scorning and berating them severely. Because of her instinctive, " organic " honesty, Mercy had some rather difficult times. This antagonism in her nature to anything which could even be suspected of not being straightforward or true, was partly attributable to the secluded life which Mercy had led, partly to a congenital moral color-blindness, and a stiff New England conscience. She hated a compliment, she suffered over the secret of her writing poetry, she would run away and hide from tiresome and disagreeable callers that she might not have to speak and act social lies to them. She would treat her friends and acquaintances with alternations of frankness and reticence, as a result of sudden misgivings which made her introspective and absent-minded. As a result of these conflicts within herself, Mercy was becoming abnormally sensitive, when she came under the influence of a teacher who became her friend. If Helen Hunt Jackson is here describing the Emily Dickinson whom she had known in young girlhood, then Emily was more serious than her letters of 1845–46 represent her to us. Probably Mrs. Jackson was over-emphasizing an aspect of Mercy's nature because of its relation to the plot of the story; but the author's characterization throughout is so remarkably interesting and suggestive for the parallels which it affords, that one likes to note everything that she has to say about Mercy Philbrick.

Mr. Allen, a young townsman who had taught Mercy for three years, tried to talk her out of some of these fancies. He was only a few years older than Mercy, yet she seemed to him to be but a child. He had very early seen in her a strong poetic impulse which he tried to stimulate and develop. He believed that in the fostering of this talent she would find an outlet for her loneliness and sorrows. He recognized in her that exceptional nature to which a certain amount of isolation would be inevitable always. Mercy had, says the author, that deepest loneliness in the world, "the loneliness of intense individuality," which is increased when in crowds of people, and only partly cured by the happiest companionship.

Her teacher's fear was lest her delight in what the
senses received from the sheer pleasure in existence,
her abounding vitality, her eager participation in surface activities, would dwarf the intellectual side of her
nature. He felt that she would develop into an unusually attractive woman, and a true poet if she fell into
the right hands. She was showing a tendency to adapt
herself docilely to her surroundings, to be satisfied with
the little demands of every-day life, bread-making, care
of her flowers, obedience to the wishes of her parents
— a tendency which was not usual in one who had
the poetic temperament. Her teacher found that Mercy
was not only very childlike in her acceptance of whatever position in which she was placed, but she was also
childlike in her attitude toward God. She was not religious. With all her morbidly sensitive conscience she
had " no strong sense of a personal God." Mercy was quite
unlike anyone Mr. Allen had ever known before. She was
an interesting and absorbing personality. He inspired her
to apply herself more diligently to her books; he compelled
her to think and to write. He felt that her mind must not
be allowed to remain inactive, that she had in her the ability
to write poems which would one day be found among the
enduring poetry of the world. Mercy's teacher sent two of
her poems to a friend of his who was a magazine editor.
The editor was very enthusiastic over her work and
printed the poems. But in spite of all her teacher could
do, it seemed that Mercy Philbrick was going to be perfectly contented to settle down among her few little books,

her pinks, and her sweet-williams, thrilled with the natural beauties of each passing day.

Then Mercy fell in love. Here the author grows somewhat sharper. Of course all who read *Mercy Philbrick's Choice* with an idea that Helen Hunt Jackson may have had Emily Dickinson as a prototype for her heroine are going to wonder just how she handled that love-affair. Obviously Mrs. Jackson could not, would not give a recognizable description of Major Hunt, presuming that he belongs to the story. But she analyzes the affair interestingly.

Stephen White is something of an æsthete whose feeling toward human relationships and what constitutes crime or sin was based upon instinct and taste rather than upon conviction and moral principle. He loved Mercy. Though he knew he could not marry her so long as his mother lived, he accepted Mercy's love for him and took the initiative in many a little subterfuge that the woman who stood between the lovers might not know of their meetings. The relation between Mercy and Stephen was, in the opinion of the author, " unfortunate " and " abnormal," for their natures were so diametrically opposite that one was certain to cause the other a very keen sacrifice and suffering. Mercy had little realization of her true position, little knowledge of the language and the currency of true love, says the author, in substance. If anyone had pointed out to the young woman, who was so easily accepting the situation, that the man was not doing an honorable thing in encouraging her to love him when he could not marry her, that he was placing her in a wrong position, was perhaps ruining her whole life, Mercy would have become indignant. Her reply would have been that he needed her, that even his kiss had been " brotherly," and that she had a right to love whom and when she pleased, regardless of circumstances; that she was perfectly justified in devoting her entire life to him, without ever being his wife, if she chose to. There was, in Mercy's opinion, an unselfishness in such a devotion that made it an even holier bond than that of marriage. Her devotion to Stephen gave a ruling motive to her life. She was very happy. Hindrances, sacrifices, difficulties arising out of her relation to Stephen seemed less than nothing.

At this crisis in her life Mercy met a preacher, many years older than she, who was to have almost as powerful an influence upon her as had Stephen. Parson Dorrance was a man eminent in his community (which was not far from Penfield), a lover of poetry and of astronomy, a man of simplicity and power, who put everyone at ease in his presence. His wife had been a woman of mental brilliance and great personal beauty; she was said to have been as clever and as cultured as her husband. He was now a widower. Mercy had heard him preach twice, and had been so impressed by his face, his voice, and his words that she had longed to know him. She was, therefore, particularly pleased when the parson was introduced to her at a picnic by her friend Lizzie Hunter.

Lizzie had already shown him some of Mercy's poems and had told him something of Mercy's life. The parson seemed venerable to Mercy, but his interest in her writing and his friendship and advice meant much to her. The parson found in her poetry an almost masculine quality — a " condensation of thought " which charmed him as much as did its beauty. He talked with her about the old English poets, especially his favorite, Wordsworth; but Mercy declared that she had not lived where there were many books, and that even her tutor's enthusiasm for Wordsworth had not aroused in her a love for that poet. Mrs. Jackson analyzes the relationship between Mercy and Parson Dorrance very clearly. One wonders if she may not have had a friendly purpose in this. Though Mercy had been strongly attracted to the clergyman from the beginning, there was never anything of the personal in her feeling for him. It was rather a thirst for moral and intellectual guidance. The author comments upon the difference between the sentiment which Mercy Philbrick felt for Parson Dorrance and " that absorbing conscious-ness which passionate love feels of its object." Had the good preacher been from another planet, adds Mrs. Jackson, Mercy could not have felt less of passionate love for him. But the gossips in the village could not understand it so. Because the parson called upon Mercy, tongues began to wag. No one dreamed of Mercy's feeling for Stephen. She never mentioned his name to any of her friends, and he avoided her in public. Stephen was not at all jealous of Parson Dorrance, for, like Mercy, Stephen considered the good man too venerable and Godlike for serious considera-tion as a rival to him. Stephen understood what the

preacher meant to Mercy. His years of experience, his
culture, his firm moral rectitude which so appealed to
Mercy's inexorable nature, his keen spiritual vision which
cleared up and set at rest her old doubts and perplexities,
made the Parson Mercy's strongest friend. How eagerly
she questioned him! Her acquaintance with him was a
turning-point in her life. The preacher, in turn, was impressed with Mercy's talents and charm.

Men understood Mercy better than did women. Indeed,
she made all other women seem dull and flavorless by
comparison, so unique and incalculable was she. She had
a certain impersonality of interests and enthusiasms; she
could look on each chosen friend as merely an expression
of ideas or narrations. She was misunderstood by the
world in general, was often accused of heartless flirting.
The blending in her of the capacity for viewing persons
quite objectively with the capacity for loving individuals
very deeply was analogous somewhat to the combination
in her of the practical and the poetic. In contrast with the
starlike quality of Mercy, Helen Hunt Jackson mentions
Lizzie Hunter, the nestling kitten type of woman who
loves to cling and to caress and be fondled; who had,
moreover, a deep maternal instinct and great loyalty of
affection. " More women like her would mean happier
children and husbands," remarks Helen Hunt Jackson,
spiritedly.

Lizzie could not understand why Mercy did not marry.
It seemed to Lizzie that it would be better to take any man
who offered himself rather than never marry at all.

Mercy's eyes filled with tears whenever she was reproached for her idealism. It was impossible for her to explain to a woman like Lizzie what love meant to her, to explain what it meant to her, a poet, just to be alive. "Why not the parson?" proposed Lizzie, the little match-maker. Mercy replied indifferently that Parson Dorrance no more needed personal ministrations to make him happy than did God himself. But Lizzie continued to hope.

Then came a break in Mercy's friendship with Stephen. The latter did something that outraged Mercy's moral sense. Stephen suffered acutely at Mercy's treatment of him, for he could see no reason at all for it. Mercy's art was becoming more to her all the time, and strangers who saw her poems were writing words of praise and en-couragement. She was building up about her a circle of appreciative friends, an audience for her poetry. That consciousness that there is always some one ready to listen is an exquisite happiness to a true artist, says the author; it is more stimulating to him than all the flattery and com-ment that the world at large can give.

Mercy had now so many new interests and occupations, her thoughts were so healthfully and engrossingly filled, that there was no room in her mind for morbid brooding and passionate longing. Separation from Stephen did won-ders for her. She began to outgrow him, though she did not realize it. The test of time began to adjust the rela-tions between them to what it should always have been, declared the author. Mercy continued to live for Stephen, to consider that she and he belonged to each other forever, in spite of the moral lapse on his part that had physically separated them. Mercy was really giving Stephen's name to an ideal personality, in the opinion of the author, a personality which had actually never existed. She poured her affection and loyalty into her poems. Helen Hunt Jackson raises the question, could Mercy have really loved Stephen and remained satisfied with a daily life apart from him? Could she have loved him and at the same time have been so busy and happy with plans and aspirations which excluded him? She gives Mercy's probable answer — Why brood, and waste one's life merely because one cannot see the object of his love? But, insists the author, was it truly love for Stephen himself, or was it not rather a blending of the poet's idealization of love with the reality of Stephen? In the beginning of the affair Stephen has seemed weak; Mercy, the sufferer; in the end, Stephen suffers deeply while Mercy gradually drifts from him, absorbed in her songs of love. On the whole Mrs. Jackson seems to blame Stephen for the inception of the love affair and to sympathize with Mercy because of the blighting effect which such a secret affair will have upon her life. Then when she sees that Mercy's life is *not* blighted her sympathies are with Stephen.

For thirty years Mercy lived a rich and uneventful life. Her sunshiny nature, her overflowing joy so outweighed her loneliness and sorrow, that people often commented upon the apparent lack of any tragedy in her life. This, in the opinion of the author, was the twofold result of her true poet's temperament and her " ever-increasing spirituality of nature." Her religion did not take the form of church or creed. It was deeper than that. It was expressed in her realization of the true significance of being alive, in her " spiritual communion " with the universe. Mercy's poems became more subjective as she grew older, and seemingly so personal that the poet often had to explain that they were purely dramatic and fancied. But, says Mrs. Jackson, the intensity of Mercy's words might have revealed to one who analyzed the poems carefully that they had come from the depths of a profound and very real experience.

When Mercy first left Penfield she suffered over her experience with Stephen. As time passed she began to feel doubt and remorse, then gradually the sense that perhaps the affair had been a mistake. With the development of her art she made literary material of her experiences. In the fictional conclusion to *Mercy Philbrick's Choice* the parson dies, and after his death Mercy begins slowly to transfer her allegiance to him. In retrospect he seemed to be a high white peak of morality on the distant horizon. Other men loved Mercy and wished to marry her, but there was no one of them who did not feel himself withheld, separated from her essentially, in spite of her frank and loving ways. Her fame and influence as a poet mounted higher with the succeeding years.

So much for Helen Hunt Jackson's interesting novel.

Can we wonder that Emily Dickinson turned white when one of the ladies in her family, bearing the anonymous book in her hand, doubtless, came into Emily's room with the breathless question, " Why, Emily! Did you write this book ? "

*

Chapter Seventeen

CALLED BACK

*

ONE summer's day, shortly after the death of her father, Emily Dickinson was working with her lilies and heliotropes in her old-fashioned garden. Her sister called to her. Emily turned, and must have dropped her shears and watering-tin in her astonishment. There stood a ghost in her garden — a ghost with a deep voice that spoke. It was Dr. Wadsworth, now sixty years of age, and heavier since his seven years in the far West. In spite of a partial paralysis which interfered with clearness of utterance, he had accustomed himself to speaking so as to throw his voice a long distance. As he stood before Emily Dickinson he had a twinkle in his eye but a very solemn countenance as he made a little joke out of the twenty years that had passed since their last conversation.

Sometime during these twenty years Emily's father had introduced to her Mr. James Dickson Clark, possibly in the late 'sixties when Mr. Clark was spending some time in his country home near Northampton in an effort to regain his health. To her surprise, Emily found that Mr. Clark was a life-long friend of the noted Philadelphia preacher, and together with other members of his family

287

had often spent Thanksgiving Day with the Wadsworths. It was upon his Thanksgiving sermon that Dr. Wadsworth usually expended his greatest effort. Mr. Clark had no doubt told her something of the clergyman's sojourn in San Francisco. Now she heard more from her friend's own lips.

Dr. Wadsworth had won so wide a recognition in Philadelphia that he had been given calls to most of the older large cities — New Orleans, New York, Brooklyn, Boston, and Baltimore — but he had declined. His success in building up church congregations, however, made him feel it his duty to attempt a new and more virgin field, and so in the early summer of 1862 he had moved with his wife and two children to San Francisco, where he became pastor of Calvary Church. It is said that Artemus Ward made a comical bow to him as the head preacher of the West. There certainly was a Californian who traveled one hundred and twenty miles every Saturday just to hear him, while the young Dutch missionary to Japan, Guido Fridolin Verbeek, " citizen of no country," wrote that he would gladly walk twenty miles to hear Mr. Beecher or Dr. Wadsworth preach. Many incidents are related of how his chance conversation in country or city, in street or train, had changed lives. Rendered nervous by the earthquake indications in San Francisco, Dr. Wadsworth had returned with his family to Philadelphia in 1869, where he had preached for a time in the Third Reformed Dutch Church, and then in the (Clinton Street) Immanuel Presbyterian Church.

But, as Emily Dickinson had once remarked, there was a special meat in the mind of each one of her friends toward which she burrowed. The kernel in the mind of every preacher, for Emily, was his conception of immortality. Of this we have ample evidence in her letters. She wrote to Mr. Higginson between 1874 and 1875, asking him if he would explain to her his idea of immortality, and added, in the manuscript letter now in the Galatea Collection, that she had introduced the subject because she had heard that Mr. Higginson himself had been a preacher in years past. Death had been the chief event in Emily Dickinson's life since she last saw her friend, but to outward appearance she was the same brilliant, birdlike personality. Nothing could dim her sheer joy in existence. Her mind was as supple, her expression perhaps more cryptic, at forty-four or so. Dr. Wadsworth told his family, so that it is now a tradition with them, how eagerly Emily Dickinson questioned him as to the nature of immortality and the mystery of death. The clergyman's idea of heaven seems to have been the conventional one, but the poet in him made of the process of dying but another form of poetry.

Her second conversation with the clergyman came at a time when his thoughts would be most likely to color Emily Dickinson's own mind and his firmness of belief would be of greater moment to her; for during the next ten years all her remaining major friendships were swept away by death. Eliza Coleman Dudley, Mr. Bowles, Dr. Holland, Judge Lord, and deaths that came almost as

near to her — Maggie's brother, the little daughter of
Dick, the workingman — each in turn gave her some new
aspect of the great theme which became absorbing to her.
We do not find anyone in literature who drew so much
from the experience. Where a lesser would have been cut
down under the swinging sickle, this poet made songs
from her scrutiny of death. The mind of a Dr. Wadsworth, or a Mr. Higginson, or a Major Hunt never really
changed the mind of Emily Dickinson. The strong and
sympathetic intellect of a friend served, rather, to stimulate her own mind to its particular expression.

It is likely that Major Hunt had had the greatest influence of any. We have not only Mr. Higginson's opinion
in the matter, but there is internal evidence, as well. The
publication of further poems, letters, or any documents
that would serve to throw light upon this friendship
would be of interest and value to those who wish to come
to a true understanding of the mind and poetry of Emily
Dickinson. When Emily went down to Washington and
Philadelphia in 1854 she had much of New England theology in her speech, as the two or three published letters
of 1854 and 1855 suggest. But during the next five or six
years we can see a change. It is dangerous to judge from
so few letters, but from the material that we have we must
conclude that Emily was becoming irreverent, delight-
fully so. Perhaps Mr. Bowles, to whom she was writing,
encouraged her in this freedom of expression; though one
of the most religious of men, he was in his way as independent as was Major Hunt. The major's unusual mind

Because ~~That~~
you are going
And never
coming back
And I, however
absolute
May overtake
your ~~track~~.

Because ~~That~~
~~Death~~ is Final,
However First
it be
This instant
be suspended
Above Mortality

UNPUBLISHED POEM

Dear friend,

I heard you had found the Lane to the Indies Columbus was looking for.

There is no one so happy her Master is happy as his grateful Pupil. The most noble Congratulation it ever befell me to offer is that you are yourself.

Till it has loved—no Man or Woman

Unpublished Letter

had infinite attraction for Emily Dickinson while he lived, because his thoughts were so different, so new. He died. She was left to grapple alone with his profound conceptions. The war was going on. Dr. Wadsworth was too far away to make even correspondence of much help to her, if there were letters. It was to Mr. Higginson that she turned during these years. In an unpublished letter to him she includes a short poem in which she indicates that she has been trying to get at a conception of heaven through the use of logic. In one of her recently published poems she speaks of having tried to use a formula in understanding the divine. In another unpublished poem, to Mr. Higginson, which the handwriting seems to place in the very late 'sixties or else it was a copy of a poem written earlier, she writes that her lover is going from her and that death will be the end. She says that this meeting and parting are above everything mortal to her because she has a premonition that she may not be able to follow along the intellectual pathway which he has blazed. Something may in time have blown like a fine obscuring cloud between her and that pathway.

Though Mr. Higginson *had* been a preacher, he was a man of letters when Emily Dickinson was writing to him. He was very busy and the correspondence frequently lagged painfully. With the passing of time Emily's premonition was coming true. The major had represented distraction, confusion to her. Her father died. Dr. Wadsworth came back. He brought solution into her confusion. It was the certainty and the joy inherent in his philosophy that had most influence upon her. She finally says that God (presumably the God with whom the clergyman was familiar) is more easeful in the extremity of death than formula. Formula had failed. And in another poem, recently published, she admits that something had come like an obscuring cloud between her and the track toward heaven left by her lover.

There are at least one hundred and forty poems illustrative of Emily Dickinson's various ideas on death: expressions of awe, of respect, a feeling for the dignity, the *éclat* of death, its dramatic finality, its nonchalance. At times she was conscious of the relative unimportance of dying as compared with living; this earth was too beautiful to leave for any other promised. But in another mood, death seemed to hold a prospect of security and tenderness that made it preferable to much in life. She felt courage, and assurance and curiosity, and the unscalable mystery of the experience. Again, death might be a deception; she sometimes feared for others, felt haunted. She measured her time by the deaths of those she loved. There were moments when she was aware only of the agony of separation, or that death would mean reunion. There are poems on death as emancipation, a return to one's native land; and a poem in which she feels death to be something which gives distinct value to life. Once only she suggests the idea of reincarnation. Toward the close of her life death was morning, it was joy and compensation. Read Emily Dickinson's letter to Dr. and Mrs. Holland in the autumn of 1876 for a fantastic prose revelation of her

thoughts upon death in which her favorite figure of a
play is used.

At 1:30 A.M. on the 5th of July, 1879, the night watchman, looking up by chance at the Baptist Church steeple,
saw shadows thereon thrust like tongues of flame. He took
one glance in the direction of the Amherst House and
ran to give the alarm. In less than ten minutes a hundred-
thousand-dollar fire was leaping from roof to roof along
the west side of the village green, from the Amherst
House to the post office, the savings bank, the town offices,
the public library, to the largest livery-stable in western
Massachusetts. There was wild running from every direction, and no Edward Dickinson to take charge. Above the
din sounded the whips of the hostlers and the cries of
thirty-eight horses fighting. Mr. Stebbins himself came
quickly to order that each horse be led out by the bridle,
and then there was no further difficulty. At 2 A.M. Charles
Fay mounted a Kentucky horse at the corner of the Amherst House, and in seventeen minutes was in Northampton, six miles away. After twenty minutes the water in the
reservoir gave out, and the John Tappan steamer, sent
with half a dozen men as Northampton's aid, did not
reach Amherst until daybreak.

Down at one end of Main Street, in the Dickinson
home, Emily was awakened by the clinking of the bells.
She sprang to the window and saw a setting like the first
act of a great drama; the sun and the high moon were
shining at the same time, and the birds were singing with

brazen throats. A flutter outside her door, and an agitated Vinnie came, soft as an Indian in the undergrowth, to comfort Emily, to assure Emily that the Fourth of July was still at its climax. All of those distant sounds were but echoes of the Fourth of July. She led Emily away into their sleeping mother's room, where mighty Maggie, flushed and wild, sat with a finger at her lips. Emily wrote to her cousins afterward that she felt it as well to say nothing, since Vinnie had gone to so much trouble to deceive her; but Emily took care to seat herself where she had a good view of the performance. So bright was the night that she could see a caterpillar on a leaf in the orchard. In the distance there was confusion of crashing timber and exploding oil, voices and footfalls, and cannon soft as plush. And Emily, who calmly thought that they were burning up, reveled in a summer night with footlights and pronounced the whole experience like a playhouse, or a night in London, or perhaps like the beginning and the end of All.

The little domestic scene in the Dickinson household, illuminated by the great Amherst fire of 1879, seems to have been a perfect miniature of life in that household from 1874 to 1886. Emily had stayed with her father because he so needed her. What was the story of the pretty, fun-loving, and socially active sister? Why didn't Lavinia marry? What of her self-denial, or did she make a real sacrifice in staying at home always to relieve Emily from disturbing influences?

It was Lavinia who sent the news in her letters; who

wanted more murders in her newspapers; who made up
her mind that she would go to war herself; who drove a
good bargain with the tin-peddler for a watering-pot
with which Emily could sprinkle her geraniums; who
trained the honeysuckle vines with strings that were taken
by the birds almost as fast as she held them up; who was
inclined to counsel delay when Emily wanted immediate
action; who, whatever her progress in nature and in art
under the tutelage of her elder sister, could not make
a departure without the scientific aid of both Emily
and Maggie; whose return was a tumult; who bustled
about in the big sunny kitchen, supervising the preparation of the more substantial part of the meal, while
Emily prepared the "julep food," of which she
was fonder; who must have poised her needle many a
time above her sewing in pleased expectation, only to
hear the distinguished visitor ask, "Is Miss Emily at
home?"

When Emily stayed alone for many hours day after day,
Lavinia was awed, and proudly told her friends that
Emily wrote poetry, though the poems were never shown
to her. She was too close, too special a personality for that.
She protected the more sensitive sister from all the harsh-
ness that she could. Once when asked by one of the
frantic crowd if she could not induce her sister to go out
occasionally, Vinnie had replied: "But why should I?
She is quite happy and contented as she is. I would only
disturb her." And the elder sister sometimes shielded
Lavinia. When a friend of the two lay critically ill, we

find Emily writing a second time for final word before she could break the news to Vinnie.

Emily wrote poetry; Lavinia kept cats, even in the back yard after their demise. One day a stray kitten that Lavinia had been nursing ran out like a little wraith as an Amherst student was passing. Miss Lavinia came to the gate and told him how she had doctored the sick animal with medicines, but that it was growing steadily more thin and wasted. She asked the student's advice. With a serious face and smiling eyes he replied, " If I were you, I should give that kitten a large bowl of rich cream three times a day." Her eyes grew brighter than ever. His prescription was a happy one, and the kitten throve.

On April 1, 1882, Dr. Charles Wadsworth died of pneumonia in Philadelphia at the age of sixty-eight years. On his last earthly Sabbath (March 26th), he had preached on " Paul as a Sailor," saying, " Life is a voyage; and with this thought I close," ending his final sentence with the words, " Going home, going home! " little thinking that for himself the voyage was almost ended, the harbor almost reached. Both Mr. J. D. Clark and his brother, Mr. Charles H. Clark, who had also met Miss Dickinson, were impressed with her unusual personality and her brilliant mind. Mr. C. H. Clark printed at his own expense one of the four published volumes of Dr. Wadsworth's sermons, a copy of which appears to have been sent by Mr. J. D. Clark to Emily Dickinson in the spring of 1883, and the brothers, in turn, wrote to her from time to time. To them

she now sent poems on immortality that she once had sent
to the clergyman. It may possibly have been in April, 1882,
that Emily wrote, " I never lost as much but twice."

In November, 1882, the long seclusion and devoted attendance upon their mother was brought to an end for
the sisters. Mrs. Dickinson "ceased." Emily writes tenderly of her mother's death to the cousins, to Miss Whitney, to Mr. Clark. It is suggested in the letters that Emily
received from Mr. Clark shortly afterward a letter which
Dr. Wadsworth had written to console Mr. Clark upon
the death of his own mother. It seems that her mother's
was the only death that Emily had witnessed. She says
that for a time thereafter she did not write much " intuitively "; but when she did resume her creative work the
death of her mother stimulated her to the writing of a
larger number of personal poems on this abstract theme
than did the death of any other in her circle of intimate
friends, except the man to whom she wrote her love
poems. Some of the poems probably inspired by the
mother were, " The last night that she lived," " Her final
summer was it," " She went as quiet as the dew," " We
cover thee, sweet face," " From us she wandered now a
year," " So proud she was to die."

One of the effects of her mental isolation in the later
years is an increasing obscurity in expression and ellipsis.
Another is the excess of emotion which she seems to put
into her more personal communications to friends. Yet
even when she makes an extravagant statement that must
have quickened the heartbeats of the recipient, we find

that she has said almost exactly the same thing to another and sometimes in almost the same mail. If any of the friends to whom she wrote overestimated the degree of her affection for him, he had his eyes opened when he read the full body of her collected letters. We are not permitted to make quotations to illustrate the point, but he who reads the letters will note identical statements to Sue and to Mrs. Holland, to Mr. J. D. Clark and to Mr. Higginson. She wrote of Dr. Wadsworth to Mr. Clark in almost the same words which she had used when writing of Mr. Bowles to his son upon the death of the father. She makes an identical reference to a gift of a book to Miss Whitney and to Mr. J. D. Clark. She uses very similar terms in eulogy of Dr. Wadsworth and of Dr. Holland. Such expressions in the years when she was a recluse seem to be the interaction of emotion, the creative faculty, and physical strain due in part to such close application to her work. When we consider her tremendous literary output, the heavy correspondence which she carried on, her constant little courtesies and attentions to her neighbors by mail, so much of which was done at night, thus breaking her rest so largely, we must wonder that she did not have nervous prostration long before a break did come to which she refers in an unpublished letter to Mr. Higginson, presumably about 1880, though we cannot know.

In June, 1884, Mrs. Jackson was injured by tripping upon the stairway in her Colorado home and was thereafter rendered inactive. In the same month and year

Emily Dickinson lost consciousness while at work in the kitchen, and after many hours awoke to find herself confined to her room indefinitely. The doctor told her that her nerves were having their revenge. Revenge upon whom but death, thought Emily. She was not now Mrs. Jackson's most intimate friend — the circumstance of their residence in itself made that impossible; but they corresponded occasionally throughout the winter of 1884–85 when both were ill. Helen Jackson, who had gotten away from the repressive New England atmosphere very early in her life, and who was unbound by those filial demands for which she had the deepest respect, had grown increasingly impatient with Emily's continued refusal to publish, her apparent idleness and shrinking. The very few letters between these women that have been given to the public suggest a certain formality, a self-consciousness on Emily's part. Perhaps each sometimes wondered to what extent she had been responsible for the bent of the other; but neither had yielded an iota of her course.

In the spring of 1885 Emily Dickinson, who had been alternately worse and then convalescent, wrote a carefully composed letter to her friend. She made at least two drafts; there were erasures, and eight substituted words. This letter as edited by Mrs. Todd (1894) is the more interesting version, not only because it is undivided, but also because both erasures and substitutes are given, which affords a study of Emily's afterthoughts. Both women used formal signatures. There was one more exchange of notes between them in that same spring. Emily wrote to ask again if her friend could walk, and Helen replied that she could fly.

Upon the advice of her physician, Mrs. Jackson went to California, but she grew steadily, though imperceptibly worse, complications having developed. "What a beautiful place in which to die!" she is said to have remarked as she was placed in a sunny room in a quiet neighborhood in San Francisco. Her presence in the city was said to have been kept from the public at large that she might not be unduly annnoyed by inquiries.

One would not have known that she was dying. There was white in her hair and a nobility of countenance remembered long by a young writer who afterward left a record of her last visit with Mrs. Jackson. The famous writer was in her fifty-fourth year. Her room was filled with flowers and her tray was piled with notes from admirers. A stiff wind from the crescent bay swept across the hilly city. Sometime during that winter Helen Hunt Jackson wrote a short story, her last, so far as we know. It was published in the *Century* in May, 1885, three months before her death. It was an exquisitely written little story which aroused more than usual interest among the readers. " The Prince's Little Sweetheart " was felt to have some deep meaning. A writer in San Francisco spoke to the author of her story. Did not Mrs. Jackson have a purpose, some message, as it were?

" Just dreamed it," replied the noted woman, smiling.

The story, in substance, was as follows:

She was a very young girl who had never been made love to by any man. The Prince found her in a stuff gown among the common people, loved her, whirled her away to the palace, dressed her up in white and gold, married her, and they went floating away in a maze of music. Some new beautiful thing to see, some new beautiful thing to do, and if the Prince left her even for one moment he brought her a gift and he kissed her. The day ended so. The lights dimmed into moonlight. She was put to bed in a gold bedstead with gold silk sheets.

"I'm going to stay awake forever . . ."

"You're talking in your sleep," murmured the Prince, close by her side, kissing her.

In the broad daylight she awoke — alone, deserted. She wound the gold sheet around her and started to explore the palace, thinking (foolish, Little Sweetheart!) that the Prince would miss her. . . . To her surprise she came upon a room full of girls in stuff gowns, all sweeping spiders, and at sight of the Little Sweetheart they laughed unpleasantly.

"Who are you?" she quavered.

"We're all Prince's Sweethearts," said the spider-sweepers.

"What! Is it only for one day, then?" said the Little Sweetheart.

"Only for one day."

Just then her own Prince came hurrying by, all in clinking armor.

"Oh, how d'do!" he said, kindly. "I was wondering

what had become of you. Good-bye! I'm off for the grand review today. Don't tire yourself out over the spiders." And he was gone.

"I hate him."

"Oh no, you don't!" exclaimed the spider-sweepers. "That's the worst of it. You love him all the time after you've once begun."

"I'll go home."

"You can't."

"I'll die!"

"Oh no, you won't. Some of us, in some of these rooms here, are wrinkled and gray-haired. The most of the Sweethearts live to be old."

"Do they?" said the Little Sweetheart, and burst into tears.

The roses were blooming. Mrs. Jackson's windows were opened wide to let in the warmth of early summer. She took up her pencil to begin another poem — "Habeas Corpus: a Farewell to My Body." Summer deepened. Through the mail, from coast to coast, there went a note to her publishers, closing:

"Good-bye. Many thanks for all your long good will and kindness. I shall look in on your new rooms some day, be sure, but you won't see me. Good-bye.

"Affectionately, forever,

"H. J."

Dear Friend,

May I ask

the delight in

advance, of sending

you the "Life

of Mr⸱ Cross

of her Husband

which the

LETTER, ON READING OF MRS. JACKSON'S DEATH, AUGUST, 1885, ONE YEAR
BEFORE HER OWN DEATH

When Emily Dickinson opened her *Springfield Republican* and saw there an editorial on " H. H. and Saxe Holm " that reviewed the life of the well-known writer who had died in San Francisco on August 12, 1885, she was greatly shocked, for she had not known that her friend was fatally ill. Emily wrote at once to Mr. Higginson. He replied, giving her such information as he had, and enclosed a sonnet that some one had written in elegy. He asked Emily Dickinson if she had seen the obituary notices, reviews of the career of Helen Hunt Jackson. He had written one in which he had declared Mrs. Jackson to be " the most brilliant, impetuous, and thoroughly individual woman of her time."

In November Emily was so ill again that the doctor forbade books or " thought " for a while, so she wrote to her friend. Aside from *Ramona,* there are two books which Emily mentions with special emphasis. How eagerly she read the new biography of George Eliot by Mr. Cross! She was delighted that there were fresh revelations so that she got the full figure of her gallant fellow-writer. In January, 1885, Emily had received as a gift from a friend a little book, *Called Back,* by Hugh Conway.

The story is told in the first person by a wealthy young Englishman who was blind as a young man. One night he had wandered out into the London streets for the air. In trying to retrace his steps he inadvertently got into a strange house. Attracted by music, he went farther into the house and came to a room in which there were evidently several people. A woman was singing at the piano. Her lovely voice rose to an exquisite note, when without warning the note broke. There was a scream of anguish, a falling body, confusion, and several voices. Before the Englishman had left the house he was made aware that a murder had been committed. He regained his sight. While traveling in Italy he saw and fell in love with a beautiful young woman, Pauline March. In London, where the two later met, he married her, only to discover that she was docile, obedient, but somewhat strange. Then he saw. Her mind was absent.

The young husband traveled to Italy, retraced her history, and found that she had suffered a severe shock in the death of her brother, the best-loved person in her orphaned life. One night, after the husband had returned to London, an Italian ex-soldier, who was a guest of the couple, recounting some of his army experiences, suddenly seized a knife to illustrate a point. Pauline fainted. When she was revived she arose, as in a trance, passed from the house, and (followed by her agitated husband) went to an old untenanted house (which was the scene of the murder attended by the blind Englishman). She went to a room in which there was a piano. She sat down, struck the bars, and began to sing — that same song of years ago. Her lovely voice rose to an exquisite note, that climax note. She started wildly to her feet, expression coming into her face. " To her, as to me, all the occurrences of that dreadful night were being reproduced," says the author. " The past had come back to Pauline — come back at the moment it left her." This crucial chapter is also entitled,

"Called Back." When the reader finally closes the book, "Called Back" is associated in his mind definitely with the words, "The past had come back, come back at the moment it left her." In a letter to her cousins, Louisa and Fannie Norcross, Emily says that she has been impressed with the story, that it haunts her.

In fifty-five years Emily Dickinson seems to have completed that oriental circuit which she ascribes, in one poem, to her favorite fellow, the bee. She had realized in successive stages a very active social life, love, knowledge, power, and circumference. What a long and crowded life was hers! She uses the term "prison" to describe her outward circumstance, in a reply to Helen Hunt Jackson, but what matter, when every atom of it was of magic. To her sensitive and richly endowed nature it seemed that beauty "jostled" her. How she had loved the wild things — storms, and angry winds, and March because of what it heralded!

In such a poem as "The going from the world we know" there is a suggestion that in her later years the question sometimes came into her mind, "Would the future hold compensation for her having climbed the hill alone?" A question seems also to be suggested in an unpublished second stanza to the poem, "The sea said 'come' to the brook." In the two-stanza version which Emily Dickinson sent to Mr. Higginson (now in the Galatea Collection) the thought is this: the Sea saw a little Brook and wanted her, but the brook held back and argued. The Brook wanted to grow larger, to attain wisdom, to be "a scholar," shall we say? But the Sea answered, " Then you will be like me. I like you as you are. I want you now. . . ." Time passed. The Sea looked up to find himself confronted by another Sea. " Go away," the first Sea commanded. Said the second, wistfully, "I am he who was once that Brook that you loved. Learning and wisdom seem now unprofitable. I have come."

The Seeker after Beauty had faced her Goliath world with a magic pebble. Goliath seemed to have won. Her shot had made little impression. Austin and Lavinia were by her side. There was the house next door. . . .

April, 1886. Times were indeed changing outwardly. Along the road where little Helen Fiske had once skipped hand-in-hand with a glittering tin-peddler, a modern Miss M—— had grown romantic over a strolling conjurer, and got poisoned for her amorous intents. Back in 1840, young Parson Colton had sat in his hotel room in the waning moonlight, and tried to choke down the subtle effect of a pedigree. Now in April, 1886, a man had suddenly risen up over in the " shire town " and had murdered a Dickinson!

The cherry trees were in bloom. The peach blossoms were blowing. Yonder in a corner of her room stood the bureau, holding her mind and her heart. There was nothing more to do. The body was willing to let go. Emily took up her pencil. " Daybreak " was at hand. On May 15th, the day before her death, she sent to the cousins in Cambridge those significant words, " Called back." . . .

Four days later there descended from the train in Amherst a distinguished-looking gentleman with scholarly countenance, friendly eyes, and sideburns. He was the only one of Emily Dickinson's " silver shelf " who had outlived her. As he walked down Main Street to the brown brick house, half-concealed by the pines, he might have been contrasting the scenes of his three visits. He had come to Amherst first on a dry, hot August day in 1870. Then he had had occasion to come again in December, three years later. Now he was seeing Amherst in May, and it was beautiful! . . .

He walked into the wide, cool parlor to see his friend for the third and last time. How young she looked! so he noted a little later in his *Journal*. She was fifty-six and she looked but thirty; not a wrinkle, not a gray hair, and " perfect peace on the beautiful brow." There were violets and a pink cypripedium at her throat and two heliotropes in her hand, which Vinnie had put there " for Emily to take to Judge Lord." In the living recollection of one of her townsmen it was Vinnie who said that Emily should be taken to her grave by way of the flowering fields rather than the usual way, because Emily herself had not gone through the village streets for so many years.

Afterward Mr. Higginson made an entry in his *Journal*. He missed Emily Dickinson. He was outliving many of his most interesting friends. What a bundle of strange gifts she was! The Emily he knew was " summer turned to autumn in an instant." In safe keeping for future public stewardship were her manuscript letters and poems to him. There was also the note to Mrs. Mary Channing Higginson, written in August, 1870. He had somehow managed to get the date of Emily Dickinson's birth, and had written in pencil at the top of the first sheet to Mrs. Higginson, —

"b. Dec. 10, 1830
d. —— "

and kindly Mr. Higginson, wise Mr. Higginson, never filled in that date.

*

Chapter Eighteen

"MY LETTER TO THE WORLD"

*

Two of Emily Dickinson's greatest pleasures had been her annual search for spring wild flowers, and her piano. She had played the piano in a most individual manner, we are told, delighting her friends especially with her improvisations, but she had given up the practice many years before her death, though retaining her love for music. It is said that she had despaired of acquiring perfection in the art after having heard Rubinstein play in Boston.

During her last years, 1880–86, by rare good fortune both pleasures were brought to her. There had come to live in Amherst Mrs. Mabel Loomis Todd, wife of Professor David Todd, a world-famous astronomer. Mrs. Todd had lived in Washington, D.C., before her residence in Amherst. She was, at the time of her friendship with Emily Dickinson, very young, beautiful, a talented musician, painter, and writer who apprehended the nature of the brilliant and secluded Amherst poet as few did at that time. Mrs. Todd had painted a panel of the Indian-pipe as a gift for Emily Dickinson and had received from the poet a note saying that it seemed almost supernatural that the painter should have chosen "the preferred flower." Emily kept the panel in her room, where she could see it constantly, and from that time Mrs. Todd was one of the few who could be termed an intimate friend, one of those whom Emily personally received.

In Vol. II of the *Letters of Emily Dickinson* which she edited Mrs. Todd tells of unforgettable occasions when she would play and sing at the square piano in the old-fashioned room — sunshiny modern airs, and old favorites of her hostess, while Emily sat near by, beyond the door, not always visible, but always showing her appreciation afterward in a little note accompanying some gift, of flowers or a poem or a delicacy which she had prepared. Once she sent in to Mrs. Todd a prune whip with the line, " Whom the Lord loveth he chasteneth."

After Emily's death her sister Lavinia found in the bureau the poems tied up in little fascicles bound with pink and blue ribbons. The quantity of the work was amazing, as the world now knows. She consulted Mr. Higginson and Mrs. Todd, and intrusted to them the responsibility for final disposition of Emily's literary work. We read in the correspondence now made available to the public that there were difficulties attendant upon the preparation of the volumes for publication, as frequently happens when several members of a family are involved in an undertaking; nevertheless, Lavinia insisted that the work go forward, so she writes Mr. Higginson in letters in the Galatea Collection in the Boston Public Library.

MABEL LOOMIS TODD

She adds that her discouragement has been such that she feels like Joan of Arc in bringing Emily's poems before the public.

Upon Mrs. Todd fell most of the physical burden of the editing. She copied in longhand every poem before it was read by Mr. Higginson. This alone must have been a stupendous task. Mrs. Todd devoted herself unsparingly to the work of introducing Emily Dickinson's poems, and later, the letters, to the public. It was for her a labor of love. She worked at her task for eight and ten hours a day and often late into the night. It was Mr. Higginson who thought the poems should have titles. Lavinia and Austin could see no reason for the titles, so the correspondence reveals, but yielded to the judgment of the literary man.

In addition to the fascicles in the bureau, we hear also of a " box of Emily's scraps." In her very interesting prefaces to the volumes Mrs. Todd describes the material with which she worked. She says of the " scraps ": " Some of Emily's rarest flashes were caught upon the margins of newspapers, backs of envelopes, or whatever bit of paper was nearest at hand, in the midst of other occupations. There were changes for a different word or phrase in hope of making the thought clearer but not in a single instance merely to smooth the form (*i.e.,* to improve the rhythm or rhyme)." Not only did Emily Dickinson indicate a choice of words on these manuscripts, but she had sent to various friends copies of her poems, which sometimes differed from one another. Therefore one should not be too quick to accuse the editors of making deliberate changes, for at times they merely made a selection from the two or three versions which Emily Dickinson had left, or they had to make an original interpretation of her handwriting.

For the cover of the first volume an impression of Mrs. Todd's panel of the Indian-pipe was used with charming effect. It is interesting to note that Mr. Niles, who had tried to induce Emily to publish, was now the member of the publishing firm into whose hands the edited manuscripts were placed. The first volume was an instant and remarkable success. It went into eleven editions (*Book Buyer,* May, 1892). A second volume was immediately prepared. One of the pleasant features of those books was their pocket size. Lavinia wrote to Mr. Higginson, thanking her two kind friends and expressing delight at the world's reception of " Emily's wonderful poems." She adds that, so long as the public cares for more, the work of publication is to be continued and trusts entirely to her two efficient friends to present the work properly.

Mr. Higginson wrote to Mrs. Todd soon after the work began:

" I can't tell you how much I am enjoying the poems. There are many new to me which take my breath away."

A year later he wrote to her:

" You are the only person who can feel as I do about this extraordinary thing we have done in recording this rare genius. I feel as if we had climbed to a cloud, and pulled it away, and revealed a new star behind it. . . ."

Mrs. Todd wrote to him:

"18 May, 1891.

"I find I have a good many of those whose first lines you sent me, but not all by any means. That exquisite 'The Nearest Dream' I do not find — which you read so thrillingly in Boston. The others that I have not are these [naming eighteen poems sent to Mr. Higginson].

"One or two of these first lines sound very familiar, but they are not with the six hundred others — that mine from which I always expect to draw unlimited riches. I do not think my 'Blue Jay' is yours, either. It begins, 'A bold, inspiriting bird is the jay,' and I have one beginning, 'It sounded as if the air were running, and then the air stood still,' which may be identical with yours using 'streets' instead of 'air.' Have you anything on the Indian-pipe? I have heard of one, but cannot get hold of it. I think she wrote it many years ago.

"The scraps written in pencil which I have recently begun to arrange and copy are, some of them, very fine. I will put in a few before I send the poems back to you. I enclose a sonnet written to E. D. out of pure enthusiasm, by one of our students here."

"9 July, 1891

"Many in this volume will be far finer than most of the first. Miss Lavinia wishes to look over the volume once more with me, to be sure none of her special favorites are omitted."

" 13 July, 1891

" I send you this afternoon the MS. second volume of
E. D.'s poems. I think it is really better than the first. . . .
I suppose you will not wish to change the line in the
'White Heat' — only as she makes 'blaze' and 'forge'
as rhymes in the last stanza. I thought it might be good
not to have them in that relation twice. Few changes
seem necessary anywhere. . . ."

" 18 July, 1891

" If ' The flower must not blame the bee ' seems too
enigmatical, let us leave it out. There is a sufficient number, certainly, although Mr. Niles said he did not in the
least object to a larger number than the first volume
showed, since the public certainly wants them. In ' The
Sleeping Flowers,'

> ' She rocked and gently smiled,
> Humming the quaintest lullaby
> That ever soothed a child.'

is the way it appeared in the June *St. Nicholas,* put so in
order to have the rhyme perfect in a child's magazine. It
reads in the original E. D.'s handwriting thus —

> ' Her busy foot she plied,
> Humming the quaintest lullaby
> That ever rocked a child.' "

"22 July, 1891

"I send 'She laid her docile crescent down.' I do not understand it, and although it is beautiful, I omitted it because there were already so many more for Vol. II than had appeared in Vol. I. If you care to include it, I shall approve. You would be almost incredulous if I should tell you that there are over 500 more already copied, in addition to the two volumes, and in addition to a box of 'scraps' in pencil, some of which are gems. Yet such is the case. One volume more? Yes, half a dozen.

"I am classifying them all now, and I have made an alphabetical index of first lines.

"In 'The night was wide,' the 'dog's belated feet *were* like intermittent *plush.*' She wrote the word unmistakably, every letter distinct and separate.

"I had put, in Nature, as perhaps you noticed, all the dawn and sunrise and spring poems at the beginning, then noon and summer, and sunset and autumn, and snow last! Probably your way is better — to have the *day* ones first, and the *seasons* after, as you describe.

"The love poems are certainly growing less in number. I might find two or three more, perhaps, for this volume, but on the whole I think they will be needed more in a subsequent one — when we use finally, 'The flower must not blame the bee,' with its rather confused metaphors!

"The line in 'He put the belt around my life' reads, 'A member of the cloud,' in the original, and I suppose simply means to express the great loftiness conferred by the love given, which made her 'fold up' her lifetime, 'henceforth a dedicated sort.'"

"25 July, 1891

"In [this preface] I have tried to answer point by point, the things said of her by the critics. . . . Most of the [newspaper and magazine notices of the first volume] say she was an invalid, that she was cruelly disappointed in love, that she was irreverent, that she never had left Amherst, that she was a recluse from childhood, and other nonsense; and then some friends have wondered at variations in the printed poems from those she sent them, and I have been questioned about her handwriting and manuscripts. Indeed, there seems an endless curiosity, both printed and verbal, about her. . . ."

Because of the great interest in Emily Dickinson's personality a collection of her letters was edited by Mrs. Todd and published in two volumes by Roberts Brothers in 1894. The undertaking must have been an unusually difficult one for the editor, since Emily did not date any of her letters and her handwriting was at times so difficult to read. Not only did Mrs. Todd painstakingly search out the dates, with the assistance of Emily's sister and brother, but she interspersed the volumes with valuable and charming paragraphs of additional information, so that her volumes constitute actually the first *Life of Emily Dickinson* so far as the family were willing that it be revealed. The family may be pardoned their reticence, for it was then obviously too soon for a definitive biography of this poet to be given to the public. The *Letters* were well received. It is doubtful if a *Life of Emily Dickinson* ever could have been written but for this careful and enduring work by Mrs. Todd. May we not be pardoned an expression of regret that these volumes published in 1894 were allowed to lapse? And a wish that we might now have Mrs. Todd's *Letters by Emily Dickinson* as well as a *Life of Emily Dickinson* by her niece, with hitherto unpublished letters appended, — some of the hundreds of letters, perhaps, which are said to be now in the possession of relatives of the poet?

Mr. Higginson wrote to Mrs. Todd, while she was editing the letters:

" I feel half sorry to hear that the book is nearly ready; it will be the last, I suppose, and will not only yield the final news of Emily Dickinson, but take from me a living companionship I shall miss."

And on Nov. 29, 1894:

" Emily has arrived. They sent her to Sever's book store where I rarely go and where she might have hid in a cupboard. . . . It is extraordinary how the mystic and bizarre Emily is born at once between two pages. . . ."

Emily Dickinson was fortunate in having as her editor one who was so sensitive and sincere a lover of nature and of the beautiful. In the year in which Mrs. Todd edited a third volume of Emily's poems, 1896, she also edited and published, through Roberts Brothers, *A Cycle of Sonnets*. The sonnets had been bequeathed to her by one the tragedy of whose life she had known. They were written in the mature years of the poet (one not known to the literary world, it seems), " in the splendor of his first great love for the girl who died during the second year of their engagement. . . . He saw her in the awakening of nature in the spring-time, and through her the summer was transfigured with magical light. The short winter days were no more dull and cold. Then the great darkness fell. . . . When she died, those who knew him knew that he died also" (Preface). A friend of Mrs. Todd's remarked that the sonnets might have been edited with Emily Dickinson in mind.

Mrs. Todd also wrote *Footprints,* Amherst, 1883; *Total Eclipses of the Sun,* Roberts Brothers, 1894; *Corona and Coronet* — a narrative of the Amherst eclipse expedition to Japan in Mr. James's schooner-yacht *Coronet* to observe the sun's total obscuration, August 9, 1896, published by Houghton Mifflin, 1896. Later books by her included *A Cycle of Sunsets,* Small, Maynard & Co., 1910, and *Tripoli, the Mysterious,* Small, Maynard & Co., 1912.

Through the kindness of the niece and biographer of Emily Dickinson her poetry is still being given to the public. In that most poignant poem in American literature, " This is my letter to the world," Emily Dickinson tells us that she is leaving behind her a message from nature which she has devoted her life to inditing. She asks that her countrymen be tender in their judgment of the poet.

One hundred years after her birth this poet's life is still

in a half-shadow. An Emily Dickinson mystery is being perpetuated. There is confusion in interpretation of her. Opinions range all the way from that of a relative of the poet who deplores any further attempt to interpret " that little life, lived in the cellar," to that of the seventeen-year-old immigrant boy who bent above his high-school English examination papers and wrote in answer to the question on Emily Dickinson: " If I could meet Miss Dickinson, I'd ask her just one question, ' Do you neck?' "

For our generation mystery has its place, but not in biography where results important to posterity are co-existent with the life. Nor can the anonymity of anyone important to Emily Dickinson be accepted as the best policy. Anonymity arouses curiosity and speculation which almost invariably result in overemphasis.

If a strange and beautiful vase were excavated from beneath a plain surface trodden by workingmen under everyday conditions, the attention of the world would be centered upon that broken ground. The vase has burning color, simple but lovely lines. There are rough edges, a crack, a nick or two, some unintelligible inscriptions. The vase had been handled not always with care in that unknown past from which it had been lifted. At once the world would begin to dig for knowledge of the factors that produced that vase. From what civilization had it come? What hands had wrought it? What was the history of those nicks and cracks? The mind must read the scroll. To do less — worse yet, to want to do less — would indicate an inadequacy in the civilization to which the vase was given. The beautiful work of art would in itself remain unchanged by such knowledge of its past, it is true. But more attention would be attracted to that vase. More people would come to look at it, to admire it. Æsthetic pleasure would be increased. Culture would be advanced. Is it not so with the poetry of Emily Dickinson and its human background?

Not only are the poems of Emily Dickinson of great value to us; her life, also, is an important life. She maintained her own high standards, unafraid of singularity. Her countrymen should know everything there is to know about her as a human being. Then only can they be in a position to judge her as sympathetically as she asked.

APPENDIX

*

APPENDIX

*

Sources for the material as a whole are:

Letters of Emily Dickinson, 2 vols. Edited by Mabel Loomis Todd. Published by Roberts Brothers, 1894.

Poems by Emily Dickinson, Series One. Edited by Mabel Loomis Todd and T. W. Higginson. Published by Roberts Brothers, 1890.

Poems by Emily Dickinson, Series Two. Edited by Mabel Loomis Todd and T. W. Higginson. Published by Roberts Brothers, 1891.

Poems by Emily Dickinson, Series Three. Edited by Mabel Loomis Todd. Published by Roberts Brothers, 1896.

The Single Hound; Poems of a Lifetime, by Emily Dickinson, with an Introduction by Martha Dickinson Bianchi. Published by Little, Brown & Co., 1914.

The Life and Letters of Emily Dickinson, by her niece, Martha Dickinson Bianchi. Published by Houghton Mifflin, 1924.

The Complete Poems of Emily Dickinson, with an Introduction by Martha Dickinson Bianchi. Published by Little, Brown & Co., 1924.

Further Poems by Emily Dickinson. Edited by Martha Dickinson Bianchi and Alfred Leete Hampson. Published by Little, Brown & Co., 1929.

The files of the *Springfield Republican,* 1840–1886.

The files of the *Hampshire Gazette,* 1840–1855.

The manuscript letters and poems of Emily Dickinson which were sent by her to T. W. Higginson, in the Galatea Collection of the Boston Public Library.

The manuscript letters and journals of T. W. Higginson, in Harvard University Library.

The collection of manuscript letters and poems given by Mr. Higginson to the Boston Public Library before his death, so I am informed by Mrs. Mary Thatcher Higginson, and placed on public exhibition in December, 1923, is a very valuable contribution to the subject. The manuscripts are in themselves fascinating to one who is interested in Emily Dickinson, but the collection is most valuable for the many suggestions which it offers. Here we find the originals of letters that have been published, and in full, with no impeding little dots. Here, also, are thirty letters and brief notes to both Mr. and Mrs. Higginson, from about 1868 to 1886, and half a dozen or so messages of a sentence or two, all unpublished material. With the letters are the envelopes and some of the pressed flowers and leaves which Emily Dickinson sent to Mrs. Higginson.

There are, in this collection, forty-four poems, four of which are in *Further Poems of Emily Dickinson,* and seven of which have not yet been published. One of the unpublished poems is a forty-line love poem, next to the longest love poem by Emily Dickinson that we have.

There are two letters from Lavinia Dickinson to Mr.

Higginson, the letter from Mr. Higginson to Mrs. Mary Channing Higginson written from Amherst on August 16, 1870, and there are letters from Mrs. Todd to Mr. Higginson at the time of her work as co-editor with him of the *Poems*.

Included also in this collection are a picture of Edward Dickinson which Emily had evidently sent to her friend; a newspaper clipping of " The Snake "; a newspaper notice of the marriage of Helen Hunt to Mr. W. S. Jackson; and an article on Emily Dickinson by Ella Gilbert Ives, from the *Boston Transcript,* October 5, 1907.

The items in the manuscript letters and journals (Harvard Library) which are of particular interest to us are: an additional sheet of the letter from Mr. Higginson to Mrs. Higginson in August, 1870; a letter to his sisters, December 9, 1873, in which he refers to his second call upon Emily Dickinson in Amherst; and several references to Helen Hunt in his unpublished journals (1866–1870).

CHAPTER ONE

The material in Chapter One is based upon the following:

> *The History of the Town of Amherst, Massachusetts.* Amherst, Carpenter & Morehouse, 1896.
> Reminiscences of Aaron Colton taken from *An Historical Review. One hundred and fiftieth anniversary of the First Church of Christ in Amherst, Mass.* — Nov. 7, 1889. Amherst, 1890.

The Genealogies of the Hadley Families, Embracing the Early Settlers of the Town of Amherst. Northampton, 1862.

Reunion of the Dickinson Family at Amherst, Mass. Aug. 8 & 9, 1883, with an appendix. Binghamton Publishing Co., 1884.

Discourses and Speeches Delivered at the Celebration of the Semi-Centennial Anniversary of Monson Academy, July 18 & 19, 1854. New York, 1855.

In *The History of the First Church of Amherst* Reverend Dwight, who succeeded Aaron Colton in 1853 as pastor of the Dickinsons; also gives a reminiscence in which he pays a special tribute to Edward Dickinson. It was Mr. Dwight who tried to "convert" Emily, so we are told by Mrs. Bianchi. The attempted conversion occurred, therefore, after her twenty-third year.

It is not the purpose of this book to make a comprehensive study of the Dickinson genealogy, but he who does do so will find that the records are contradictory and confusing. In *The Life and Letters of Emily Dickinson* it is said that Samuel Fowler Dickinson was the first of his line in Amherst, but according to both of the genealogical sources listed above, Nathan was the first of his line in Amherst, and Samuel Fowler was born to him there on October 19, 1775. The biography of Emily Dickinson also gives the name of her maternal grandfather as Alfred Norcross, while we find him to be Joel Norcross in the *Discourses and Speeches . . . of Monson Academy.*

There is a statement made in the *Reunion of the Dick-*

inson Family that Emily Norcross was Edward Dickinson's second wife, which seems utterly unlikely.

Chapter Two

This very brief impression of Helen Hunt Jackson's personality in early girlhood is based upon references in the *Dial,* September, 1885, the *Critic,* August 22, 1885 and the *Springfield Republican* announcing the writer's death on August 12, 1885. These are the only allusions to her girlhood that I have been able to find.

The impression of Emily Dickinson's early years is based upon her own allusions to her childhood in the published letters and in the unpublished letters to Mr. Higginson. Thoughts relative to her childhood are found most frequently in the letters of her later years. The reference to the clock is made in Mr. Higginson's letter. to his wife, and also in his *Carlyle's Laugh and Other Surprises.*

When Emily was in her tenth year the family moved from her birthplace. Reverend Colton found them in March, 1840, living in the east half of Deacon Mack's house, where they remained until their return to her birthplace in 1855. There is no evidence that Emily Dickinson was irrevocably attached to one house, one garden enclosure, one window view. She was attached to her world, but not to her shell. As with all extremely sensitive people, she disliked disturbing confusion, purposeless upheaval — anything which threatened her perception.

There is a popular impression that Emily Dickinson lived as a recluse all her life in the brick house in which she was born. In her girlhood she doubtless made many short visits to Belchertown, Monson, Northampton, Springfield, where the family had relatives and friends. The records show that she left Amherst at least eight times: once to Boston for four weeks (1846); for almost a year to Mt. Holyoke (1847–48); twice to Springfield and once to Boston for a few days each time (1851–53); for seven weeks to Washington and Philadelphia (1854); for from six to eight months to Boston (1864); again for six to nine months to Boston (1865). Furthermore, she desired to go to Boston in 1868, but her father objected. Only once, so far as we have her own testimony, does she show disinclination to change.

CHAPTER THREE

Many of Emily Dickinson's letters written to Mrs. Strong (1845–50) have been omitted in part or in whole in *The Life and Letters of Emily Dickinson*. It is from the complete collection in the Todd volumes that material for the background of part of this chapter has been taken. Other sources are:

> *Reminiscences of Amherst College,* — historical, scientific, biographical, and autobiographical, by Edward Hitchcock. Northampton, Mass., 1863.
> *Religious Lectures on Peculiar Phenomena in the Four Seasons* . . . delivered to the students in Amherst College —

in 1845, 1847, 1848, and 1849, by Edward Hitchcock. Amherst, J. S. & C. Adams, 1850.

Retrospect of Western Travel, by Harriet Martineau. Harper & Brothers, 1838.

Emily signs her name, " Emilie E. Dickinson." Mrs. Todd tells us that the poet's middle name was Elizabeth, a name seldom used later. Mrs. Bianchi gives Emily the middle name, Norcross.

CHAPTER FOUR

Two interesting and sympathetic books about Mary Lyon are:

The Life of Mary Lyon, by Beth Gilchrist. Houghton Mifflin, 1921.

The Power of Christian Benevolence Illustrated in the Life and Labors of Mary Lyon, by Edward Hitchcock, D.D. and others. Hopkins, Bridgman & Co., Northampton, 1852.

It is from the latter book that a brief extract from Miss Tolman's diary is taken.

CHAPTER FIVE

The volumes of letters edited by Mrs. Todd include not only a large number not to be found in *The Life and Letters of Emily Dickinson,* but also the reminiscence of Emily's girlhood by Mrs. Emily Fowler Ford, a daughter of Professor Fowler of Amherst College. This is the only recollection by one who knew Emily Dickinson in her

girlhood of which we have any record. We are told that
Mrs. Ford had intended to revise her sketch before its
publication, but her death occurred suddenly. Her recollections of events forty-five years past seem to be somewhat
confused in certain details, but her sketch is charming
and valuable. Mrs. Ford is our only source of information
about the school paper, the Shakespeare Club, and the
Literary Club, three events in the life of Emily Dickinson
that are not to be overlooked.

It would be interesting to see some of Emily Dickinson's
contributions to *Forest Leaves,* the little paper which she
and her friends are said to have started in the Academy
and to have kept up for two years. The paper was all in
script and the contributions recognized from the handwriting. Emily is said to have been irresistible as a humor-
ist of the comic column. Mrs. Ford (Todd Vol. I, pp. 128–
129) says that one bit was reprinted in the college paper,
where Emily's touch was instantly detected, and there
were two paragraphs in the *Springfield Republican.* I have
been unable to locate these paragraphs in back files of the
paper. Mrs. Bianchi places *Forest Leaves* in Emily's second Academy period (1848–50); but Mrs. Ford mentions
Helen Fiske and Tutor Henry M. Spofford in connection
with these girlhood literary activities, and neither was
living in Amherst after 1844. It seems a little difficult,
therefore, to place *Forest Leaves* chronologically in a study
of Emily Dickinson's development. In some old New
England attics there must yet be in existence copies of
this unique school paper.

Mrs. Ford distinctly recalled that Emily Dickinson once wept violently when her favorites of the *Atlantic Monthly* were assailed by Tutor Spofford, who advised the girls " to leave Emerson and Motherwell alone. Lord Byron had a much better style." But the *Atlantic Monthly* did not make its first appearance until 1857.

Emily Dickinson refers to dish-breaking moods in a letter to Abiah and in one to Mrs. Holland. Nathan Haskell Dole in the *Book Buyer* May, 1892, gives a report of a talk on the Amherst poet by Mrs. Todd in Boston in which the speaker tells of Emily Dickinson's habit of breaking dishes to relieve her feelings.

In connection with Emily and the Shakespeare Club it may be interesting to recall that seventy years or more after her utterance of independence a young instructor was dismissed from a Western college because he used an unexpurgated version of *King Lear* in his classes; and in the spring of 1924 Mr. John Barrymore's performance of *Hamlet* was visited by a policeman at the instigation of a member of the Citizens' Committee of New York City.

The account of how Emily got her first books is taken from the manuscript letter of Mr. Higginson to his wife, though I believe he makes reference to the same in *Carlyle's Laugh and Other Surprises*. Mr. Bowdoin left his first books for Emily " when she was a little thing in short dresses, with her feet on the rungs of the chair," according to Mr. Higginson, who adds that Mr. Dickinson found *Kavanagh* in the possession of his children and was displeased.

The sources of my material on Leonard Humphrey are:

> *The Amherst College Biographical Record of its Graduates,
> and non-Graduates, 1821–1921,* published by the college,
> 1927.
>
> Mrs. Todd's biographical paragraph — *Letters of Emily Dickinson,* Vol. I, p. 50.
>
> Professor Hitchcock's *Reminiscences of Amherst College.*
>
> Emily Dickinson's allusions to him in her letters.
>
> Personal recollections of his nieces.
>
> His *Index Rerum.*
>
> Correspondence in the possession of his family.

Mr. Humphrey's notebook contains but topical references to the books that most interested him. Occasionally he would copy out a sentence or a paragraph. I have gone to the sources of these notations in an effort to synthesize the mind of Emily's tutor. Young as he was, Leonard Humphrey left his mark. One cannot go very far into the Amherst records of this period without finding Mr. Humphrey's name there. Had he lived he would have distinguished himself in his chosen field. Because of Emily Dickinson's own testimony to the meaning which association with him had for her it seems unfair to her that he should be omitted altogether from a biography of her.

CHAPTER SIX

The Life of Josiah G. Holland, by Harriette Plunkett, is the source of my impressions of Dr. and Mrs. Holland. References to Mr. Bowles in this chapter are taken from *The Life and Letters of Samuel Bowles.*

CHAPTER SEVEN

The description of the journey to Washington, the city itself, and Edward Dickinson's activities in the House during Emily's visit are based upon:

> Time-tables given in the *Springfield Republican* for March, 1854.
>
> Dickens' account of his journey from New Haven to New York (fourteen years earlier, it is true, but general conditions had not changed much as accounts of travel in 1850–55 indicate). *American Notes.* Harper & Brothers, 1842.
>
> *The Education of Henry Adams.* Houghton Mifflin, 1918. I have been influenced in my description of Washington, by Mr. Adams' impressions of that city in the spring of his visit.
>
> *Walks about Washington,* by Leupp. Little, Brown & Co., 1915.
>
> Old newspaper clippings 1850–55.
>
> The *National Era,* March–April, 1854. Washington, D.C.

In *The Life and Letters of Emily Dickinson,* Mrs. Bianchi says, p. 45, that Emily spent a winter in Washington in 1853. This is at variance with Emily's own statement in her letter to Mrs. Holland in the spring of 1854, written from Philadelphia, in which she says that she was in Washington for three weeks. Emily had written to her brother on March 17th from Amherst that her mother and sister were making their preparations to go to the capital; in May she writes to him again from Amherst. Allowing for even a very few days of preparation for the trip and the time necessary for the journey, Emily Dickinson arrived in Washington very late in March if not the first of April. The Willard register for that year is not in existence, nor is there any record of the visitors to Mt. Vernon at that time. Emily says in her letter to Mrs. Holland that she and her sister were in Philadelphia about three weeks (two weeks, and were staying longer). If Edward Dickinson accompanied his family to Philadelphia, which is not certain, the record of roll-calls fixes the time as very late in April and early in May, for from May 18th, he was again at his post. There is no question that Emily Dickinson was in the capital during the first two weeks of April and it is more than probable that it was an altogether April visit.

We know from Mr. Higginson's letter that Emily Dickinson met Lieutenant Hunt and that he called upon her afterward in Amherst. He was a man who worked hard and did not take vacations. The only occasion which even resembled a " vacation " for him was the annual meeting of the American Association for the Advancement of Science. For this occasion Lieutenant Hunt always prepared a paper, usually at the place of meeting, for which purpose he was granted time from his office duties by Professor Bache. The lieutenant was on duty in the superintendent's office in Washington from May 5, 1851, until April 4, 1855. In a letter to his chief in 1857 Lieutenant Hunt refers to his residence in Washington in 1853 and says that as a result of the effect of the climate upon his health in the summer of that year " we left Washington." The context of the letter suggests that he may mean that he and Mrs. Hunt spent no more summers there; or perhaps they moved to a cooler and more healthful place near the city, for his work in the Washington office of the Coast Survey continued until 1855. Even at the time when he tells of his residence there his name is not in the City Directory; he was evidently living in a boarding-house or a hotel.

Lieutenant Hunt addressed the meeting of scientists in Washington in April, 1854. We learn from the report of the Association for 1854 that the Willard Hotel was headquarters for the delegates and that the meetings began on April 26th. If the lieutenant were not living in the city of Washington at this time he came there and stayed at the Willard several days in advance of the opening meetings. He was accompanied by his wife. On p. 46 of *The Life and Letters of Emily Dickinson* there is a paraphrased letter written by Emily in Washington to Sue, in which Emily says that some one of whom she is very fond is coming to see her, some one whom she has not seen for a time, we must assume from her manner of expression. I have traced the careers of Emily's girlhood friends whose names we know, and Helen Hunt is the only one who was in Washington in April, 1854. Whether Helen was coming from her home to see Emily at the Willard, or she and Lieutenant Hunt were coming to the Willard to stay during the meetings, she introduced her husband to Emily Dickinson, and the three met more than once in the hotel, for many of Lieutenant Hunt's fellow-scientists and friends were staying there. I therefore feel fully justified in placing the reunion of Emily Dickinson with Helen Hunt and the introduction to Lieutenant Hunt in Washington at the Willard.

My account of the personality and various activities of Lieutenant Hunt is based upon:

> Memoir of Edward Bissell Hunt, by F. A. P. Barnard, *National Academy of Science*, 1895, Vol III, pp. 29–41.
>
> His army record in files of the War Department.
>
> His cadet record at West Point.
>
> An old history of army costumes in the West Point Library.
>
> The Coast Survey Reports, 1851–63.
>
> The Alexander Bache Correspondence, in the Library of Congress, Washington, D.C.
>
> Reports of annual meetings of the American Association for the Advancement of Science.
>
> Of the dozen or more papers by Edward B. Hunt which were printed in the *American Journal of Science*, 1852–63, those of special interest to us are:
>
> On the Nature of Forces, 1854.
>
> On Our Sense of the Vertical and Horizontal, and on Our Perception of Distance, 1855.
>
> On the Idea of Physical and Metaphysical Infinity.
>
> On an Index of Papers on Subjects of Mathematics and Physical Science, 1855.
>
> On the Dynamics of Ocean Currents, 1859.
>
> Modern Warfare: Its Science and Art — The New Englander, November, 1860.
>
> Union Foundations: a Study of American Nationality as a Fact of Science, 1862 (published as pamphlet 1863).
>
> Key West Physical Notes, 1863.

My description of his appearance is based upon Mr. Barnard's *Memoir,* an article in the *New York World,* October 5, 1863, and pictures of ex-Governor Washington Hunt.

CHAPTER EIGHT

Sources:

The Presbyterian, week ending April 8, 1882.

The Presbyterian Banner, April 5, 1882.

The Presbyterian Encyclopedia (for biographies of Dr. Wadsworth and of Rev. Lyman Coleman).

Impressions of Dr. Wadsworth as a Preacher, by George Burrowes.

In Memoriam, Rev. Charles Wadsworth, D.D. Presbyterian Printing Co., 1882.

Sermons by Dr. Charles Wadsworth. A. Roman & Co., New York and San Francisco, 1869.

Sermons by Dr. Charles Wadsworth. Presbyterian Publishing House, 1882; Vol. III, 1884.

Recollections by living members of Dr. Wadsworth's family.

Dr. Wadsworth's poems, from a scrapbook in the possession of the clergyman's family.

Letters from Emily Dickinson to J. D. and C. H. Clark.

Life of Verbeek, by Griffith.

Dr. Wadsworth's sermons are well exemplified in two of his most famous ones:

Religion in Politics, published by Martien, 1853.

Eben-Ezer, a sermon delivered at the Arch Street Church on the tenth anniversary of its organization, February 5, 1860.

For the special setting of Emily Dickinson's visit in Philadelphia my authorities are:

> *The Life and Letters of Emily Dickinson*, p. 46.
> Philadelphia City Directory, 1854.
> Genealogy of the Coleman family.

The façade of the Coleman residence of 1854 is still standing, as part of a modern structure.

> The biography of Rev. Lyman Coleman in the *Presbyterian Encyclopedia.*

I have suggested that the sermon which so impressed Emily Dickinson was one which she heard in Philadelphia. It is likely so, though it seems impossible to verify the fact. The subject of that sermon which she said, twenty years later, was the loveliest she had ever heard, was a favorite subject with the Philadelphian, according to his obituary notices. It was a subject psychologically impressive to Emily Dickinson at just that time, and she referred to the sermon later to her cousins. She also makes several references in her letters to Mrs. W—— and Miss W—— in Boston. This suggests that the Norcross sisters may have known Mrs. Wadsworth and her daughter, since the latter ladies visited in Boston frequently.

CHAPTER NINE

It is a matter of record in Dr. Wadsworth's family that he was invited to preach at Amherst College and that he accepted the invitation. I have been unable to fix the exact date by research, but one of the co-editors of the poems of Emily Dickinson distinctly recalls being told by Miss Lavinia Dickinson that Dr. Wadsworth was entertained in the Dickinson home only twice, the first time being very soon after the visit of the Dickinsons in Philadelphia. Emily Dickinson tells that her friend came directly from Philadelphia to call at her home upon the occasion of her last meeting with him, that she thought him an " apparition," and that he made a little joke about the twenty years that had passed (final letter to C. H. Clark). I therefore date the visits of her friend as probably 1854 and about 1874 or 1875.

The San Francisco Evening Bulletin for May 26, 1862, is the source of my statement that Dr. Wadsworth took up his duties in California in June, 1862, and that he did not make the journey westward until May, 1862.

The only record of Lieutenant Hunt's calls in Amherst is the Higginson letter in the Boston Public Library. This letter indicates that Emily Dickinson saw her friend at least twice after her return from Washington. In the chapter on Washington I took an impression of Lieutenant Hunt's ideas from his papers, 1850–60, with no thought of chronology of ideas; but where we know that a topic of one of the papers was discussed between Lieutenant Hunt and Emily Dickinson it is reasonable to date the conversation at or near the time of the preparation of that paper, particularly when we find that the date fits into the probable time scheme of their conversations so satisfactorily.

In the love story of Emily Dickinson as given on p. 47 of *The Life and Letters* we are told that Emily fled from Philadelphia to her home in Amherst and that she was followed afterward by the man who had fallen in love with her. We are told that Sue was upon the scene, and the inference is that she was by that time a member of the Dickinson family; but Sue Gilbert was not married to Austin Dickinson until July, 1856. Emily's friendship with the man with whom she was in love evidently extended over a period of some time, even in the story of the family recollections.

I am not trying, in this chapter, to imagine a conversation between Emily Dickinson and Lieutenant Hunt. Such could quickly become ludicrous. But it is interesting to observe, as one reads her letters, 1854–62, and his papers, 1850–63, how their minds do actually give expression, at times, to the same impressions.

Lieutenant Hunt might have stopped in Amherst on his way to the meetings rather than from them. We cannot know certainly, though I think it less likely.

CHAPTER TEN

All thoughts attributed to Emily Dickinson in this book are thoughts expressed in her own writings. Her poems have furnished such material largely for the first division of this chapter.

The *Springfield Republican* for August 12, 1860, tells of the mysterious box delivered to the treasurer of Amherst

College on the 11th and the visit of the Governor also on that date.

I have not found any reference in the histories to Captain Hunt's activities at Fort Taylor during the Civil War, nor does Key West seem to have such a record. The *New York World* on October 5, 1863, however, made such a strong statement of Captain Hunt's part in the saving of the fort for the Union that there must have been reason for that statement, which is the source of my references to the same in this chapter. It seems somewhat strange that Fort Taylor is not mentioned in the histories, in view of its strategic importance.

Mr. Higginson's letters to his mother will be found in his published *Letters and Journals*.

Chapter Eleven

Sources:

The Atlantic Monthly and Its Makers, by M. A. DeWolfe Howe. Atlantic Monthly Press, 1919.

The Atlantic Monthly, October, 1891.

The Letters and Journals of T. W. Higginson, edited by Mary Thatcher Higginson, Houghton Mifflin, 1921.

Emily Dickinson manuscripts in the Galatea Collection, Boston Public Library.

On the manuscript letters of Emily Dickinson there are penciled dates, in each case, one day earlier than the published date.

We are reminded of Emily Dickinson's use of " school "
terms in so recent an expression as that of Sir Hall Caine
who said, in returning thanks for the highest honor which
the Isle of Man can bestow — the freedom of its capital:
" This island has been my school, my university, my alma
mater, my mother. It has taught me all, or nearly all, I
know of human nature." (July 23, 1929).

CHAPTER TWELVE

My account of the death of Major Hunt is based upon
information given in the War Department records, and
upon New York and Brooklyn newspapers of the time,
particularly the *New York Times,* October 2, 1863, and
the *New York World,* October 5, 1863.

In her letter to Mr. Higginson in the summer of 1864
Emily Dickinson had inclosed her address on a separate
slip of paper, which is now in the Galatea Collection. To
reconstruct the setting for her visits in Cambridge has been
no easy matter. The neighborhood has changed and the
number, 86, is no longer to be found on Austin Street.
The street itself is directly back of the Cambridge City
Hall and one has only a short walk from that point to the
neighborhood of No. 86. Mrs. George E. Thorndike, of
Cambridge, remembers distinctly the house and garden
that were on the site of No. 86 in Civil War days. She is
my authority for the description which I have given. The
church, which she once attended, will no longer be found
across the street from 86; instead, there is a newspaper

office. " The orange stripe of city," now known as " Austin Place," remains, dimmed and dusty. In the oldest bookstore, around the corner, on the main business street I found a delightful old gentleman who drew for me a fascinating plan of the No. 86 locality. Conspicuous in the plan was the pear tree, from which he had many times been shaken in his boyhood; but when he heard that his pear tree was to go into " a history," he asked that his name be withheld from the printed page, for he remembered from his American history that a fruit tree can attain considerable notoriety.

In the Cambridge Directory of 1864–65 I found that 86 Austin Street was the residence of Barnabas Bangs, a bookkeeper, whose business was in Boston. In a letter to her cousins after her return from Cambridge (Cambridgeport, it was then called), Emily Dickinson makes a reference to Mrs. B—— and Miss B——, her hostesses. In a letter written from Cambridge in 1865 she refers to the coming of new lodgers. We know, also from her letters, that the Misses Norcross were in a lodging-house which Austin Dickinson visited. It seems reasonable to place the cousins at 86 Austin Street, for it is unlikely that they would have allowed Emily, ill and so shy, to go to a strange house. Her letters indicate that her cousins were with her. They seem to have had a suite of rooms. After 1870, Barnabas Bangs no longer lived at 86 Austin Street, according to the City Directory. In Emily's letters we learn that the cousins were at the Berkeley Hotel again for a while after Mrs. Bangs had given up her lodging-house;

but they returned to Cambridge for residence finally, and were in the famous suburb at the time of the death of Emily Dickinson.

CHAPTER THIRTEEN

In *The Christian Union,* October 24, 1891, will be found " A Child's Recollections of Emily Dickinson," by Mac-Gregor Jenkins. Might it not be worth while to gather into one section of her book all of the poems that Emily Dickinson is known to have written for children? Does not the scattering of such poems throughout her work perhaps intensify an impression of childishness beyond the point of fairness to Emily Dickinson?

The Life and Times of Samuel Bowles, by G. S. Merriam (Century Co., 1885), is a book which anyone will find interesting. Especially in his correspondence with Miss Whitney, also a friend of Emily Dickinson, one gets an insight into the mind of Mr. Bowles.

In a letter dated 1868, *Life and Letters of Emily Dickinson,* p. 72, Mr. Higginson tries to persuade Emily Dickinson to come to Boston. In a letter dated also 1868, *Life and Letters of Emily Dickinson,* p. 268, and marked in pencil on the original manuscript, June 9, there is a reference to her going to Boston, but in this letter she also alludes to the publication of " The Snake," which I find in the *Springfield Republican* on February 14, 1866. She thinks it possible that Mr. Higginson will see her poem in the paper. It seems certain, therefore, that the

letter on p. 268 must have been written in 1866, and that
Mr. Higginson in that year and again in 1868 was trying
to persuade Emily Dickinson to come to Boston, where
she could make literary contacts. The reference to her
promised visit to her doctor in May would further confirm the 1866 date, since it was at that time that Emily was
having trouble with her eyes. There is in the Galatea
Collection a letter, no part of which has been published,
and which is placed between the published letters on pp.
268 and 270. In this letter she again refers to Mr. Higginson's invitation to her to come to Boston, and it is
written after the death of Carlo. The date seems to be
about 1868 and it is probably a reply to the letter printed
in part on p. 72, *Life and Letters of Emily Dickinson.*

In addition to her chosen books and her magazines,
Harper's and the *Atlantic,* Emily Dickinson read the best
daily newspaper in the country. She read other papers, the
New York Times for one, so we note in her letters, but
the *Springfield Republican* was her daily interest. I
found the most interesting reading of my research (next
to the Galatea Collection) in the files of the *Springfield
Republican.* In Emily's day its literary department was
lively. There was a column of general literary criticism,
there were reviews of the leading new English and American publications, there were comments upon the monthly
magazines, *Harper's* and the *Atlantic* leading, the *Token,*
the *Northern Light,* etc. During these years when Emily
Dickinson was writing behind the hedge, her daily paper
carried reprints of the most famous poems in English

literature — poems by Blake, Keats, Shelley, Marvell, Herrick, Arnold, Rossetti. In one respect the *Republican* took a negative position and voiced the opinion of the multitude. Whitman had found no " wile " necessary in candor. Swinburne had appeared. The *Springfield Republican* could not take to this new form of art. In reviewing *The Life and Death of Jason,* by William Morris, on August 10, 1867, the *Republican* was vigorous in its denunciation of " such decorous indecency, soft singers of the senses . . . who lure us from true manhood. . . . Roberts Brothers' first venture into dirtier waters. . . ." The *Republican* preferred Hawthorne's treatment of mythology, and Dr. Holland's new poem, " Kathrina," to *The Life and Death of Jason.*

No one mentioned Emily Dickinson as a hard worker comparable to Mr. Edison, during the Golden Jubilee Celebration of the invention of the incandescent bulb, but when Eleanora Duse died in Pittsburgh on April 21, 1924, the writer of a special dispatch to the *New York Evening Post* did think to draw an analogy between the two women. He said:

" La Duse was destined to captivate in America, two — almost three — generations of playgoers. She gave herself wholly to her art. She avoided society. She hated publicity. The secret of her genius puzzled critics. They went, they were won, but the mystery — it eluded pens. It was moonlight, playing on strings of the spirit with filmy fingers, eluding capture by any less gauzy net than poetry.

" Her presence on the stage was like an echo of Emily

Dickinson's poetry in the mind. Sad, said the critics. To be sure. Pensive, wistful, spiritual, expressing a haunting, inward beauty, a sweet melancholy, an aching loneliness. All these things they said and more. She chimed on all the silver bells of truth and beauty in the human heart."

CHAPTER FOURTEEN

There are psychologists who are trying to find an explanation for Emily Dickinson's life in an " Œdipus complex " in her nature. I am convinced that Edward Dickinson is to be taken historically rather than as a special case. Mr. Higginson quoted a New England college president as saying, in the 'sixties, " No lawyer ever reads a book." There are three letters from Mr. Dickinson to Salmon P. Chase in the Library of Congress. They are probably typical of his letters during his political career. If so, the publication of his collected letters would give little insight into his relations with his children. Emily Dickinson's own letters seem to be the best source for that study.

CHAPTER FIFTEEN

My study of Helen Hunt Jackson is based entirely upon information which has been given to the public. Every factual statement about this talented woman is documented from the following sources:

The Atlantic Monthly (Contributors' Club), November, 1900.
The Critic, April 25, 1885.

The Critic, August 22, 1885.

The Dial, September, 1885.

Education, November, 1900.

The Nation, August 20, 1885.

The New Princeton Review, July, 1886.

The Overland Monthly, September, 1885.

Letters by Helen Hunt Jackson in the Manuscript Division of the New York Public Library.

The published and unpublished *Journals* of T. W. Higginson.

    Mrs. Jackson's own works, published usually by Roberts Brothers:

Verses, by H. H., 1873.

Sonnets and Lyrics, by Helen Hunt Jackson, 1886.

Bits of Travel, 1872.

Bits of Talk about Home Matters, 1873.

Bits of Talk for Young Folks, 1876.

The Saxe Holm Stories, 1873–78. Scribners.

Mercy Philbrick's Choice, 1876.

Hetty's Strange History, 1877.

Bits of Travel at Home, 1878.

A Century of Dishonor, Harper & Brothers, 1881.

Ramona, 1884.

" *The Prince's Little Sweetheart,*" a short story, *Century,* May, 1885.

There are contradictions as to the date of Mrs. Jackson's first marriage. Many of the obituary notices state that Mrs. Jackson was married to Lieutenant Hunt when she was twenty-four years old; but the notice in the *Springfield Republican* at the time of her first marriage, and a copy of the marriage license which is in the Pension Bureau in

Washington, D. C., give the date as October 26, 1852, when she was but twenty-one. Helen Fiske Hunt Jackson was born on October 18, 1831, in Amherst.

The date of the birth of Warren Horsford Hunt is carved upon his tombstone as December 2, 1857, but in her application for a pension Helen Hunt gave the age of the child as eight years at the time of his father's death in 1863, and his birth date is given as December 2, 1855, in practically all of the biographical dictionaries and reference works.

It is said that Mrs. Jackson had chosen Mr. Hamilton Wright Mabie for her biographer, but no full-length book about Helen Hunt Jackson has yet been published.

CHAPTER SIXTEEN

It should be clear that I have attempted to show something of Mrs. Jackson's, rather than my own, analysis of Mercy Philbrick's character.

CHAPTER SEVENTEEN

The *Springfield Republican,* July 5, 1879, has a full account of the Amherst fire which Emily Dickinson describes so brilliantly in a letter to her cousins.

A Reminiscence of Emily Dickinson, by Clara B. Green, *Bookman,* November, 1924, gives a charming description of the author's impressions of Emily Dickinson and her sister as Mrs. Green saw them in her own girlhood. She remembers Emily as small, with delicate features, large, dark eyes, a beautiful voice, and a breathless way of speaking.

Professor Thompson of Amherst College has many a pleasant recollection of Miss Lavinia's kindness to him in his student days, when he probably gave her more than the one bit of advice as to doctoring a kitten.

Called Back, by Hugh Conway, was published by Henry Holt & Co., 1884.